THE NARRATIVES OF ČAPEK AND ČEXOV

A TYPOLOGICAL COMPARISON OF THE AUTHORS' WORLD VIEWS

THE NARRATIVES OF
ČAPEK AND ČEXOV

A TYPOLOGICAL COMPARISON OF THE
AUTHORS' WORLD VIEWS

PETER Z. SCHUBERT

Library of Congress Cataloging-in-Publication Data

Schubert, Peter Zdeněk
    The narratives of Čapek and Čexov : a typological comparison of
    the authors' world views / Peter Z. Schubert.
      p. cm.
    Includes bibliographical references and index.
    ISBN 1-57309-061-1 (hc): $69.95 - ISBN 1-57309-060-3 (pbk.): $49.95.
    1. Čapek, Karel, 1890-1938--Philosophy. 2. Chekhov, Anton Pavlovich,
    1860-1904--Philosophy. I. Title.
    PG5038.C3Z84 1996
    891.72'3--dc20   95-49592
                                          CIP

Editorial Inquiries:
International Scholars Publications
7831 Woodmont Avenue, #345
Bethesda, MD 20814

To order: (800) 55-PUBLISH

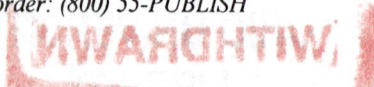

To my family—Sue, Misha, and Danny

❦

TABLE OF CONTENTS

PREFACE

A comparative study examining the affinities between Čapek and Čexov is long overdue. The parallels were first observed almost half a century ago, and commented on *in passim* by no less than seven scholars. The critics' allusions would suggest that similarity exists in the stories' quality, in the authors' artistic method, stylistic structure, and language, as well as in the atmosphere, or mood, of the narratives. The affinity found in the similar treatment of analogous subjects has remained until now an entirely unexplored field.

The two authors' prose fiction, as well as the dramatic *oeuvres*, offer numerous examples of identical, or very similar, themes, which often have been given analogous treatment. The present treatise centers on the prose, which offers a broader basis for comparison. To investigate both genres would entail extending the examination and paying the price of repetitiveness. The conclusion, however, applies to both the fiction and drama. The method used is that of a typological comparison, rather than an investigation of contactual relations. This approach is justified by the establishment of the affinity between the world views espoused by Čapek and Čexov. The Czech writer's *Weltanschauung* is expressed more explicitly, this being a reflection of his philosophical training. This typological study then not only fills a gap in literary criticism by demonstrating the similarities between the works of Čapek and Čexov, but also, by revealing the affinities apparent in the two authors' ideas, supplies a basis for the eduction of Čexov's philosophy, the integrity, and even existence of which, has so often been denied. A proper understanding of this philosophy provides insight into numerous stories by Čexov which have so far eluded satisfactory explanation.

The study opens with a recapitulation of the observations critics have made with regard to this relation. This is followed by a brief summary of the biographical similarities. Čapek and Čexov's similar treatment of analogous subjects, or their overall similarities, are demonstrated in the main part of the first chapter. The examination subsequently deals with the major themes treated by both writers. Once the similarities between their literary works have been established, an attempt can be made at educing the world view they respectively espouse. Thus far, the treatise belongs to the sphere of literary typology. The thesis of the study is, however, the claim of affinity between Čapek and Čexov's philosophical thought. Since this topic is extremely controversial, a survey of the voluminous criticism dealing with their *Weltanschauung* constitutes the next subdivision of the work. Although the critics arrived at their views through literary analyses, this part of the study can be classified as a social-typological comparison. Since dependable reference material regarding this topic is lacking, this survey of critical views provides a good research tool. The actual discernment of the philosophy adopted by Čexov and Čapek is presented in the final chapter. Their world views are analogous and, although not specifically labelled, they are shown to be akin to pragmatism. be akin to pragmatism. are analogous and, although not specifically labelled, they are shown to be akin to pragmatism.

Introduction

Ivan Bunin reminisces how "[o]dnaždy, čitaja gazety, on [Čexov] podnjal lico i, ne speša, bez intonacii, skazal:—vse vremja tak: Korolenko i Čexov, Potapenko i Čexov, Gor'kij i Čexov."[1] Valerij Alekseevič Gejdeko refers to this incident and observes that Čexov's displeasure is easily understandable, for, with uncommon persistence, critics kept finding his "doubles."[2] At times, according to Gejdeko, the subjects of comparison were mediocre, such as the now almost forgotten Ignatij Nikolaevič Potapenko; at others, they were talented and interesting, each gifted and attractive in his own manner, and deserving of independent attention. Such treatment on the basis of his own unique qualities was also, no doubt, Čexov's due. Nevertheless, instead of exploring two individualities, critics studied a strange symbiosis, and thereby Čexov's originality as well as that of the writer to whom he was compared disappeared from view. In spite of this observation, Gejdeko adds to the number of studies analyzing parallels between Čexov and other writers in his own *A. Čexov i Iv. Bunin.*

The present study also compares Čexov with another author. Its purpose goes, however, beyond that of a simple juxtaposition. The affinity between Čexov and Čapek, when established, provides a solid basis for an examination of their respective world views. Because of the Czech author's philosophical background, his *Weltanschauung* is presented clearly. Armed with this knowledge, one can educe similar and frequently the same ideas from Čexov's voluminous works.

The overabundance of comparisons involving the Russian writer constitutes another reason why a number of additional similarities between the two men of letters are not investigated in this work. A discussion of Čexov and Čapek in the context of their respective national literatures in order to establish their *Stellenwert* is, for instance, a potentially significant area of study, but would contribute little to the educing of their *Weltanschauungen*. Other possibilities include their involvement with various literary genres. Thus, for instance, both Čexov and Čapek were involved in journalism, the former, as a regular contributor of the *feuilletons* "Oskolki moskovskoj žizni" to *Oskolki* between 2 July 1883 and 12 October 1885, and the latter, publishing his "Sloupky" in *Lidové noviny* from 9 April 1932 to 25 December 1938. Both gained world recognition through their plays, but their stories—as renowned as their plays now—form the greater part of their literary production. Moreover, both excelled in the short prose genres, but encountered difficulties in their attempts at writing novels. Čexov worked on a novel entitled "Rasskazy iz žizni moix druzej" for over two years (1887-1889) but probably destroyed the unfinished manuscript. His "Drama na oxote" and "Duèl'" are long narratives but not novels. Similarly, Alexander Matuška comments on the brevity of Čapek's "novels:" "The novels that he wrote are . . . . brief. Some are, in essence, short stories or novellettes or story cycles—like *Hordubal* and *The Meteor [Povětroň]*."[3] Čapek confirms this observation in the preface to *Věc Makropulos* by stating that the subject seemed ideal for a novel, but that he does not care for this form.[4]

No less than seven scholars mention a similarity between Čexov and Čapek, but only one actually discusses the analogy at length.[5] That article is, however, limited to a study of the similarities perceived in the language used in two dramas. The present study centers on prose works, which offer a wider basis for comparison. To investigate both genres would entail extending the examination and paying the price of repetitiveness. The conclusion, however, applies to both. The method used is that of a typological comparison, rather than an investigation of contactual relations. The evidence of these direct contacts cannot, however, be entirely disregarded. William Harkins, for instance, does not hesitate to speak of Čexov's influence upon Čapek's work."[6] Moreover, the Czech writer himself does not refute such claims. As a matter of fact, referring to the influences in his *oeuvre*, Čapek says: ". . . je to *embarras de richesse*. . . . Mohl bych snad uvésti tři nebo čtyři autory, kteří na mne neměli vliv."[7] Nevertheless, this being a typological study, the idea of a potential influence serves one purpose only, namely, to strengthen the argument of an affinity between the two authors in the spirit of Viktor Žirmunskij's observation: ". . . a literary influence is not an accidental and mechanical impulse from outside . . . . The preconditions for adoption are the need for ideological importation and the existence of more or less parallel tendencies in the adopting society and literature."[8] No attempt to prove Čexov's influence on Čapek is made in the present work, but the very fact that such a relation is considered in critical literature indicates a certain affinity between the two authors. The term affinity is herein understood as it is used by Ihab Hassan in his seminal article on influence:

> When we say that A has influenced B, we mean that after literary or aesthetic analysis we can discern a number of significant similarities between the works of A and B. We may also mean that historical, social, and perhaps psychological analyses of the data available about A and B reveal similarities, points of contact between the "lives" or "minds" of the two writers. So far we have established no influence; we have only documented what I [Hassan] shall call an affinity.[9]

Thus, according to this scholar,

> Literary analysis can reveal all the techniques of a writer and much of his sensibility. And it can provide a sound basis for comparisons between different works and different writers. But alone it can go no further than to demonstrate similarities, and if these similarities be more than technical, literary analysis may uncover some phase of an affinity.[10]

This suffices for the purpose of this study, the first aim of which is to establish the existence of an affinity between Čexov and Čapek.

The treatise opens with a recapitulation of the observations critics have made with regard to this relation. The biographical similarities are briefly summarized next, for, as discussed by Claudio Guillén,[11] "the writer's experience" is a source of his creative work. Čapek and Čexov's similar treatment of analogous subjects, or their general similarities, are demonstrated in the main part of the first chapter. The examination then deals with the major themes treated by both writers. Once the similarities between their literary works are established, an attempt can be made at educing the world view they respectively espouse. Thus far, in Dionýz Ďurišin's terminology,[12] the treatise belongs to the sphere of literary typology. The thesis of the study is, however, the claim of affinity between Čapek and Čexov's philosophical thought. Since this topic is extremely controversial, a survey of the voluminous criticism dealing with their *Weltanschauung* constitutes the next subdivision of the work. Although the critics arrived at their views by literary analyses, this part of the study can be classified as a social typological comparison.[13] The actual discernment of the philosophy adopted by Čexov and Čapek is presented in the final chapter. The application of the extrinsic analogy *ad tertium*[14] is useful here. Unfortunately, it has been employed erroneously in several critical works. Biographical information provides a basis for a psychological[15] typological analogy *ad tertium*. The established affinity between Čapek and Čexov's world views enables the author to present a picture of the Russian writer's *Weltanschauung*, which for almost a century has remained so controversial. The direction of the analogy from the later to the earlier writer justifies the typological approach and simultaneously precludes any attempt at a search for influences. The subject of the concluding chapter forms the most important contribution the present dissertation wishes to make to the literary scholarship concerning these two writers, for, as G.K. Chesterton observes, " . . . . the most practical and important thing about a man is still his view of the universe . . . . [F]or a general about to fight an enemy, it is important to know the enemy's numbers, but still more important to know the enemy's philosophy."[16]

Notes

1. I.A. Bunin, *O Čexove: Nezakončennaja rukopis'* (New York: Izd-vo im. Čexova, 1955), p. 113.

2. V.A. Gejdeko, *A. Čexov i Iv. Bunin* (Moskva: Sovetskij pisatel', 1976), p. 5.

3. A. Matuška, *Karel Čapek: An Essay*, trans. C. Alan (London: G. Allen & Unwin Ltd., 1964), p. 152, cf. p. 156.

4. K. Čapek, *Věc Makropulos* (Praha: Aventinum, 1922).

5. These critical comments are discussed in the ensuing chapter.

6. W. Harkins, *Karel Čapek* (New York and London: Columbia Univ. Press, 1962), p. 69.

7. K. Čapek, "O sobě," *Rozpravy Aventina*, 1, No. 1 (Sept. 1925), 1-2; rpt. in *Poznámky o tvorbě*, ed. M. Halík (Praha: Čs. spisovatel, 1960), p. 79.

8. V.M. Žirmunskij, "On the Study of Comparative Literature," *Oxford Slavonic Papers*, 13 (1967), 7-8.

9. H. Hassan, "The Problem of Influence in Literary History: Notes Towards a Definition," *Journal of Aesthetics and Art Criticism*, 14, No. 1 (1955), p. 68.

10. Ibid., p. 73. The term "similarity" is used here as defined by the OED, namely, the state or fact of being similar; likeness, resemblance. Another term encountered in scholarly work on the concept of influence and on the idea of parallels in literature is that of an "analogy." Its meaning is again derived from the dictionary and employed (cf. Weisstein's works on the topic) as a likeness in one or more ways between things otherwise unlike or unrelated.

11. C. Guillén, "The Aesthetics of Literary Influence," in *Literature as System* (Princeton: Princeton Univ. Press, 1971), p. 30.

12. D. Ďurišin, *Problémy literárnej komparatistiky* (Bratislava: Slovenská Akadémie Vied, 1967), pp. 96-99.

13. Ibid., p. 96.

14. The comparison of two analogates to something external to both, but which both somehow share. The term is defined in U. Weisstein, "Influences and Parallels," in *Teilnahme und Spiegelung*, ed. D. Gutzen (Berlin and New York: Walter de Gruyter, 1975), p. 602.

15. Ďurišin, p. 100.

16. G.K. Chesterton, "Introductory Remarks on the Importance of Orthodoxy," *Heretics* (London: The Bodley Head, 1905), pp. 7-8. The quotation is also used as an opening to W. James, *Pragmatism* (Cambridge: Harvard Univ. Press, 1975), p. 9.

❧

CHAPTER I

GENERAL SIMILARITIES

René Wellek, in his essay "Karel Čapek," discussing the Czech author's *Trapné povídky*, claims that: "There is an atmosphere of heavy, melancholy fatality in those stories, which can be very well compared with some of the 'painful' stories in Maupassant or Chekhov."[1] Oliver Elton, writing about Čapek's literary production, refers to Čexov twice,[2] the first time in his essay "Karel Čapek: Short Tales and Fantasies," where he asserts that "the *contes* rank with those of Chekhov;"[3] and the second time, in "Karel Čapek: Later Novels," when he refers to the ending of *První parta*: "Čapek, like Chekhov, well knows where to stop."[4] These three sentences comprise the entire scholarship on the similarity between Čapek and Čexov for a quarter century. Then, like Wellek, William Harkins, in his monograph on Čapek, speaks of *Trapné povídky* as reminiscent of the Russian writer's works: "With their melancholy mood, coming from introspective reminiscence, and with the *pointe* of the tale usually blunted they recall the stories of Chekhov."[5] He does not stop at this observation, however, and comments also on Čexov's influence in Čapek's *Loupežník*: "A number of influences can be detected in the play. Chekhovian is the mixture of styles: comedy, farce, tragedy, and melodrama."[6] Thomas Winner finds a similarity between *Loupežník* and Čexov's *Ivanov* in the stylistic techniques by which the *dramatis personae* are characterized by traits of speech, and his examination constitutes the only comparative study dealing with the two writers to date[7] In the introduction to this study, Winner asserts that Čexov's writings affected Čapek, and that similarities to Čexov's works may be detected in Čapek's literary production. Moreover, he notes that "[t]he problem of the relationship of *Trapné povídky* to Čexov's stories has not yet received the attention it deserves."[8] At the same time that Winner makes these observations, Alexander Matuška, a Slovak critic, publishes a monograph on Čapek, in which he describes the atmosphere in the Czech writer's works with a reference to Čexov: "It was a mourning and a melancholy that bordered on the Chekhovian, that developed into anxiety."[9] Hence, the affinity in the mood of their stories becomes a commonplace observation by 1965. This could have been one of the reasons that led Oleg Malevič, a Soviet Bohemist, to write an article entitled "Karel Čapek i Rossija." The orientation of the study provides the author with wider perspective. Thus, Malevič notes that the Čapek brothers considered "pravdoiskatel'stvo, postojannye razdum'ja nad smyslom žizni" to be a distinct feature of Russian literature."[10] Čexov is, according to this scholar, intrinsically close to Karel Čapek.[11] Malevič further develops this notion, when he writes: "Čapeku byl blizok glubočajšij demokratizm Čexova, ego vnimanie k prostomu čeloveku. Razrabatyvaja temu malen'kogo čeloveka, Čapek po-Čexovski složen v otnošenii k nemu: tut i sočuvstvie, i ironija, i dobrodušnaja usmeška, i gor'kij sarkazm."[12] In the conclusion of his article, the Russian critic mentions Čexov's name once more, speaking "...o vozdejstvii xudožestvennogo opyta russkoj literatury na ego [Čapeka] tvorčeskij metod."[13] Karel Čapek justifies Malevič's observation in his reaction to Pavel Eisner's claim that the Czech author knows and therefore presents well only the country, the educated proletariat, and the life of the city scum and of the middle class up to the level of departmental councillor: "Kdyby tomu tak bylo, tedy chválabohu obzíral by důkladný kus života, a nemuseli bychom se trápit proto, že nepíše o mravech plutokratické vrstvičky, které se u větších a bohatších národů říká hořeních deset tisíc. Pokud vím, Hamsunovi stačí norští sedláci a nějaký ten nesrstný inteligent; Anton Čechov nedospěl ani k společenským výšinám odborových radů ... a přece se to říká světová literatura."[14] Hence, Čapek approves of the Čexovian hero, and, as stated by Malevič, he has the same attitude toward man.

Malevič further substantiates his claim of the effect Čexov has on Čapek by a reference to three notes that the latter published concerning the former in *Lidové noviny* during 1926-1927.[15] Two years later, Malevič again refers to the similarity between Čapek and Čexov. This time he notes an analogy in the structure of narrative in *Boží muka*, but does not elaborate on the topic."[16] Malevič's fellow Soviet Bohemist, Sergej Vasil'evič Nikol'skij, is the last critic to have commented on the similarity between the two writers. He refers to it twice in his 1973 book *Karel Čapek-fantast i satirik*, and both times the association is with Čapek's later works. According to Nikol'skij, "[o]tdel'nye kuski romana [*Krakatit*] svoej real'noj nagljadnost'ju napominajut . . . kartiny iz proizvedenij . . . Čexova."[17] Further, he quotes a sentence from the first chapter of *Válka s mloky* and relates it to the Čexovian method: "Ona [kakaja-to plotina] byla tem Čexovskim 'ruž'em,' kotoroe teper' v četvertoj glave 'vystrelilo.'"[18]

In spite of all the above observations, only Winner has even attempted to compare the Czech writer with his Russian counterpart, and his study is strictly linguistic. The similarity between Čapek and Čexov exists, however, on a far more general basis, and this study aims at probing the dimensions of the relationship. Certain parallels exist already in their biographical data, although Anton Pavlovič Čexov was born in 1860, spent his life in czarist Russia and died in 1904, while Karel Čapek was born in 1890, lived his creative life in the democratic republic of Czechoslovakia, and died in 1938. They both were writers as much as playwrights, became famous in both genres, loved nature and gardening, married actresses, were terminally ill, and died prematurely in their forties. The biographical similarities are, however, only marginally important. Their writings, as noted by the above critics, can provide a good foundation for comparison of the type carried out by Winner. Although a linguistic analysis would further substantiate the claim of similarity between the two writers, the author of the present study does not consider himself qualified to undertake a meaningful discussion of this type.

The scholars who observe an affinity between Čexov and Čapek, most often point out the similarity between *Trapné povídky* and the work of the Russian writer. One of the tales from this collection, "Na zámku," offers itself for comparison with two of Čexov's stories, namely "Spat' xočetsja" and "Van'ka." "Na zámku" is a story of a poor girl working as a governess on a country estate. She suffers from the humiliating behaviour of the count who refuses to believe that his daughter, her pupil, is rude and stupid. The daughter, in her turn, hates the teacher. The countess increases the girl's abasement when, suspecting the governess of stealing, she

searches her room. The son's English tutor torments her with his impudent
love-play. She determines to put an end to her suffering and give up her
position. A letter from home terminates her plans, however, and she, a
virgin, seeks self-destruction in submission to the tutor's advances. At
first glance, the story may seem to have little in common with either of
Čexov's stories. In "Spat' xočetsja" a very tired child, while working
during the day, watches over her employers baby at night. As she is at the
end of her strength, in despair, she strangles the infant. The other story,
"Van'ka," describes the Christmas evening of a nine-year-old orphan who
is apprenticed to a cobbler in Moscow. The boy takes advantage of his
master's absence to write a letter to his grandfather complaining of
mistreatment, and asking that he be taken home. The letter, addressed only
"Na derevnju deduške Konstantinu Makaryču," is dropped in the mailbox.
Jan Mukařovský, in his "Úvod" to *Výbor z prózy Karla Čapka* discussed
the conflict between a "hidden" private evaluation of the facts of the story
by the characters themselves on the one hand and the superficial,
conventional view of things on the other.

> Vidíme . . . událost, o které se vypravuje, současně "zevnitř"
> i "zevně." Tento protiklad a rozpor dvojího hodnocení se vždy
> uplatňuje v celém průběhu děje, ba zpravidla se na konci
> naznačuje, že přetrval událost o které se vyprávělo. "Skryté"
> hodnocení je představováno jako vyšší; nevyrovnaný rozpor
> mezi ním a konvencí je pocit'ován jako cosi bolestného a
> nespravedlivého: odtud název *Trapné povídky.*[19]

One of his examples is the story "Na zámku:"

> *pohled zevnitř*
> vychovatelka žijící
> v šlechtické rodině
> v mnohem lepších poměrech,
> než jaké by jí mohla
> poskytnout chudá rodina
> vlastní, ale zároveň . . .
>
> *pohled zevně*
> hrdá bytost, bez ohledu

a bez omluv ponižovaná
svými chlebodárci.²⁰

Such oppositions are not new in literature. The conflict is traditionally resolved, however, either way, in the *dénouement*. It is not so in the *Trapné povídky*. Čapek himself claims that:

> *Trapné povídky* se zase vracejí k thematu: každý má pravdu. Nebot' tady lidé jednají špatně, zbaběle, krutě nebo slabošsky, jedním slovem trapně; a celý vtip je v tom, že nikoho z nich nemůžete odsoudit; po nikom hodit kamenem; podařil-li se mi aspoň trochu tento povídkový cyklus, musel jsem docílit *mučivého* [Čapek's italics] dojmu, že není koho soudit. Chtěl jsem ukázat člověka v ponížení a slabosti, aniž by byla snížena jeho lidská hodnota.²¹

Naturally, the above can be applied to Čexov's stories. The entire monograph *The Chameleon and the Dream: The Image of Reality in Čechov's Stories* by Karl D. Kramer is based on the multiplicity of perspective in Čexov's writings.²² Mukařovský's distinction between the external and the internal views is maintained in both writers. Van'ka, for instance, recalls his idyllic village, but these memories are related by the narrator. This is made clear by contrasting Van'ka's semiliterate style with the correct Russian of the flashbacks into his happy past. The alteration of styles permits the unobtrusive transmission of the "external" information. Thus, while Van'ka is full of love for his grandfather and Miss Ol'ga Ignat'evna, the reader learns that his grandfather is a "starikaška s p'janymi glazami," who has not shown any interest in him in the past three months, and Miss Ol'ga took interest in Van'ka "ot nečego delat'." In "Spat' xočetsja," the contrast between the "internal"—Var'ka's view of the murder of the baby and the implied "external" view of the event provided by the reader himself, is clear. We find the same duality of meaning, which Mukařovský, in the case of *Trapné povídky*, calls the method of twofold reflection of the event through which the author achieves a special impression of oppressive fatality. The two stories of Čexov have been brought together by Thomas Winner as the most significant of the stories of children with "Van'ka" anticipating "Spat' xočetsja."²³ They both deal with children exploited by their employers, their despair and an attempt at a resolution of their problem. Inasmuch as the

heroine of "Na zámku" can be considered a child, this description can be
applied to Čapek's story as well. Nathan Rosen offers a more substantial
basis for relating two Russian stories. According to him,

> "Spat' xočetsja" (Sleepy) is similar in theme and structure to
> "Van'ka." There is the same situation of a friendless, exploited
> child, the same alternation between the past and the present in
> the child's mind, and a surprising action at the end by the child
> to resolve his unbearable situation. "Van'ka" could easily be
> regarded as a preliminary "daylight" version of "Sleepy,"
> lacking only the demonic element of the latter.[24]

When these terms are applied to Čapek's story, the overlap is obvious. The
protagonist, exploited by the employer, is left among strangers with no
person she can relate to. Similar to Čexov's children's reminiscences of the
past are Olga's memories of her home, the only refuge in her intolerable
suffering. The final resolution of the heroine of "Na zámku" can also be
related to the unexpected action in the *dénouement* of the Russian stories. As
a matter of fact, the very points Rosen makes in his discussion of Čexov's
stories are stressed in Čapek's tale. Olga is explicit about her being left
alone among strangers: "jsem cizí a najatý člověk, nikdo na mne nemyslí.
Jsou jen takoví, bože, nikde není člověk tak sám jako mezi cizími lidmi!"[25]
While Van'ka reminisces about the cruelty of his master, and the reader gets
only a glimpse of the actual behaviour of Var'ka's employers, the conduct—
or misconduct—of every member of the count's household in relation to
Olga is of primary importance in the Czech story. Var'ka's suffering is
increased by her memories of the past and by the irritating "krik" of the baby
and the cricket.[26] Olga's suffering is augmented after every meeting with
any of the people around her, and this too is made explicit by the author.
Practically every paragraph of the story contains one or more references to
her pain. Like Van'ka, she derives her only happiness from the decision to
go home. While Van'ka does not know that his letter will not bring him the
happiness he seeks, however, Olga's hopes are shattered by a letter from
home. The common motif of the letter is strengthened by the fact that Olga
had intended to use it as an excuse for her giving notice. Left to despair she
cannot cope with, Olga, like Var'ka, indirectly seeks total destruction,
which in her case is the submission to the tutor's advances.

    One of the causes of Olga's anguish is the abasement she suffers when she finds the countess searching her room. This theme is developed in less than two pages of the nineteen-page story. Singled out, it too has a remarkably close parallel in Čexov's work. As early as 1886 the Russian author published a story entitled "Perepolox," in which a rich lady, who has lost a brooch worth two thousand roubles, unceremoniously ransacks the room of a poor governess in the mistaken belief that she is the thief. The similarity of, particularly, the first half of Čexov's story, to Čapek's treatment of the motif is quite remarkable. In "Perepolox" "Mašen'ka vošla v svoju komnatu, i tut ej . . . prišlos' ispitat' vo vsej ostrote čuvstvo, kotoroe tak znakomo ljudjam zavisimym, bezotvetnym, živuščim na xlebax u bogatyx i znatnyx. V ee komnate delali obysk. Xozjajka Fedos'ja Vasil'evna . . . stojala u ee stola i vkladyvala obratno v rabočuju sumku klubki, šersti, loskutki, bumažki . . . "[27] Olga in Čapek's story enters her room under the same circumstances. When she opens her door, "Tu stanula v úžase, stěží chápajíc co se děje; prostřed pokoje seděla na židli paní hraběnka, a komorná před ní přehrabavala její, Olginu šatní skříň . . ."[28] This startling encounter is not the only affinity between the two stories. Mašen'ka's "feeling, common to people living at somebody else's expense" agitated by a servant's remark, "V čužix ljudjax živete, baryšnja,"(IV, 333) develops into a sense of loneliness: "V stolice ona odna, kak v pustynnom pole, bez rodnyx i znakomyx."(IV, 333) Exactly the same sentiment is expressed by Čapek's heroine: "Jsem cizí a najatý člověk, nikdo na mne nemyslí. Jsou jen takoví, bože, nikde není člověk tak sám jako mezi cizími lidmi!"[29] Both girls suffer so much from the humiliation brought upon them by the search that they decide to give notice, and start packing. Both are interrupted by being called to the dining room, but neither is able to finish her meal. Mašen'ka completes her packing, however, while Olga is forced to realize that she must stay.

The similarities between "Na zámku" and Čexov's stories may have been the indirect cause for the exchange between the protagonist of Čapek's "Povídka starého kriminálníka," Mr. Jandera, and his friend: "Člověče, tak se mně zdá, že ta má poslední povídka je od někoho kradená.—To jsem přece poznal na první pohled, řekl kamarád tos ukradl z Čechova."[30] This interlocution could also refer to "Zločin v chaplupě." This is even more likely, as the story is a part of a collection *Povídky z jedné kapsy*, while the above quote comes from the story included in the continuation of this book, namely, *Povídky z druhé kapsy*. "Zločin v chalupě" bears a strong resemblance to Čexov's "Zloumyšlennik." The hero of Čapek's story is a peasant who

kills his father-in-law because the latter wanted to sell a piece of the
family's fields. The entire village approves of the murder as the only
possible course of action to be taken. As a matter of fact, even the judge, who
is of peasant background, recognizes that the murder may be justified in
terms of practical peasant common sense and love for the land.
"Zloumyšlennik" for some reason has not found favour with English
translators, although Lev Nikolaevič Tolstoj considered it one of Čexov's
fifteen best stories (together with "Van'ka" and "Spat' xočetsja"),[31] and
although it was translated into six languages (among them Czech) during the
author's life time.(IV, 479) The "Zloumyšlennik" is tried for stealing nuts
from railroad ties, because he needs them as sinkers for his fishing gear. The
protagonist is a simple peasant who is unable to understand that there is
anything wrong with taking the nuts. There is an obvious difference in the
crimes committed by the two peasants. Yet the stories are almost identical
in every other regard. Two simple men stand trial for an act they do not
preceive as a crime. Both stories begin with the appearance of the peasant
in court. Denis Grigor'ev, Čexov's protagonist, is acquainted with the
details of his crime and asked whether he unscrewed the nut, to which he
replies: "Koli b ne nužna byla, ne otvinčival by."(IV, 84) Questioned
further, he explains: "My iz gaek gruzila delaem . . .—Kto èto—my?—My,
narod . . . Klimovskie mužiki, to est'."(IV, 84) Čapek's hero, Vondráček, is
asked whether he killed his father-in-law: "Zabil jste ho?' 'Jo.' "Tedy se
cítíte vinen?' 'Ne!'"[32] There is nothing wrong with the murder in his eyes,
because his father-in-law, the victim, mismanaged the farm. He too, looks
for approval from his fellow villagers, and this is wholeheartedly given:
"'To nejni žádný hospodářství, no že jo?' Auditorium zabručelo na
souhlas."[33] Both peasants try to explain their arguments for taking "the only
possible" course of action. The court does not accept their reasoning and
they cannot comprehend the inferences of the judge. Denis Grigor'ev is
shocked when told that he could kill people by his deed: "Razve ty ne
ponimaeš, glupaja golova, . . . ljudej by ubilo! Ty ljudej ubil by!—Izbavi
gospodi, vaše blagorodie! Začem ubivat'? Nešto my nekreščenye ili zlodei
kakie?"(IV, 85) Similarly, Čapek's hero tries to explain: "'Dyt' říkám, že to
bylo skrz to pole,' vybuchl Vondráček téměř vzlykaje. 'To přece není žádná
vražda! Ježíšmarjá, tomu přece každej musí rozumět! Milostpane, dyž to
bylo v rodině! Cizímu bych to neudělal—Já jsem nikdy nic neukrad . . . a
voni mě sebrali jako zloděje, jako zloděje,' sténal Vondráček duse se
lítostí."[34] Their defense is also similar in the fact that Čexov's peasant, as

cited above, explains that he is not a heathen of a criminal, while Čapek's murderer sobs that he was arrested like a thief. Čapek completes his story with a short appendix in which the judge speaks to a clerk: "Poslouchejte, pane kolego, ten člověk se cítí tak v právu jako vy nebo já. Mně to připadá, jako bych měl soudit řezníka za to, že porazil krávu, nebo krtka za to, že dělá krtiny."[35] Then the judge continues, saying that only God himself should be permited to pass sentence in cases like this one. The story ends with the return of the jury. No sentence is passed. Čexov's protagonist is sentenced, but he does not understand why: "Za čto? I ne kral, kažis', i ne dralsja . . . Nado sudit' umejuči, ne zrja . . . Xot' i vyseki, no čtob za delo, po sovesti . . ."(IV, 87) Both stories resound with a call for justice, in Čapek's case even divine fair-mindedness. Thus, it does not come as a surprise that the adjacent story in the Czech collection deals with precisely this topic. The fundamental idea of the story, "Poslední soud," is very simple. God refuses to judge a criminal, for he knows everything about him and his life; He can serve at the Last Judgement solely as a witness. Only men are capable of judging each other because their knowledge is limited. This idea of relativity in justice was already expressed in the concluding story of *Trapné povídky*, "Tribunál." A military judge, who has justly condemned a soldier for killing and robbing a wounded comrade, hears suddenly an inner voice telling him that there is no law, justice, conscience or God, and he, unable to argue against this nihilist concept, is on the verge of despair. The chief magistrate in Čexov's "Rasskaz starzego sadovnika" follows the same train of thought as Čapek's judges when unable to sentence a convicted murderer: "—Obvinjaemyj!—obratilsja glavnyj sud'ja k ubijce.—Sud priznal tebja vinovnym v ubijstve doktora tokogo-to i prigovoril tebja k . . . Glavnyj sud'ja xotel skazat': 'k smertnoj kazni,' no vyronil iz ruk bumagu, na kotoroj byl napisan prigovor, vyter xolodnyj pot i zakričal:—Net! Esli ja nepravil'no sužu, to pust' menja nakažet bog, no, kljanus', on ne vinovat! Ja ne dopuskaju mysli, čtoby mog najtis' čelovek, kotoryj osmelilsja by ubit' našego druga doktora! Čelovek nesposoben past' tak gluboko." (VIII, 346)

The idea of the inability of absolute knowledge to judge has not been exclusively Čapek's either. Mašen'ka's employer in "Perepolox" defends himself with the French: "Tout comprendre, tout pardonner."(IV, 337) This phrase, usually attributed to Madame de Staël,[36] or rather the idea expresed therein, permeates Čexov's *oeuvre* just as much as the works of Čapek.[37]

Another feature common to both writers is a dislike of empty words. Čexov ridicules the "speech-makers" in his "Orator."(V, 431-35) "Zapojkin, the 'orator,' who is able to produce a speech for any occasion, is asked to speak at the funeral of a high official. His beautiful, flowery speech is filled with rhetorical clichés. In the end, it becomes clear, however, that the speaker has mistakenly described the wrong individual who is still alive, and present among the guests. A similar instance of mistaken identity is presented in "Jasnovidec" by Čapek.[38] A clairvoyant examines a manuscript taken from a murder file. His precise description of the murderer's character is also presented in high-flown language. The public prosecutor is greatly impressed with the clairvoyant's ability, until he finds out that he accidentally submitted a sample of his own handwriting. Then he realizes that the beautiful description is independent from the truth.

The inverse problem, namely, that of an inability to act or even speak in spite of possessing the correct information, is the theme of Čexov's "V more"(II, 268-71) and Čapek's "Historie dirigenta Kaliny."[39] Moreover, in both these stories, the narrator is given the role of a hidden observer. Čapek's hero overhears a conspiracy to commit a murder but is unable to prevent it. The sailor in Čexov's story is powerless when he observes a passenger selling his newly-wed bride to an English banker. This work was reprinted under the title "Noč'ju" in 1901. At that time Maupassant enjoyed great popularity in Russia, and the critics claimed to see the French writer's influence in the story.(Cf. II, 532) The idea was readily accepted by the readers ignorant of the publishing history of the work, for, at the turn of the century, Čexov was often compared to Maupassant.(See II, 532) The reason for such confrontations is the mood in Čexovian stories and the writer's attitude toward man. The approach to humanity and the treatment of the literary material in the Russian author's work is juxtaposed, for instance, by Leonid Grossman.[40] The fact that the themes of the first two stories in Čapek's *Trapné povídky* have their counterparts in Maupassant's work is of interest here. The first one, "Otcové," is reminiscent of "Monsieur Parent." A little girl has died and her father mourns for her. The reader learns from the narrator that the father, who loved her immensely, was not her real parent. It is he who suffers the most, however; the natural father of the child jokes at the funeral. The theme of the story is simple, yet it leaves the reader in a stunned state with a heavy weight on his heart. A similar mood is evoked by the second story, "Tři." Čapek's treatment of the theme of "two husbands" brings to mind Maupassant's "Le Retour," but it is more tragic in conception. In "Tři," a husband forces his unfaithful wife to request from her lover his share in supporting her. Still the husband loves her, and he is very unhappy.

There is no direct equivalent for these two stories in Čexov's *oeuvre*. It is only the atmosphere of heavy melancholy which, as observed by Harkins[41] and Wellek,[42] brings Čexov to mind. Jan Kuipers claims that it is not the theme of everday life or of the common people that disinguishes Čexov from other writers. According to him, "Tschechow ist . . . der Schöpfer der Stimmungsgerschichte."[43] It is on this basis that these stories of Čapek can be compared with Čexov's "Toska," "Strax," or even "Skučnaja istorija." There is the same mood of impasse and despair. The affinity of the tales can also be illustrated by the fact that "Strax" has also its counterpart in Maupassant. The French story bears the same title ("La Peur") and was compared to Čexov's version by G.V. Ivanov.[44]

The third story of Čapek's collection, "Helena," begins as an idyll with the meeting of a girl with a man older than herself. She has exalted notions and mistakes their intimacy for love. Oliver Elton finds a parallel to this story in Puškin's *Evgenij Onegin*, thus emphasizing the relationship with the Russian literature. "In Helena there is a sudden explosion of hopeless passion. She comes to the man and confesses it and he has to undeceive her. She is no Tatjana, but he talks to her somewhat like a bourgeois Evgenij Onegin. She goes off, they never meet again; she thinks he has done her a grievous wrong."[45] It is surprising that Elton, who considered Čapek's *contes* comparable to Čexov's in quality, did not choose an example from the work of that author. After all, Čexov's "Veročka" treats the same failure of communication. Ivan Alekseevič Ognev has completed his task in a provincial town, and is about to leave, when Vera, the younger daughter of his landlord, suddenly declares her love. Similarly to Čapek's hero, Ognev does not know how to reply so as not to hurt the girl and not to deceive her at the same time. The outcome is the unhappiness of both protagonists.

Next in *Trapné povídky* is the already discussed "Na zámku," followed by "Peníze." The latter story has a thematic parallel in Čexov's "U znakomyx." The protagonist of Čapek's story loves his two sisters and is willing to sacrifice himself to help them. But their hypocrisy, envy and lies become unendurable for him. Therefore he turns his back on them. The situation is not as acute in Čexov's story. Miša Podgorin is invited to visit with friends. Upon his arrival, the protagonist is exposed to demands made so obvious that he cannot bear it, and knowing that he will never be able to return to the place he used to love, he leaves prematurely. As in the other "painful tales," the similarity is largely rooted in the atmosphere of the

stories. The strong characters of the type of Čapek's Pelikán or Vojta are
hard to find. There is Nikolaj, the proagonist of "Kryžovnik," for instance,
but in general, Čexov's heroes behave differently. For example, the
situation in "Strax" could have developed along the same lines as in
"Surovec," had Dmitrij Petrovič Silin, the protagonist of the former story,
the strength of Pelikán of the latter. Čapek's hero ignores the possibility
that his wife could give up the comfort he provides for the sake of love, and
he manages to drive her suitor off, although it utterly exhausts his mental
strength. Silin, in the same situation, realizes that his wife does not love
him, and considers his marriage a terror, but at the same time wants it to
be preserved. His wish is granted only by the voluntary compliance of the
suitor who never comes back. The second of Čapek's strong personages
mentioned above is Vojta in "Uražený." His brother, an official, is unjustly
accused of an error and insulted by his superior. This causes a real change
in his life. He refuses to go home, claims that he does not love his wife and
stays the night with his brother Vojta. The brother saves the situation by
talking to the superior. Čexov's hero does not have such a brother. He,
faced with a situation similar to that of Čapek's official, has to leave the
service. That is a theme in "Sosedi," for instance. Vlašič has behaved
decently but, in the eyes of his army superiors, he has made an error. Like
Čapek's official, Vlašič writes a letter to his superiors, and, as there is no
Vojta to stop him, Vlašič resigns his commision.

The only story in Čapek's *Trapné povídky* not yet dscussed is
"Košile." This story tells about a widower who, suspecting his housekeeper
of stealing, searches her closet. When the protagonist confronts the lady
with the evidence of her theft, she takes offense at his invasion of her
privacy. He is powerless when faced with her reaction. This theme was
treated by Čexov in chapters vi and ix of "Rasskaz neizvestnogo čeloveka."
Zinaida Fedorovna Krasnovskaja discovers thievery on the part of her
maid Polja, yet the most she manages is to say "Ona mne protivna, i ja
bojus' ee. Mne tjaželo ee videt'."(VIII, 162) When Polja continues her
pilferage, Zinaida Fedorovna tries to dismiss her, but she is as powerless
as Čapek's protagonist. The maid retorts: "Posmotrim, kto iz nas pervaja
ujdet! Da!"(VIII, 175)

As already demonstrated, the affinity between the works of Čapek
and Čexov is not limited to the stories collected in *Trapné povídky,* where
it has been noticed by critics the most often. Even Čapek's fairy tales have
a parallel in the Russian writer's *oeuvre.* Thus, in one of his early stories, the

"Vint," Čexov ridicules the bureaucratic hierarchy and its valuation of people solely on the basis of rank. His characters play a game of vint, in which each card is substituted with a photograph of an official, his rank corresponding to the value of the card. In other words, human beings are reduced to the level of professional status. The clerks playing the game "napominali skazočnyx gnomov."(III, 69) Čapek proceeds from this point. In his "Pohádka pošt'ácká,"[46] the gnomes actually play the game. They are post-office sprites and the card game is played with letters. The value scale differs, however, from that in Čexov's story. The rank of the sender is irrelevant. The only recognized value consists in the sentiments expressed in the letter, with indifference ranking the lowest, and sincere love, a letter into which a person puts his whole heart, the highest. Naturally, the implication is the same as that of Čexov's work.

Čexov's parody "Švedskaja spička," which deals with a murder mystery and is full of complications, including misleading clues (a traditional device of the genre at the time) is also echoed in Čapek's story "Smrt barona Gandary," in which the police councillor Pitr, having solved a murder case by his simple methods, says: " . . . když si pomyslím, že by ten případ dostal Mejzlík, co ten be z té látky udělal! Ale já nemám tu fantazii, to je to."[47] A different side of justice is revealed in Čexov's "Vor." The author speaks sympathetically of a condemned criminal's predicament in the story, an unheard-of attitude at the time. Thus, Čexov is forced to defend his stand. In a letter to the editor of *Oskolki*, Nikolaj S. Lejkin, he writes "Upasi bože ot suši, a teploe slovo, skazannoe na Pasxu voru, kotoryj v to že vremja i ssylnyj, ne zarežet nomera."[48] The same problem is encountered by the musician Jevíšek in Čapek's "Hora." The pursuing party encircles a mountain on which a murderer is hiding. Jevíšek is the only person who manages to talk to him, and he finds that the criminal, far from being terrible, is weak and pitiful. This theme recurs in Čapek's "Muž, který se nelíbil." The embezzler Rosner, who has been in hiding for three years, when arrested, admits: "Ale já vám povím, že už bych to byl dýl ani nevydržel. Jezus, vždyt' já jsem si po ty tři roky s nikým od srdce nepromluvil, až tady!"[49] Both authors, Čapek as much as Čexov, seek in every person, even a criminal, his sympathetic features; one only needs to realize the multiplicity of human character. Karel Čapek wrote to that effect in the *feuilleton* "Co je pravda?" He attended a trial and saw witnesses giving testimony regarding the defendant's personal character. To Čapek this is meaningless, as they knew the defendant from one of his life functions only. He says about the

witnesses and their testimony: "Chci tím říci, že nemluvili o různých
chováních, různých projevů jednoho a téhož člověka, nýbrž zcela určitě *o
jednom* jeho chování."[50] Yet, even then, the individual testimonies differed.
Čexov wrote a story on the same topic. In his "Dvoe v odnom"(II, 9-11) a
personage of high station takes a streetcar, something degrading for him, so
he tries to be as inconspicuous as possible. To his amazement, the most
outspoken passenger, loud and self-confident, turns out to be the bashful
clerk from his office. Sometimes a simple change of clothes causes a total
change of character. This is illustrated in Čapek's story "Šaty dělají člověka"
in the collection *Podpovídky*.[51] A policeman in civilian clothes is an entirely
different man; even his voice changes. The life of any individual is composed
of several distinct life functions, accepted by the fellows of this individual
as his life. Even the premise of life being the sum of its functions is not
satisfactory, as there are other potential lives embodied in every life. For
instance, Jakov Ivanov of Čexov's "Skripka Rotšil'da" dreams of these
potential lives while looking at the river: "Ved' reka porjadočnaja, ne
pustjačnaja; na nej možno bylo by zavesti rybnye lovli, a rybu prodavat'
kupcam, činovnikam i bufetčiku na stancii i potom klast' den'gi v bank;
možno bylo by plavat' v lodke ot usad'by k usad'be i igrat' na skripke, i
narod vsjakogo zvanija platil by den'gi; možno bylo by poprobovat' opjat'
gonjat' barki—èto lučše, čem groby delat'; nakonec, možno bylo by razvodit'
gusej, bit' ix i zimoj otpravljat' v Moskvu . . . A esli by vse vmeste—i rybu
lovit', i na skripke igrat', i barki gonjat', i gusej bit', to kakoj polučilsja by
kapital! No ničego ètogo ne bylo daže vo sne."(VIII, 303) Similarly, Mr.
Karas in Čapek's "Sbírka známek" finds that: "Kdyby se člověk hrabal ve
své minulosti, našel by, že v ní je dost látky na docela jiné životy. Jednou .
. . buïd' omylem, nebo z náklonnosti . . . si vybral jenom jeden z nich a dožívá
jej až do konce; ale nejhorší je, že ty druhé, ty možné životy nejsou tak
docela mrtvé."[52] Misail Poloznev, the protagonist of Čexov's "Moja žizn':
rasskaz provinciala," tries to select from these "possible lives," but the
choice is not an easy one. Furthermore, whichever walk of life Misail opts
for, at its end he may turn back and look at his life as critically as the
professor does in "Skučnaja istorija." Čapek's Mr. Karas says that the
choice was made either by mistake or by inclination and agrees with Father
Voves's statement: " . . . co je to platno, ted' už se to nedá napravit, nedá se
začít znova—"[53] The question of the potential lives comes up also in
Čapek's novels (*Povětroň, Obyčejný život*), and with its recurrence one
begins to ask whether man really has a choice. The protagonists in the works

of Čapek and Čexov are so often unable to do what they wish. For instance, in "Rasskaz staršego sadovnika," Čexov does not let his chief magistrate complete his sentence: "Glavnyj sud'ja *xotel skazat'* [italics mine, P.Z.S.]: 'k smertnoj kazni,' no vyronil iz ruk bumagu . . . i zakričal:—Net! . . . on ne vinovat!"(VIII, 346) Also the professor, in "Slučaj iz praktiki," does something other than what he wants to do: "On *xotel skazat'* [italics mine, P.Z.S.] ej, čto u nego v Moskve mnogo raboty, čto doma ego ždet sem'ja; emu bylo tjazelo provesti v čužom dome bez nadobnosti ves' večer i vsju noč', no on pogljadel na ee lico, vzdoxnul i stal molča snimat' perčatki."(X, 78-79) It is no different in the case of Nadja, the protagonist of "Nevesta:" "Ej, Nade, bylo uže 23 goda; s 16 let ona strastno mečtala o zamužestve i teper' nakonec ona byla nevestoj . . . "(X, 202) Yet, later, she says: "Ja ne ljublju ètogo čeloveka,"(X, 212) and does not get married. Čexov's heroes want to say or do one thing, but what they actually say or do is something different. So it is in the works of Karel Čapek, too. Olga, in "Na zámku" decides: "Dám výpověd' na hodinu a odjedu zítra ráno v pět hodin."[54] Naturally, she does not leave at five or at any other time. Karel in "Uražený" asks his brother: "Vyřid' mé ženě, že jsem vystoupil z úřadu,"[55] because he does not want to come back home. At the end of the story, Karel returns to the office, and the brother calls his wife that he, i.e., Karel, will return home. A final example is presented in Čapek's story, "Čintamani a ptáci." The hero, Doctor Vitásek, tells about his discovery of a priceless oriental carpet in a little store: "Tedy já jsem si vzal do hlavy, že musím ten koberec lacino dostat a že jej pak daruju muzeu, protože taková věc jinam nepatří."[56] Naturally, his resolution never materializes. Although this last example does not deal with a choice which would change the entire course of the life of the person concerned, it does say something about the capability or freedom of man to make his own decisions.

The evidence indicates that there are three possible choices in store for Čexovian heroes. They all imply, however, that the protagonists cannot do what they want, unless they select what fate assigns to them. Thus, Olen'ka, the protagonist in "Dušečka," or Očumelov in "Xameleon" can accommodate themselves to the situation, because their wishes change with the conditions. The two other types of heroes in Čexov's works are unhappy Either they do something they do not want to do, like Van'ka, in the story bearing his name, Var'ka in "Spat' xočetsja," and Nastas'ja Kanavkina in "Znakomyj mužčina," or they do what they wish and are discontent with their choice just as much as the former, like Katja and Nikolaj Stepanovič in "Skučnaja istorija: Iz zapisok starogo čeloveka," Misail in "Moja žizn'," or Zinaida Fedorovna in "Rasskaz neizvestnogo čeloveka." A detailed analysis of the behaviour of the protagonists necessarily requires a discussion of such issues as freedom, justice, truth, and lack of communication, and these will be discussed in the next chapter. It is in these topics that one can meaningfully seek the affinity between the two writers.

Notes

1. R. Wellek, "Karel Čapek," *Slavonic and East European Review*, 15 (1936), 195.

2. The transliteration of Russian words, names, and titles follows Professor Shaw's "System III" (J.T. Shaw, The transliteration of Modern Russian for English-Language Publications. If, however, the transliteration given in the quotation differs from this table, this dissertation retains the spelling of the former.

3. "Karel Čapek: Short Tales and Fantasias," in Essays and Addresses (London: E. Arnold, 1939), p. 153; cf. Elton, "Karel Čapek's Stories," *Life and Letters Today*, 21, No. 2 (1939), 35.

4. O. Elton, "Karel Čapek: Later Novels," in Essays, p. 189.

5. W. Harkins, Karel Čapek (New York and London: Columbia Univ. Press, 1962), p. 62.

6. Ibid., p. 69, and cf. p. 70.

7. T.G. Winner, "Speech Characteristics in Čexov's Ivanov and Čapek's Loupežník," in *American Contributions to the Fifth International Congress of Slavists, Sofia* The Hague: Mouton, 1963), II, 403-31. Professor Winner expressed his support for this project in a personal letter dated August 11, 1977. At the time, he was not aware of any work on the topic beyond his own.

8. Ibid., p. 403.

9. A. Matuška, Karel Čapek: An Essay, trans. C. Alan (London: George Allen & Unwin Ltd., 1964), p. 105.

10. O. Malevič, "Karel Čapek i Rossija," Voprosy literatury, 9, No. 7 (1965), 86.

11. Ibid., p, 90.

12. Ibid., p. 91.

13. Ibid., p. 96.

14. K. Čapek, "Žije český autor nesprávně?" *Lidové noviny,* 15 Oct. 1933, p. 9; rpt. in *Poznámky o tvorbě,* ed. M. Halík (Praha: Čs. spisovatel, 1960), p. 29.

15. Malevič, "Karel," pp. 90-91; unfortunately, these articles have not been reprinted, and the Czechoslovak authorities, in a letter I received dated June 21, 1978, denied any possibility of assistence.

16. _____, "Úloha literární tradice v knize Boží muka," Česká literatura, 15, No. 2 (1967), 142.

17. S.V. Nikol'skij, Karel Čapek-fantast i satirik (Moskva: Nauka, 1973), p. 188.

18. Nikol'skij., p. 232. The reference is to Čexov's famous statement "Esli vy govorite v pervoj glave, čto na stene visit ruž'e, vo vtoroj ili tret'ej glave ono dolžno vystrelit'." Cf. S.N. Ščukin, "Iz vospominanij ob A.P. Čexove," in A.P. Čexov v vospominanijax sovremennikov, ed. S.N. Golubov et al. (Moskva: GIXL, 1960), p. 461.

19. J. Mukařovský, "Úvod," in Výbor z prózy Karla Čapka, ed. J. Mukařovský (1934; rpt. Praha: Státní nakl., 1946), pp. 12-13.

20. Ibid., p. 12.

21. K. Čapek, "Musím dále," Lidové noviny, 18 June 1922, pp. 1-2; rpt. in Poznámky o tvorbě, ed. M. Halík (Praha: Čs. spisovatel, 1960), p. 94.

22 K.D. Kramer, The Chameleon and the Dream (The Hague: Mouton, 1970).

23. T. Winner, Chekhov and his Prose (New York, Chicago, San Francisco: Holt, Rinehart and Winston, 1966), pp. 27-28.

24. N. Rosen, "The Unconscious in Čexov's 'Van'ka' (With a Note on 'Sleepy')," Slavic and East European Journal, 15 (1965), 451.

25. K. Čapek, Boží muka—Trapné povídky (Praha: Mladá fronta, 1967), p. 148.

26. Note, that the cricket "kričit" in the original, rather than chirrs ("treščit," or "strekočet") as it is usually translated. The fact that the cricket emits "the same sound" increases the girl's suffering. Prof. Struve uses "shrills" or both sounds, cf. G. Struve, "On Chekhov's Craftsmanship: The Anatomy of a Story," Slavic Review, 20 (1961), 473-74.

27. A.P. Čexov, Polnoe sobranie sočinenij i pisem v tridcati tomax (Moskva: Nauka, 1976), IV, 331. Hereinafter, all quotations from Čexov's work will be taken from the same edition, and will be incorporated in the text. The volume number will be given in Roman numerals and the page number in Arabic.

28. K. Čapek, Boží, p. 151.

29. Ibid., p. 148.

30. _____, Povídky z jedné kapsy—Povídky z druhé kapsy (Praha: Čs. spisovatel, 1973), p. 163. The Czech writer refers to Čexov twice in his fiction. The other mention is in the feuilleton "Kdy se co čte," Věci kolem nás (Praha: Čs. spisovatel, 1970), p. 145.

31. V.Ja. Lakšin, Tolstoj i Čexov (Moskva: Sov. pisatel', 1975), p. 128.

32. K. Čapek, Povídky, p. 123.

33. Ibid., p. 125.

34. Ibid., p. 126.

35. Ibid., p. 126.

36. B. Stevenson, *The Home Book of Quotations: Classical and Modern* (New York: Dodd, Mead, 1934), p. 710.

37. Beside the above introduced examples, it can be found in Čapek's "Hora," "Obyčejná vražda," or "Ukradený kaktus," and in Čexov's "Ispoved'," "Vor," or "Košmar."

38. Čapek, *Povídky*, pp. 23-28.

39. Ibid., pp. 205-09.

40. L. Grossman "Naturalizm Čexova," in *Sobranie sočinenij v pjati tomax: Mastera slova* (Moskva: N. A. Stolljar, 1928), IV, 199-236.

41. Harkins, p. 62.

42. Wellek, p. 195.

43. J. Kuipers, *Zeitlose Zeit: Die Geschichte der deutschen Kurzgeschichtenforschung* (Groningen: Wolters-Noordhoff, 1970), p. 19.

44. G.V. Ivanov, "Čexov i Mopassan," *Russkaja literatura*, No. 1 (1977), 175-77.

45. O. Elton, "Karel Čapek: Short Tales and Fantasias," in *Essays and Addresses* (London: E. Arnold & Co., 1939), p. 158.

46. Čapek, *Devatero pohádek* (Praha: Dilia, 1972), pp. 201-28.

47. _____, *Povídky*, p. 213. Thus far, only actual parallels in Čapek's and Čexov's works have been discussed. Some notes in the Russian writer's "Zapisnye knižki" have, however, their equivalents in Čapek's *oeuvre*. For instance, the idea "Smert' strašna, no ešče strašnee bylo by soznanie, čto budeš' žit' večno . . . "(XVII, 67) is developed in *Věc Makropulos*, and Čexov's note regarding an unprovable murder(XVII, 110) is the motif of "Zmizení herce Bendy."

48. Letter to N.S. Lejkin, dated "later than April 17, 1883," No. 40 (XIX, *Pis'ma*, I, 67).

49. Čapek, *Povídky*, p. 62.

50. _____, "Co je pravda?" *Místo pro Jonathana* (1922; rpt. Praha: Symposium, 1970), p. 79.

51. _____, *Bajky a podpovídky* (Praha: Čs. spisovatel, 1970), pp. 211-13.

52. _____, *Povídky*, p. 264.

53. Ibid., p. 268.

54. Čapek, *Boží*, p. 152.

55. Ibid., p. 208.

56. _____, *Povídky*, p. 175.

꘎

CHAPTER II

FREEDOM, LACK OF COMMUNICATION, JUSTICE, AND TRUTH

The parallels between the works of Čapek and Čexov discussed in the previous chapter, although numerous, might be attributed to the fact that the Russian author wrote such a quantity of stories that there is bound to be a number of similarities with the works of other writers, if the workings of mere chance were not precluded by the obvious affinity in the choice and treatment of major issues such as freedom, lack of communication, justice, and truth.

Freedom

The question or theme of freedom in the works of the two writers calls for a more detailed discussion of the ability of their protagonists to decide on the course of action they will take. One of the earliest examples of the treatment of this theme in Čapek's work is the story "Povídka poučná," written in collaboration with his brother Josef as early as 1908. It is divided into three parts, each of them headed with the same motto, signed "O. Wilde:" "Jaká škoda, že svou lekci od života dostáváme teprve tenkráte, když ji už nemůžeme potřebovat,"[1] and each part of the story reflects this sentiment. Henri Louis Jacquet Droz, the main character in the "Povídka poučná," cannot change anything in the choice he has made. His path of life is closed. Neither can Čapek's other heroes act upon their discovery of the potential lives concealed in their actual life.

The protagonists of *Obyčejný život* (1934) and "Sbírka známek" (1929), for instance, realize only in retrospect the possibility of choice they once had. This is no accident; they never really had a choice. A key to the problem is revealed in the discourse of the hero of *Obyčejný život*. He describes a number of his potential lives, but is aware of the continuity of actual life. The meaning of the continuity is implied in *Boží muka,* written between 1913 and 1917. Karel Čapek explained the title of this collection of stories as being purposely ambiguous: "Název *Božích muk* je dvojsmyslný, i znamená jednak rozcestí, jednak sebetrýzeň těmi vyššími věcmi a tím hledáním."[2] The word *rozcestí* (crossroads) again indicates the possibility of choice. It is not, however, left to man to make it. One of the stories, "Lída," can serve as an illustration of man's prospects. The heroine of the story disappears and the author offers three possible ways of finding her. Lída's mother relies on Divine Providence; her brother believes in chance and intuition; and a friend of the family, Holub, deduces that she has run off with a lover. Her actions are typical and statistically predictable. Holub explains his reasoning to Lída's brother in the following manner:

> Martinče, s důvody nelze počítat, je jich možno množství bez konce; ale skutků je daleko méně a proto jejich logika je jednodušší. Je nekonečný počet motivů, kterých se můžeme u Lídy domyslet, ale skutků, které mohla udělat, nebo které se s ní mohly stát, je výběr omezený. Jednáním se vlastně končí každá neomezenost. Činy nejsou už tak osobní jako pohnutky k nim; je v nich uniformnost, opakování a pravidelnost, která nezávisí na našich pohnutkách a která se vůbec vymyká našemu přání a motivování. Skutky jsou fatální.[3]

Oleg Malevič has noted this phenomenon. In his analysis of the story, the Russian scholar says that "Pisatel' ubežden, čto po svoej suščnosti čelovek dobr. V mire že carit zlo. Sledovatel'no ljud'mi rukovodit kakaja-to vnešnjaja, ne zavisjaščaja ot nix sila."[4] Holub's hypothesis proves to be right. Malevič also comments on this fact: "Lída okazalas' 'vešč'ju,' passivnoj igruškoj 'železnoj slučajnosti,' a ne svobodnym v svoem povedenii čelovekom."[5] According to Malevič, it is the "iron rule of chance" which governs Lída's behaviour.

Unfortunately, this explanation leaves us in the dark with regard to that continuity of life discussed by the protagonist of *Obyčejný život*. Indeed, he is not the only character in Čapek's writings to refer to it. For example, the hero in "Ztracená cesta," another story in *Boží muka*, tries to explain to his friend how he found an answer to his quest: "Něco, co jsem hledal po celý život, i když jsem na to nemyslil. Ó Bože, je to strašně složité! Tím se mění můj celý život —Všechno souvisí."[6] The consequences of this discovery are shattering:

> Za prvé z toho plyne, jak bědné a nesmyslné bylo všechno, co
> jsem dosud žil. Rázem mne to proniklo jako nůž, zděsil jsem
> se sama sebe a pochopil jsem, že tolik let, ó Bože, jsem žil jen
> nevýslovnou a netušenou bolest. Tolik let! To tedy mi vysvitlo,
> co jsem byl, a jak jsem nevěda trpěl; a všechno bylo marné a
> mylné, a úzké jako vězení; a mně bylo strašně, když celý můj
> život se mi vytratil jako nalezená chyba.[7]

Čapek's protagonist sees his life as a prison, and this is not the only instance of such a sentiment. Oldřich Králík quotes the above excerpt from "Ztracená cesta," and he also stresses the comparison of life and prison: "Co vytýká tato Čapkova kritika životu? Prostě to, že je to vězení, pustý mechanismus, tupé cihly dní."[8] He goes on to claim that there are numerous variations on this theme in *Boží muka*.[9] For example, he cites from the same story:

> Kdo jde po cestě, tomu je svět napravo i nalevo kulisou bez
> významu a stěnami dlouhé chodby ... tvé přemýšlení je jenom
> cesta jedním směrem jako chodba mezi stěnami. Tvé myšlení
> jde jenom kupředu po některé z mnoha cest ... tvá logika je
> utkána ze zvyků a tvé cesty z tisícerých minulých kroků ...[10]

Another of Králík's examples of the development of this motif is a rather extensive quotation taken from "Pomoc!" As it describes the monotony of the days which slowly build up the walls of the protagonist's prison, it is cited in its entirety:

Nic se už nezmění; co také měnit? Události prchají a léta
ubíhají; ale den po dni se vrací, jako by se vůbec nic nedálo.
Uplynul den: co na tom? Vzdyt' stejný den, týž den přijde mi
zítra jen když zas uplyne!
A denně si mohu říci: Neztratil jsem nic než den. Nic víc než
den! Proč tedy ta úzkost? Brož si tvrdě mnul čelo. Abych se
probral. Jsem nevyspalý. Zastavil jsem se, a dny narostly
kolem mne jako zdi; den po dni se hladce a těžce nakladly jako
stěny. Už záhy se probudím: ale bude to nový den a nebývalý,
jejž naleznu dokola? Nebo den složený z tisíců minulych—
jako stěny? A řeknu si opět: tož to je zas další den mezi tisíci
narovnanymi—jako stěny? Proč přibyl? vzdyt' bylo včera jen
o jeden den méně! Stálo to za to, vzbudit se pro ten jediný den?
Veškerá ospalost se od něho rázem oddělila. Vždyt' je to
vězení, pochopil zděšen; tolik let žil jsem jako ve vězení!
široce utkvěl očima; bylo mu, jako by se všechna ta léta
smutně rozsvětlila: divně cizí, divněji známá; vše, nic, dny
bezpočtu . . .[11]

Life is like a prison. Everyday is determined by the previous day, and
one can only go forward. The flow of life is like a river; there are banks
which limit the stream and unless a miracle happens, it will follow its
course; it cannot go back, stop or turn. Such an image is employed in the
story "Odrazy." Even the possibility of a miracle is considered by the invalid
watching the surface of the river. He relates his observations to a chance
acquaintance:

"Chvílemi," pokračoval chorý, "viděl jsem tak podivné zčeření
na vodě, že nelze pochopit, odkud přichází. Někdy se zlomí
vlna a zaleskne se krásněji než jiné; a jsou i úkazy na nebi—
Stává se to velice zřídka. A tu si myslím: proč by to nemohl být
bůh? Snad je právě tím nejprchavějším na světě; snad i jeho
skutečnost je náhlé zlomení vlny a záblesk; nepochopitelně,
výjimečně se vyskytne, a zajde—Často jsem o tom přemýšlel;
ale hled'te, mám tak malý obzor, po léta jsem nedošel dále než
sem. Je možno, že i mezi lidmi se přihodí takové zčeření nebo
záblesk, a zase se zlomí. Musí se zlomit. Pravá skutečnost se
musí zaplatit zánikem."[12]

The citation is rather lengthy, but it is necessary in order to comprehend the invalid's idea of God and of the fact that true reality must be paid for with doom. The latter thought is embodied in many of Čapek's heroes. They live the life to which they have been condemned by circumstances. It is too late for them to change anything when they become aware of this fact. There may be salvation in God, who, according to the above quotation, is very volatile. Perhaps it is better to speak of divine moments, and this idea is also developed in the story "Elegie: Šlépěj II." Two of the protagonists discuss the disappearance of the third one, and the only explanation for the phenomenon they can come up with is a miracle. Then the problem of the purpose of such a wonder arises:

> "I kdyby to k ničemu a pro nic nebylo přec je to div—I v nás jsou takové události a případy, jež snad nemají cíle ... než vlastní svou dokonalost. Náhlé okamžiky svobody—I když jsou to jen okamžiky! Kdyby se věci děly tak, jak je přirozeno naší duši, dály by se zázraky."[13]

Králík, in his analysis of *Boží muka,* brings the last two stories together. He describes the "Elegie" in terms of the "Odrazy:" "Existuje jen vlna pozemského života, spějící k zániku, a zázrak, odsouzený víc než co jiného k okamžitému zániku, k nepokračování, je výjimečným." [14] The broken waves, the divine moments, or the miracles—for they are identical concepts—are synonyms for the freedom which cannot, however, be achieved through normal means. This is well illustrated by the story "Zázrak na hřišti" in the collection *Podpovídky*. The hero prays for his team, and through the miracles which follow, the team is victorious. The praying boy is noticed and a member of the rival team explains to him the rules of the game. The boy still prays, but now for help "within the rules," and no miracles happen. As Čapek concludes the story: " . . . jakmile platí pravidla, nedají se dělat žádné zázraky."[15] This is also exemplified in "Muž, který dovedl lítat." Tomšík, the hero of the story, discovers in himself the ability to fly. Since he does not keep it a secret, he is invited to appear before a committee of experts. It comes out that Tomšík does not start or take off properly. The experts explain to him how it is properly done, with the result that he is unable to fly again.[16] Miracles and rules mutually exclude each other. Freedom cannot be regulated. The same idea comes out in Malevič's description of the story "Hora:" "Čapeka vskryvaet konflikt ličnosti i obščestva, individual'noj svobody i podavljajuščix ètu svobodu organizacii, zakona, gosudarstva s ego apparatom nasilija (policija, armija)."[17] The Russian scholar interprets the basic clash of freedom and organization differently, but he clearly demonstrates that he too is aware of this conflict. Further on in his analysis Malevič speaks of the solution to the problem presented in the story as unveiled by one of the characters:

> Vmesto zagadočnogo zlodeja on naxodit bol'nogo, odinokogo čeloveka, moljaščego o spasenii. Presleduemyj otvergaet protjanutuju emu ruku pomošči i pogibaet. No u presledovatelej ne ostaetsja inogo čuvstva, krome oščuščenija viny pered nim. I presleduemyj i presledovateli ediny v svoem proteste protiv posjagatel'stv na ix vnutrennjuju svobodu, protiv toj čuždoj čeloveku sily, instrumentom kotoroj vol'no ili nevol'no oni stali.[18]

This force prevents most of Čapek's protagonists from ever exercising their freedom of choice. These characters can be compared with those of Čexov, who do something different from what they wish to do.

Čapek's protagonists too can be divided into three groups. There is the above-discussed group of characters who are committed by some not precisely determined force to live, or at least to act, in a manner contradictory to their wishes. Naturally, the representatives of this group are not happy. The remaining two groups, like those of Čexov, are made up of people who act according to their decisions. Some of them do not find happiness as a result of their choice, others do. The protagonists of the former type find their direct counterpart in Čexov's works, for instance the "Muž, který se nelíbil," the hero of "Ušní zpověd'," or the officer in "Tribunál." The characters who avoid discomfort by indulging in an activity which they themselves have chosen differ from those of Čexov in that the latter's protagonists allow circumstances to dictate their choice, i.e. the result in a way precedes the selection. Očumelov in "Xameleon" and Olen'ka in "Dušečka" are such characters. Čapek's protagonists do not find peace of mind in such an accommodated choice, unless they disregard the limitations imposed upon them. In order to do that they must be insane (for instance Klára in "Modrá chryzantéma") or fanatics (such as the cactus collector in "Ukradený kaktus").

Čexov's heroes of the first type, those who act against their wishes, are many. Again, there is some compelling force which makes them act in a certain manner, although they are later surprised or sorry. The "Xoristka," for instance, acts on impulse when she gives away her jewels, and she is sorry about it soon afterwards: "Paša legla i stala gromko plakat'. Ej uže bylo žal' svoix veščej, kotorye ona sgorjača otdala, i bylo obydno. Ona vspomnila, kak tri goda nazad ee ni za čto, ni pro čto pobil odin kupec, i ešče gromče zaplakala."(V, 215) The reaction of Kunin in "Košmar," when he realizes his mistake, is different, but he too regrets what he has done on the spur of the moment: "Tut vdrug Kunin vspomnil donos, kotoryj napisal on arxiereju, i ego vsego skorčilo, kak ot nevznačaj naletevšego xoloda. Èto vospominanie napolnilo vsju ego dušu čuvstvom gnetuščego styda pered samim soboj i pered nevidimoj pravdoj..."(V, 73)

The protagonists of the above two stories regret a single action of the past. There are characters in Čexov's work, however, who regret their entire way of life. The turner in "Gore" recollects his past life and dreams of a possibility to start all over again: "'Žit' by syznova' . . .—dumaet tokar'. Vspominaet on, čto Matrena let sorok tomu nazad byla molodoj, krasivoj, iz bogatogo dvora. Vydali ee za nego zamuž . . . Vse dannye byli dlja xorošego žit'ja, no beda v tom, čto on kak napilsja posle svad'by . . . i do six por ne prosypalsja. Svad'bu on pomnit, a čto bylo posle svad'by—xot' ubej, ničego ne pomnit, krome razve togo, čto pil, ležal, dralsja. Tak i propali sorok let."(IV, 233)

There were all the makings of a good life, yet it turned out differently. The hero, Grigorij Petrov, is discontented with his life, without understanding why it has taken such a bad turn. His life has been afflicted by the same undetermined force that made Kunin in the above quotation write his letter, or the "Xoristka" give up her jewels. Jakov's memories and regrets in "Skripka Rotšil'da" parallel those of Grigorij Petrov in "Gore," but there are also direct examples of the activity of this power. One is found in "U znakomyx:" "Podgorin xotel skazat', čto on sam stesnen v den'gax, i podumal, čto lučše èti dvesti rublej otdat' kakomu-nibud' bednjaku ili prosto daže proigrat' v karty, no strašno skonfuzilsja i, čuvstvuja sebja . . . kak v lovuške, . . . stal bystro iskat' v karmanax svoju zapisnuju knižku, gde byli den'gi.—Vot . . ."(X, 19) Other examples of involuntary action include the "Niščij," who was asked to chop some wood: "Po ego poxode vidno bylo, čto soglasilsja on idti kolot' drova ne potomu, čto byl goloden i xotel zarabotat' a prosto iz samoljubija i styda, kak pojmannyj na slove."(VI, 26)

He does not in the end chop the wood, although initially he went against his will to do so. This character had been taken at his word. But the words are also said against the speaker's wishes. For instance, the chief magistrate in "Rasskaz staršego sadovnika" wanted to deliver the death sentence, but pronounced the murderer free instead.(VIII, 346)

Čexov does not speak of prisons. There are no walls limiting his protagonists, at least not apparent ones, but they feel the restrictions imposed upon their lives as much as Čapek's heroes. Vera in "V rodnom uglu" experiences this type of confinement and searches for a way out. "Ona moloda, izjaščna, ljubit žizn'; ona končila v institute, vyučilas' govorit' na trex jazykax, mnogo čitala, putešestvovala s otcom,—neuželi vse èto tol'ko dlja togo, čtoby v konce koncov poselit'sja v gluxoj stepnoj usad'be i izo dnja v den', ot nečego delat', xodit' iz sada v pole, iz polja v sad i potom sidet' doma i slušat' kak dyšit deduška? No čto, že delat'? Kuda devat'sja?"(IX, 316) There is a great potentiality in Vera, but it will never be realized. She feels trapped and has nowhere to go. When her aunt dismisses a worker because he was illegitimate, Vera is upset, but does not act accordingly: "V grudi u Very kamnem povernulos' tjaželoe, zloe čuvstvo. Ona negodovala, nenavidela tetju; tetja nadoela ej do toski, do otraščenija . . . No čto delat'? Oborvat' ee na slove? Nagrubit' ej? No kakaja pol'za? Položim, borot'sja s nej, ustranit' ee, sdelat' bezvrednoj . . ."(IX, 322.) She contrives various measures to be taken, but none is executed. Moreover, after some time, Vera discovers, within herself, the same cruel tendencies towards the servants that she criticizes in her aunt and grandfather. In order to avoid the impasse into which she feels drawn, she decides to marry a man she does not love. This should solve her problem: " . . . ona rešila, čto vyjdja zamuž, ona budet zanimat'sja xozjajstvom, lečit', učit', budet delat' vse, čto delajut drugie ženščiny ee kruga, a čto postojannoe nedovol'stvoi soboj, i ljud'mi, ètot rjad grubix ošibok, kotorye goroj vyrastajut pered toboju, edva ogljaneš'sja na svoe prošloe, ona budet sčitat' svoeju nastojaščeju žizn'ju, kotoraja suždena ej, i ne budet ždat' lučšej..."(IX, 324) There is nothing Vera can expect from the *life fated to her*. She has no choice but to accept that which is predetermined. It is only in retrospect, when nothing can be altered, that Čexov's heroine is able to see the choice she once had. Ol'ga Ivanovna in "Poprygun'ja," for instance, does not realize her mistake until her husband dies. At this time, it is too late to change her life: "Ona xotela ob"jasnit' emu, čto to byla ošibka, čto ne vse ešče poterjano, čto žizn' ešče možet byt' prekrasnoj i sčastlivoj, čto on redkij, neobyknovennyj, velikij čelovek i čto ona budet vsju žizn' blagogovet' pered nim, molit'sja i ispytyvat' svjaščennyj strax..."(VIII, 31)

These examples illustrate that the protagonists of the Russian author are as limited in their freedom as those of the Czech. Čapek's characters, if they wish to enjoy freedom, have to be either insane or fanatics. For Čexov's heroes, there are also two possibilities: firstly, they choose that which is allotted to them by fate and accept the outcome; secondly, they may abandon all claims on life. The old Semen in "V ssylke" is an example of the latter. He is content with his life because, as he says: " . . . teper' ja dovel sebja do takoj točki, čto mogu golyj na zemle spat' i travu žrat'. I daj bog vsjakomu takoj žizni. Ničego mne ne nado i nikogo ne bojus', i tak sebja ponimaju, čto bogače i volnee menja čeloveka net."(VIII, 43) Not every man would accept freedom and happiness at such a price. Thus, the Tatar to whom Semen explains his idea of freedom rejects it for the hope of a fuller life.

The other way to avoid anxiety is for the characters to "select" that which is destined to happen. This can lead to frequent changes in outlook, but on the other hand it does bring satisfaction with life. This approach to life is found in Očumelov in "Xameleon" and Olen'ka in "Dušečka." Police inspector Očumelov, informed that a dog has bitten a man, decides that the dog must be destroyed and its owner punished. When told that the dog belongs to a general, Očumelov finds a reason to accuse the victim instead. The Inspector reverses his opinion in this fashion three times. In the first instance after learning that it is the General's dog, in the second instance, when the General's ownership is refuted, and finally, when he is told that it belongs to the General's brother. One might disregard the story as an example of a necessary tribute to a higher rank, if it were not for the other story, "Dušečka." Although in this case there is no difference in rank, the heroine, Olen'ka, also tends to have rather transient opinions. This is manifested in her frequent changes of spheres of interest. She married Ivan Kukin, who was in the entertainment business because "Ona postojanno ljubila kogo-nibud' i ne mogla bez ètogo . . . I ona uže govorila svoim znakomym, čto samoe zamečatel'noe, samoe važnoe, i nužnoe na svete—èto teatr . . . I čto govoril o teatre i ob akterax Kukin, to povtorjala ona."(X, 104) Her husband died prematurely, however, and after three months of mourning, Ol'ga Semenovna met Vasilij Pustovalov, manager of a timber-yard. She married him soon afterwards. Olen'ka's interests were transferred to a new sphere. "Ej kazalos', čto ona torguet lesom uže davno—davno, čto v žizni samoe važnoe i nužnoe èto les . . . Kakie mysli byli u muža, takie i u nee."(X, 106) Unfortunately, after six years Ol'ga was widowed again. Approximately six months later she met a veterinarian, Vladimir Smirnin, and was heard to say: "U nas v gorode net pravil'nogo veterinarnogo nadzora i ot ètoto mnogo boleznej. To i delo slyšiš', ljudi zabolevajut ot moloka i zaražajutsja ot lošadej i korov. O zdorov'e domašnyx životnyx v suščnosti nado zabotit'sja tak že, kak o zdorov'e ljudej. Ona povtorjala mysli veterinara i teper' byla obo vsem takogo že mnenija, kak on."(X, 108) When the veterinarian left with his regiment, Olen'ka had no views on anything and she maintained this amorphous personality until his return, when she transferred all her love to his son Saša. With a new centre of attention Ol'ga again develops opinions. "I ona uže imela svoi mnenija i za užinom govorila s roditeljami Saši o tom, kak teper' detjam trudno učit'sja v gimnazijax, no čto vse-taki klassičeskoe obrazovanie lučše real'nogo, tak kak iz gimnazii vsjudu otkryta doroga: xočeš'—idi v doktora, xočeš'—v inženery."(X, 111-12) The above record of Olen'ka's views might seem rather too detailed, but it will be needed for later reference. Ol'ga Semenovna had the freedom to make decisions, but she accepted the opinions of those she loved. Similarly, Očumelov adapted his decisions to what he expected to be the views of his superiors. Neither of them did anything in which he did not believe. Their statements were always sincere. Therefore, both of them could be content.

Čapek reflects on such ideas in his story "O fantazii." [19] His protagonist, a cobbler, explicates the concept of imagination, and in the process, speaks about the potential lives of all people. We live only one of them, but all the other lives are lived by people around us. We imagine ourselves living the lives we like. This is not enough, however. According to the cobbler, other people live our lives—our potential lives—for us. We should look at their lives as if they were our own. "Dušečka" does not do anything else. There are, however, no characters of the type of Olen'ka in Čapek's *oeuvre*. Ráček in "Ukradený kaktus"[20] is contented because he is such a fanatical cactus collector. He is so obsessed with his cacti that no rules exist for him. Ráček lives an ascetic life, steals cacti and is ready to go to jail rather than return them, he makes up new cacti in his dreams, even dies stuck to a cactus, completely happy. He has chosen such a life and is free because he does not recognize limitations such as the law. To be capable of disregarding the restrictions imposed on the individual's life, one must be either a fanatic like Ráček or insane. An example of the latter possibility is Klára in "Modrá chryzantéma." She is always happy. Čapek describes her mood as joyful: "Klára radostně zabučela . . . nadšeně kdákala a řehtala se . . ." [21] The reason she was always in a pleasant state of mind is very simple. As an idiot, she did not have any restraints, she was free. Her superiority in this regard to the people around her is made clear by the fact that Klára achieves something the others cannot; she does so because of her total lack of concern for regulations. Klára is the only person who can find a chrysanthemum of a new colour, for it grows at a location to which entry is forbidden. The idea of her "superiority" is strengthened still further by the fact that when by chance the narrator of the story discovers the plants, they will never bloom again. Čapek and Čexov differ in the presentation of the characteristics of this type of protagonist who is capable of choosing his objectives and of attaining satisfaction, but the type is clearly present in the works of both authors.

The last category of characters classified according to their freedom consists of the heroes who excercise their freedom of choice, but who do not find happiness. They are very conscious of this liberty, as exemplified, for instance, when Zinaida Fedorovna in "Rasskaz neizvestnogo čeloveka" expresses her appreciation of freedom directly: "Net vyše blaga, kak svoboda!"(VIII, 154) With this credo she leaves her husband to go and live with her lover. Zinaida Fedorovna feels the fact that she exercises her freedom lifts her above the common people who are not free. Unfortunately she does not find such superiority in her lover. She tells him that he is afraid of freedom: "Vy boites' svobody i nasmexaetes' nad čestnym poryvom iz straxa, čtoby kakoj-nibud' nevežda ne zapodozril, čto vy čestnyj čelovek."(VIII, 179) At this moment, the heroine identifies freedom and honesty. She is disappointed in her lover, and realizes her mistake before he defines this concept for her: "Svobodno sledovat' vlečenijam svoego serdca—èto ne vsegda daet xorošim ljudjam sčast'e. Čtoby čuvstovat' sebja svobodnym i v to že vremja sčastlivym, mne kažetsja, nado ne skryvat' ot sebja, čto žizn' žestoka, gruba i bespoščadna v svoem konzervatizme, i nado otvečat' ej tem, čego ona stoit, to est' byt' tak že, kak ona, grubym i bespoščadnym v svoix stremlenijax k svobode."(VIII, 185-86) This is easy for Orlov to say, but there is no one with whom Zinaida can be harsh and pitiless. She is powerless and unhappy in her "freedom."

Perhaps she wanted too much when she asked for Orlov's love, since, as Semen in "V ssylke" says, one is really free only when he gives up any claim on life. This sentiment is echoed in Maša's letter to Misail in "Moja žizn': Rasskaz provinciala:" "Vse proxodit, projdet i žizn', značit, ničego ne nužno. Ili nužno odno liš' soznanie svobody, potomu čto kogda čelovek svoboden, to emu ničego, ničego, ničego ne nužno."(IX, 272) This statement has its irony, since Maša is supported by her father, who will satisfy all her demands as long as she obeys him. Misail is not happy. At the end of the story he has occasional conversations with a friend, in which they discuss the sadness of life.(IX, 280) Another example of people who freely follow their inclinations is the character Katja in "Skučnaja istorija." Thomas Winner, in his analysis of the story, speaks of her as the ideal of freedom for the old scientist: "The professor is constantly drawn to Katya. In Katya, the artist, he sees an escape from the constrictions of his own life, something free, unconventional, natural, and beautiful." [22] The professor is unhappy because of the restrictions imposed on him, but Katja is not happier with her freedom. She would gladly relinquish it in exchange for happiness.

Some of Čapek's characters share this sentiment. The officer in "Tribunál," for instance, would be delighted if he were relieved of the necessity of decision. Pelikán in "Surovec" always enforces his will but it does not make him happy. The discontent of the criminals in "Ušní zpověd'," "Závrat'" and other stories may be attributed to their remorse, but they too belong to the protagonists who follow their inclinations without finding happiness. The importance of this type of hero for Čapek is illustrated by the fact that they became the protagonists of his novels. *Hordubal* is such a hero, and up to a point so is Prokop in *Krakatit*. The best example is found, however, in *Povětroň.*

An unknown man has been fatally injured in an airplane crash. He cannot be questioned or identified. All that is known about the stranger is his medical record, the facts about the accident and the coins from various countries in his pockets. There are three persons present in the hospital whom the mystery surrounding the patient compels to attempt a reconstruction of his life. The first, a nun who watches by his bedside, dreams of him on successive nights. According to her, the stranger did not remember his mother, and the relation between him and his father had never been good. "Ba, po pravdě řečeno, leželo mezi námi tiché a nesmiřitelné nepřátelství. Můj otec byl totiž nadmíru řádný muž; zastával důležité místo ve svém působišti a pokládal svůj život za vyplněný tím, že v každém ohledu konal svou povinnost.[23]

The background of Čapek's protagonist is remarkably similar to that of Misail in "Moja žizn'," and the similarity is strengthened as the nun continues: "Se mnou nemluvil jinak než napomínaje a dávaje sebe za příklad; nejspíš považoval lidský život za něco předem hotového . . . Náramně si vážil sebe sama, svých zásad i svých zásluh; jeho život zdál se mu hoden toho, aby se v něm pokračovalo jako v odkazu."[24] Similarly to Misail, he revolts against the father and leaves home. Then he meets a girl, the daughter of an engineer, and decides that she must be his. The parallelism with "Moja žizn'" ends here, since as soon as the girl submits to his advances, the hero begins his escape from responsibility, which he fears as a threat to his freedom. After a life of hard labour, which takes him all over the world but does not bring him the peace of soul he seeks, the hero identifies the abandoned girl with happiness, and crashes on the way back. The price of his freedom was paid by the absence of happiness in his life. The second narrator, also a patient in the hospital, is clairvoyant and uses his gift to form his version of the stranger's story. It is interesting to note that the account of the patient's youth is identical with that given by the nun. No conflict with a girl, however, occures in his rendition. The hero becomes a chemist and makes a discovery which is not accepted by an authority. As a result, the young man discards his past and leaves on a voyage reminiscent of the escape in the first version. Eventually he gets hold of a journal in which a part of his discovery is published. The desire to defend his priority is the cause for his sudden return, but before it can be satisfied, the plane crashes. The last narrator is a poet. In his version the hero, again motherless, leaves home only to spite his father. Their conflict, caused by the same protest against the father's idea of life as in the other two versions, results in the son's leaving home. The story is complicated by the hero's amnesia. His speedy return is motivated by the hope of reconciliation with the father, of regaining his position in society and of the possible resulting happiness. This hope is destroyed by the accident. There are three different perspectives, and all of them meet in the same assumption that the stranger did not know his mother and that he rebelled against his father. The reason for the rebellion is always the same: the son refuses to follow in his father's footsteps which lead to acquiring wealth and a high position in society. The hero preserves his independence or freedom, but does not find happiness. The stories diverge widely in detail, but there is a common theme, which is strongly reminiscent of the story of Misail in Čexov's "Moja žizn'."

The theme of freedom, i.e. the personal freedom of every individual, is one of the major themes in the writings of Anton Pavlovič Čexov as well as in those of Karel Čapek. Moreover, in both cases the protagonists, who are conscious of this freedom, can be divided into three groups based on the manner in which they use it. Some of them make their decisions and are unhappy as a result; others, also discontented, are unable to behave according to their choice; and only the members of the smallest group find happiness when they exercise their freedom. The unhappiness of the majority of characters in the works of the two writers must be shared.

Lack of Communication

The worst misery is that which one has to keep to oneself. This is a problem for many of the protagonists in Čexov's stories. The lack of communication among the people is another of the major themes in the work of the Russian author. As Thomas Winner writes: "The theme of individual isolation is suggested in many of Chekhov's early stories, including the children's stories and 'The Lady of the Manor' [Barynja, 1882], but it is first fully developed in the brief sketch 'Misery' (Toska, 1886), the tale of the cab driver, Iona Potapov, whose son has just died and who has no one to tell of his sorrow." Although Winner speaks of the theme of individual isolation only in terms of Čexov's early stories, it is not so limited as this perspective would imply. As a matter of fact, Winner's example, "Toska," is one of the stories which, according to Sergej Mitrofanovič Petrov's *Istorija russkoj literatury XIX veka* marks the beginning of a new period in Čexov's creative work. The same idea is expressed by Prince Mirsky: "In 1886 . . . Chekhov was able to free himself from the comic papers and would now develop a new style . . . "Moreover, this scholar lists "the principal stories" written by the Russian author after 1889 with the conclusion that "No writer excels him in conveying the mutual unsurpassable isolation of human beings and the impossibility of understanding each other. This idea forms the core of almost every one of his stories . . . "The example Mirsky singles out is "Skučnaja istorija," where "The leitmotiv [sic] of mutual isolation is brought out with great power."[29] Mirsky's claim that the unapproachable isolation of men is an essential part of almost all Čexov's writings is supported by the observations of Arnold Hauser. This Hungarian scholar calls Čexov the purest representative of impressionism[30] and his conclusion is based largely on the fact that

> . . . die Weltanshauung Tschechows dreht sich um das für den Impressionismus charakteristische Erlebnis der

Beziehungslosigkeit der Menschen zueinander, ihrer Unfähigkeit, die letzte Distanz, die sie voneinander trennt, zu überbrücken, oder wenn dies ihnen auch einmal gelingt, in einer distanzlosen Nähe zueinander zu verharren. Es ist das Gefühl der vollkommenen Hilflosigkeit und Hoffnungslosigkeit . . . das die Menschen Tschechows erfüllt.[31]

The question of purity in Čexov's impressionism is not the issue here. What is more important is the prominence of the theme of lack of communication, which Hauser finds in the works of Čexov and the sentiment he observes in the protagonists. It is also remarkable how well this statement can be applied to some works of Karel Čapek, although the Czech writer has never been described as an impressionist.

Isolated characters with the feeling of absolute helplessness and hopelessness are found in every story in Čapek's collection *Trapné povídky* and also, for instance, in the novel *Hordubal*. The significance of the theme in the works of both authors is enhanced by the fact that the works dealing with the lack of communication are among their best. Thus, for instance, the famous Czech critic František Götz praises Čapek for his presentation of the protagonists in *Trapné povídky*: "Je v nich opravdová krev, hmatáte v nich živou hmotu. Se svou bezprostředně vyjadřovanou nevírou v člověka dovedl Čapek tvořiti živé lidi."[32] *Trapné povídky* is also praised by Václav Černý as " . . . kniha, v níž je velmi mnoho umění a formální svrchovanosti a stejně mnoho pravdy."[33] The trilogy of which *Hordubal* is the first part is considered by René Wellek to be Čapek's "highest achievement."[34] and William Harkins also calls it Čapek's masterpiece.[35] Similarly, Čexov's stories dealing with human isolation and lack of communication are among this author's best. "Skučnaja istorija," for instance, is called by Winner "the most significant work of the 1880s,"[36] and he quotes Pleščeev and Gol'denvejzer to substantiate his claim. Pleščeev praised the story in a letter to Čexov dated September 27, 1889 as his most profound and powerful work.[37] Gol'denvejzer reports that Lev Nikolaevič Tolstoj during a reading of "Skučnaja istorija" ". . . vse vremja vosxiščalsja umom Čexova."[38] Tolstoj also valued highly the stories Winner chose as examples of the treatment of the theme, namely "Toska" and the children's stories.[39] "Doč' Al'biona" made a great impression on Nikolaj Semenovič Leskov, who, having read the story, urged Čexov to write more.[40]

The young author not only continued writing but he also employed the same theme. Thus, the three stories, "Čelovek v futljare," "Kryžovnik" and "O ljubvi," published as late as 1898, each deal with a special kind of constricted, isolated life, while, as noted by Winner, "[i]n most of Čexov's stories about love written in the 1880s and 1890s, emotion is destroyed . . . simply by the absence of human communication." [41] This seems to indicate that there are actually two separate themes, that of human isolation and that of lack of communication. It would be extremely difficult, however, to distinguish between the two types. "Čelovek v futljare" is certainly an example of the isolated individual, while "O ljubvi" is based on the lack of communication. But the former necessarily leads to the latter, and vice versa. Hence, Belikov, the hero of "Čelovek v futljare," is incapable of ordinary social intercourse: "Bylo u nego strannoe obyknovenie—xodit' po našim kvartiram. Pridet k učitelju, sjadet i molčit i kak budto čto-to vysmotrivaet. Posidit, ètak, molča, čas-drugoj i ujdet,"(X, 44) and Alexin, in "O ljubvi," unable to communicate, all alone and unhappy ". . . vertelsja . . . v ètom gromadnom imenii, kak belka v kolese, a ne zanimalsja naukoj ili čem-nibud' drugim, čto delalo by ego žizn' bolee prijatnoj."(X, 74) A similar conclusion can be drawn from any other of Čexov's stories on the topic; a safe assumption can be made that the theme of human isolation and that of lack of communication coincide in his work.

However, the treatment of the theme differs. "Toska" awakens in the reader the same feeling of heavy melancholy as does Čapek's *Trapné povídky*, while "Doč' Al'biona," similarly to "Muž, který se nelíbil" by the Czech writer, is a rather amusing tale. Čexov's stories dealing with human isolation, if the effect is considered, cover the entire scale of possibilities. The lack of communication leads to murder in some of them (e.g. "Barynja," "Ubijstvo," "Spat' xočetsja"), to despair in others (e.g. "Toska," "Skučnaja istorija"), to the protagonist's liberation from the impasse through his own death in still others ("Čelovek v futljare," "Gore," "Skripka Rotšil'da"), or they end without a resolution ("Doč' Al'biona," "Ogni"). Some heroes are even happy in their isolation (e.g. "Kryžovnik"), while others find relief because they believe that communication has been established, whether this is so or not ("Van'ka"). Due to the great diversity in these stories, only two qualifiers can be applied to them for a meaningful classification. One of these is the aesthetic category (humorous or tragic), the other is the protagonist's awareness or acceptance of his isolation. Thus "Doč' Al'biona," for instance, is humorous and the heroine is content (if aware) with her isolation. "Zloumyšlennik" is also humorous, but the protagonist is aware of the faulty communication. "Kryžovnik" and "Skučnaja istorija," on the other hand, are tragic, with the hero of the former contented with his isolation, and the characters of the latter driven to despair as a result of it.

Many of Čapek's works also deal with this theme and they can be classified in the same manner. Klára in "Modrá chryzantéma" is unable to communicate with people around her, but she is happy and the story is amusing. "Zločin v chalupě" has already been compared to "Zloumyšlennik" and like Čexov's story it can be considered humorous—regardless of the author's philosophical postscript and the underlying crime—with the protagonist well aware of the unsatisfactory communication. The majority of Čapek's writings based on human isolation are, however, not humorous. The protagonists of *Trapné povídky* are desperately alone, aware of the fact, and unable to escape their isolation. *Hordubal* and the hero of "Ušní zpověd'" find escape only in their own death—*Hordubal* is murdered, whereas the protagonist of the latter story dies of natural causes. As opposed to Čexov's characters, the heroes in Čapek's tragic stories treating the lack of communication are never satisfied in their situation, but some of them are able to find a way out of their isolation either alone ("Muž, který se nelíbil"), or with help ("Uražený").

Naturally, as the two authors published such a great number of works dealing with this issue, there are bound to be direct parallels. The analogies between "Na zámku" and the children's stories, "Zločin v chalupě" and "Zloumyšlennik" have already been discussed, but there are more. Besides the general similarities based on the use of the same theme, there are such parallels as the motif of sorrow for the dead child in "Toska" and "Otcové." Also interesting are the similarities between *Hordubal* and "Barynja." The former is a story of a peasant who has returned from America to his farm in Ruthenia, where he left behind his wife and daughter. While Hordubal was in America, his wife became involved in an affair with the man she hired. He refuses to accept this fact and when the peasants in the tavern speak slightingly of her, he fights to defend her reputation. Eventually, Hordubal is killed, the hired man is sentenced for the murder to life imprisonment and Hordubal's wife receives twelve years. The story itself is different in "Barynja." A young peasant is compelled by his family to betray his wife and become the lover of the lascivious female landowner in order to improve the family's material position. Unable to resolve his inner conflicts, the peasant visits the local tavern. He is provoked into fighting, and upon his return home, in despair beats his wife to death. In both stories the landlady has an affair with her hired man and these men become murderers, but the affinity does not lie in this theme. It is Čexov's peasant and Čapek's Hordubal who are blood relatives. They love their wives and wish to live with them in peace. Neither is permitted such domestic bliss. They are not able to cope with the situation into which they were drawn any more than they are able to avoid being provoked into the tavern fight. The pub scenes in the two works seem to be freely interchangeable. Furthermore, the family driving the peasant to despair with its demands is reminiscent of the family of the protagonist of Čapek's "Peníze," while the ending of *Hordubal* calls to mind the finale of Čexov's "Ubijstvo." There is no need to elaborate on this thematic similarity any further. Many of Čapek's stories with the theme of lack of communication have already been compared to those of Čexov in the previous chapter. The theme of human isolation is one of major importance for both writers.

Justice

Many of the above mentioned works involve crime. There is murder, as in "Ubijstvo," "Zločin v chalupě," "Spat' xočetsja" and *Hordubal,* thievery as in "Rasskaz neizvestnogo čeloveka," "Košile," "Zloumyšlennik" and "Ukradený kaktus," embezzlement as in "Vor" and "Muž, který se nelíbil," etc. Therefore it is only logical that both authors were also interested in justice. This is illustrated for instance in their concern with the Dreyfus affair. Čexov referred to it in no fewer that seventeen of his letters between November 12, 1897 and September 18, 1902. His involvement with the matter is well exemplified by his own statement in a letter to Sobolevskij: "ja celyj den' čitaju gazety, izučaju delo Drejfusa. Pomoemu, Drejfus ne vinovat."[42] When Zola published his "J'accuse," an open letter which denounced the judges as having obeyed orders from the authorities, Čexov praised him for it. In a letter to Batjuškov he writes that every Frenchman felt ". . . čto slava bogu, est' ešče spravedlivost' na svete i čto, esli osudjat' nevinnogo, est' komu vstupit'sja."[43] Later the Russian author commented on the same event in a letter to A.S. Suvorin: "Razžalovanie Drejfusa, spravedlivo ono ili net, proizvelo na vsex . . . tjaželoe, unyloe vpečatlenie . . . Pust' Drejfus vinovat,— i Zolja vse-taki prav, tak kak delo pisatelej ne obvinjat', ne presledovat', a vstupat'sja daže za vinovatych, raz oni uže osuždeny i nesut nakazanie." [44] Čexov believes in the writer's duty to stand up for an individual even for the guilty one once he is condemned and punished. Therefore the negative approach of *Novoe vremja* to the affair resulted in a rupture in the friendship between its editor, Suvorin, and Čexov as well as in a fierce criticism of the paper, expressed, for instance, in the letter to his brother: "Povedenie *Novogo vremeni* v dele Drejfus-Zolja prosto otvratitel'no i gnusno. Gadko čitat'."[45] Čexov's letters give evidence of his interest in the case and about his belief in the duty of an author to the culprit, so it does not come as a surprise that in the story "O ljubvi," written at the time (June—July 1898), the heroine falls in love with the narrator when he, upset about the outcome of the court session, emotionally expresses his dissent, while her husband believes that the man in the dock is always guilty. The connection with the Dreyfus affair, although unnoticed by scholars, is quite obvious:

> Èto bylo kak raz posle znamenitogo dela podžigatalej . . . V dele podžigatelej obvinili četyrex evreev, priznali šajku i, po-moemu, sovsem neosnovatel'no. Za obedom ja očen' volnovalsja, mne bylo tjaželo, i už ne pomnju, čto ja govoril, tol'ko Anna Alekseevna vse pokačivala golovoj i govorila mužu:—Dmitrij, kak že to tak? Luganovič—èto dobrjak, odin iz tex prostodušnyx ljudej, kotorye krepko deržatsja mnenija, čto raz čelovek popal pod sud, to, značit, on vinovat, i čto vyražat' somnenie v pravil'nosti prigovora možnoe ne inače, kak v zakonnom porjadke, ne bumage, no nikak ne za obedom i ne v častnom razgovore.—My s vami ne podžigali,— govoril on mjagko,—i vot nas že ne sudjat, ne sažajut v tjur'mu.(X, 68-69)

This quotation seems to be just a recapitulation of the sentiments the author expressed in his letters. Čapek, because of his age, could not become as involved in the case as Čexov did, but he too has written a story reminiscent of the Dreyfus affair. In his "Případ Selvinův" a great poet considers his major achievemnt to be the liberation of Frank Selvin, who was sentenced to life imprisonment. It is interesting to note that the stories in the collection *Povídky z jedné kapsy* were written in 1928 and the celebrated "Selvin's case" took place about twenty-nine years before that. Thus the date is brought back to the time of the Dreyfus affair. As the narrator says: ". . . můj největší úspěch byl případ Selvinův. Nu ovšem vy už ani dobře nevíte, oč šlo; vždyt' už je tomu dvacet šest, nebo ne dvacet devět let."[46] The trial was improperly conducted and the poet protested against it in a series of newspaper articles. He describes how the analysis of the trial led him even further: " . . . když už jsem byl v tom začal jsem útočit na celou justici, na trestní řád, na instituci porot, na celý netečný a sobecký společenský řád." [47] The youth stood on the side of the culprit and there were demostrations. Selvin's lawyer was upset because the case became so prominent that " . . . vyšší instance nemůže ustoupit teroru ulice, a proto zamítne všechny jeho rekursy."[48] The appeal was dismissed, but the judge was pensioned off. Then the poet became more deeply involved in the matter. He refers to what he did as "a holy war for justice," and describes the affair in the following manner: "Selvinův případ přešel do světového tisku; řečnil jsem dělníkům v hospodách a delegátům celého světa na mezinárodních kongresech. . . . Pokud šlo o mne, byl to boj jedince proti státu; ale za mnou bylo mládí."[49] It took years, but eventually Frank Selvin was re-tried and acquitted. The poet celebrated the fact as the greatest triumph of his life. It was only afterwards that he found out that the accused really was guilty. Naturally, he was disappointed, but he still insists that "Selvin's case" is his greatest achievement. If one is to paraphrase Čexov—even when Selvin is guilty, Čapek's poet is right, for it is the business of a writer not to accuse, not to persecute, but to champion the quilty once they have been condemned and undergo punishment. Neither of the two writers limited his interest in justice merely to one legal case. A number of their stories concerned with justice have already been referred to in this treatise, but there are more. Čapek, for instance, describes his *Povídky z jedné kapsy* as noetic and judicial: "První můj autorský zájem o detektivky vycházel z problémů noetických, jak se poznává a objevuje skutečnost. *Povídky z jedné kapsy* jsou tedy povídky noetické. Jakmile jsem se začal zabývati světem zločinu, zaujal mě proti mé vůli problém spravedlnosti. Asi v polovici mé knihy najdete ten přelom. Místo otázky, jak se poznává, převládá otázka, jak trestat."[50] According to this statement, Čapek began to write about the problem of justice against his will. It would seem that he did not concern himself with this theme prior to the work on the *Povídky z jedné kapsy*, but "Hora" from 1917 and "Tribunál" written in 1920 contradict such an assumption. This is demonstrated by the fact that the collection *Kniha apokryfů* contains several stories dealing with justice and dated in the 1930s. The author's hero speaks up against the prosecution of a murderer: "'Nedobré je stíhat člověka.' . . . 'Co tedy se má?' 'Nic. Všechno je stejně nedobré. Zlé je bít i nebít, soudit i promíjet—Všechno má svůj stín i svou vinu.'" [51]Both are wrong to judge as well as to forgive. Justice is relative, and if all the circumstances were known, every human action could be excused. This is implied at the end of the story, when one of the characters refers to the murderer: "Kdybyste ho jen slyšeli—Ach jak dobře byste mu mohli rozumět."[52] The relativity of justice is also the theme of the story "Věštkyně." Already in the introduction there is a subtle criticism of judicial institutions: " . . . tento příběh se nemohl stát u nás ani ve Francii ani v Německu, nebot' v těchto zemích, jak známo, soudcové jsou povinni soudit a trestat hřěšníky podle litery zákona a nikoliv podle svého rozšafného rozumu a svědomí."[53] The story itself is simple. A Detective Inspector's wife, pretending to be younger and single, visits a fortune-teller with a request for card reading. She is told that before the year is out she will get married to a very rich young man, although there will be an obstacle in the form of an elderly gentleman. After the wedding, according to the fortune-teller, the young couple will move across the ocean. The prediction is obviously wrong and the fortune-teller does not even protest when tried and sentenced. Only, about a year later the magistrate who condemned the fortune-teller meets the Detective Inspector and is told that the prediction became reality: " . . . my jsme se totiž rozvedli . . . on se do ní znenadání zabouchl jeden mladý flákač... takový milionář nebo obchodník z Melbournu . . . Já jsem jí bránil, ale . . . Před týdnem spolu odjeli do Australie."[54] The magistrate was perfectly justified in condemning the fortune-teller, yet the circumstances proved him wrong. Human justice is imperfect as it cannot take all the factors into consideration. Therefore Eupator in "Jako za starých časů," when told about the accusation against Nikomachos, remains calm and asks: " . . . jsou zákony, které jsme si dali, dobré nebo špatné? . . . A říká někdo na agoře, že úředníci, kteří vyšetřují Nikomacha, jsou špatní a nespravedliví?" [55] If the laws are good and the officials just, human justice is at its best. Similarly, officer Bartošek in "šlépěje" reduces justice to keeping order: "Spravedlnost není záhadná . . . My se vám vykašleme na záhady; nás zajímají nepatřičnosti... Koukněte se, spravedlnost musí byt nepochybná jako násobilka. Já nevím, mohl-li byste dokázat, že každá krádež je špatná; ale já vám dokážu, že každá krádež je zakázaná, protože vás v každém případě seberu."[56] Legal justice is possible because it involves only a comparison of the facts with the code. If some facts are missing, the law loses its power. An example of such a case is given in "Povídka starého kriminálníka." A murderer admits his crime but, because his victim is not to be found, he cannot be condemned. Powerless justice also figures in "Zmizení herce Bendy" and "Zločin na poště." In the former story a physician discovers that a rich industrialist killed his friend but cannot prove it. The best he can do is to tell the murderer that he knows the facts of his crime and leave the rest to the industrialist's conscience. The latter story treats the same theme. As its narrator phrases it: "...já sám usvědčil dva lidi z vraždy a sám jsem je odsoudil k spravedlivému trestu a trest jsem vykonal ..." [57] An estate steward is in love with a postal clerk from the city. In order to bring his fiancée closer to the estate the steward arranges for an embezzlement charge against the local mail clerk. It results in the girl committing suicide from shame. The narrator discovers the crime, but feels that human law is not satisfactory. His punishment takes the form of a transfer of the steward just as his fiancée arrives. Legal justice is inadequate in punitive measures as these stories illustrate, but it is also limited in its ability to forgive. Hence the protagonist in "Propuštěný" cannot be forgiven for his crime, although several lawyers seek for an excuse to allow them to pardon his offence. Záruba is conditionally discharged and acquainted with the fact that if he commits some mischief, he will have to serve the full life sentence. As he is released, the unfortunate Záruba gets involved in an anti-government demonstrtion and ends up back in prison. Before the lawyers can decide how to help him, the culprit commits suicide. The limitations of human justice are also expressed in the reflections of the judge in "Zločin v chalupě," and his conclusion is that some cases should be tried by God: "... někdy by měl soudit Bůh; víte, on by mohl uvalit takové strašné a veliké tresty—Soudit ve jménu božím; ale na to my jsme krátcí." [58] The strength of divine justice comes forth in "Balada o Juraji Čupovi." The hero, a Ruthenian peasant who has murdered his sister, tramps for hours through a blizzard in two meters of snow, to surrender himself to the police. Čup's superhuman journey is credited by the police captain to the workings of divine justice. Nevertheless, Juraj Čup is judged and convicted by the people. God cannot judge because he knows all the circumstances leading to the crime. The inability of God to condemn a criminal is elaborated upon in the "Poslední soud." The God in the story explains why he cannot judge people: "Protože všechno vím, nemohu vůbec soudit. To přece nejde. . .Kdyby soudcové všechno, ale naprosto všechno věděli, nemohli by také soudit; jen by všemu rozuměli, až by je z toho srdce bolelo ... Soudce ví jenom o ... zločinech; ale já vím ... všechno ... A proto ... nemohu soudit."[59] Absolute justice is not possible for man or God. Čexov's Nikolaj Sergeič in "Perepolox" with his "Tout comprendre, tout pardonner"(IV, 337) expresses the idea of Čapek's "Poslední soud," but the Russian author did not stop there. Similarly to his Czech colleague, he has concerned himself with justice throughout his works. As early as 1881 Čexov published his "Sud," a story in which a mayor's son is tried and condemned for theft of his father's money. While he is being flogged, the money is found in his father's pocket. A miscarriage of justice is also found in the story "V ovrage" written almost twenty years later. Aksin'ja kills Lipa's baby, and it is Lipa who is accused of taking insufficient care of the baby. Furthermore, Aksin'ja, the murderess, forces Lipa to leave the house. Naturally Čexov's interest in the theme did not find the expression in only these two stories published twenty years apart. There is "Ispoved'," for instance, in which an embezzler explains how his environment made him steal the money. "Edinstvennoe sredstvo" describes a reverse situation. The cashier is given all he requires so that he will not embezzle any money. The murderer in "Drama na oxote" cannot be convicted, while an innocent man is punished for his crime. "Zloumyšlennik" is an example of a justly condemned criminal who does not understand why his deed should be considered a crime. "Unter Prišibeev" feels that people do not have the proper respect for law and order. He tries to correct the situation and does not understand why he is sentenced for his well-meaning actions. "Mstitel'" is another example of an amusing story concerning justice. The avenger is a husband who has suprised his wife with a lover and who wants to take justice into his own hands. When he attempts to buy a gun, the shopkeeper is so enthusiastic in describing the murderous qualities of each pistol that the husband's fury gives way to uneasy embarrassment. The vengence will not take place, but the offence is not forgiven. The nobility of pardon comes forth in the Professor's talk to Katja in "Skučnaja istorija:" "Samoe lučšee i samoe svjatoe pravo korolej—èto pravo pomilovanija. I ja vsegda čuvstvoval sebja korolem, tak kak bezgranično pol'zovalsja ètim pravom. Ja nikogda ne sudil, byl snisxoditelen, oxotno proščal vsex . . ."(VII, 281-82) Unfortunately, this sentiment was not shared by the Russian authorities, and the penal colony at Saxalin island had many customers in 1890. Čexov's interest in justice was so intense at the time that he decided to visit Saxalin. Ronald Hingley questions the writer's reasons for the trip in his book: "He has explained his reasons frankly, repetitively and at length in his letters of early 1890; but the more closely we scrutinize this material the less does any single, overriding purpose emerge. The complex, self-contradictory motives which he discusses . . . are literary, scientific, humanitarian and personal."[60] Hingley is apparently searching for other reasons than the simple interest in justice, which should be a satisfactory motive. After all, one of letters to which the English scholar refers elucidates Čexov's view of the way in which the law is enforced and gives some reasons for his concern:

> . . . my sgnoili v tjur'max *milliony* ljudej, sgnoili zrja, bez rassuždenija, varvarski; my gonjali ljudej po xolodu v kandalax desjatki tysjač verst, zaražali sifilisom, razvraščali, razmnožali prestupnikov i vse èto svalovali na tjuremnyx krasnonosyx smotritelej. Teper' vsja obrazovannaja Evropa znaet, èto vinovaty ne smotriteli, a vse my no nam do ètogo dela net, èto neinteresno.[61]

Literary motives may have not been the most important incentive for Čexov's expedition, but a number of stories bear marks of the experiences undergone by the author during the trip. Thus, in his treatise *Ostrov Saxalin* is found "Rasskaz Egora." It is a story of a peasant sentenced to penal servitude in Saxalin for a murder he did not commit. The fate of the Tatar in the story "V ssylke" is similar. His two brothers and his uncle had stolen a peasant's horses, but the community court had judged dishonestly, sentencing all three brothers to Siberia while their rich uncle stayed at home. In "Vory," on the other hand, two horse thieves get away with their crime and the victim imagines how wonderful the free life of his cozeners must be. Therefore, the fear of Ivan Gromov in "Palata No. 6" of a judicial miscarriage is understandable. The man in question, was taking his morning walk, when...

> Vodnom iz pereugolkov vstretilis' dva arestanta v kandalax i s nimi četyre konvojnyx s ruž'jami. Ran'še Ivan Dmitrič očen' často vstrečal arestantov i vsjakij raz oni vozbuždali v nem čuvstva sostradanija i nelovkosti. Teper' . . . emu vdrug počemu-to pokazalos', čto ego tože mogut zakovat' v kandaly i takim že obrazom vesti po grjazi v tjur'mu . . . On ne znal za soboj nikakoj viny i mog poručit'sja, čto i v buduščem nikogda ne ub'et, ne podožžet i ne ukradet; no razve trudno soveršit' prestuplenie nečajanno, nevol'no, i razve ne vozmožna kleveta nakonec, sudebnaja ošibka?(VIII, 77)

Gromov lists several possible causes for imprisonment of an innocent man. His imagination limits the notion of detention to a jail, however. In the course of the story, he learns of another possibility, namely, the mental ward of the hospital, of which he becomes an inmate. His criticism of the legal system expressed in the statement: " . . . nedarom že vekovoj narodnyj opyt učit ot sumy da tjur'my ne zarekat'sja. A sudebnaja ošibka pri teperešnem sudoproizvodstve očen' vozmožna i ničego v nej net mudrenogo,"(VIII, 77-78) in its turn, is justified by the many stories by Čexov which describe a judicial miscarriage. In one of them, the injustice appears only on the second level of law enforcement. Jakov, the protagonist in "Ubijstvo," is justly sentenced for murder to a penal servitude in Saxalin. It is in the penal colony that he is unfairly treated. Twice he is flogged for losing prison clothing though it was stolen from him.(IX, 159) Čexov's concern with the justice in Saxalin is expressed in Chapter xxi of his *Ostrov Saxalin*. One of the examples he gives is the following case:

> V selenii . . . ukrali svin'ju. Podozrenie palo na Z., u kotorogo pantalony byli opačkany v svinoj kal. Sdelali u nego obysk, no svin'i ne našli; tem ne menee, vse-taki sel'skoe obščestvo prigovorilo otobrat' svin'ju, prinadležaščuju ego kvartiroxozjainu A., kotoryj mog byt' vinoven v ukryvatel'stve. Načal'nik okruga utverdil ètot prigovor, xotja naxodil ego nespravedlivym. "Esli my ne budem utverždat' sel'skie prigovory,—skazal on mne,—to Saxalin togda sovsem ostanetsja bez suda."(XIV-XV, 331-32)

The authority consciously upholds an unjust decision because if the verdicts of the village court were not confirmed, Saxalin would be left without any judicial authority. The picture of justice, as drawn by Čexov, is not an attractive one. The only case of forgiveness is presented in "Rasskaz staršego sadovnika," where a convicted murderer is set free with general approval: "Ubijcu otpustili na vse četyre storony, i ni odna duša ne upreknula sudej v nespravedlivosti."(VIII, 346) In this instance, however, the author stresses that it is not a real event, but merely an old legend.

The above examples make it obvious the Čexov finds legal justice as imperfect as Čapek does. Both are critical of the Penal system in their respective countries (e.g. "Věštkyně," "Rasskaz Egora"); both ask for compassion for the convicted criminal (e.g. "Hora," "Vor"); and both find the law incapable of pardon ("Propuštěný," "Rasskaz staršego sadovnika"— only a legend). Čapek is looking for a better justice in a divine court, but is disappointed even there, because absolute knowledge eliminates the possibility of judgement ("Poslední soud"). This is echoed by Čexov's hero as "Tout comprendre, tout pardonner" ("Perepolox"). In the works of both authors one finds characters who seem to be above the law. Čexov put down a case like this in his note book: the protagonist admits to a murder for remuneration, but there is no evidence to convict him. (XVII, 110) The same situation is found in his "Drama na oxote." Čapek is stricter with his heroes—they do escape the legal justice, but their fellow men take justice in their own hands (e.g. "Zmizení herce Bendy," "Zločin na poště"). Čexov describes the incomprehensibility of the law for the common people (e.g. "Zloumyšlennik") and this idea also finds its equivalent in the work of the Czech writer (e.g. "Zločin v chalupě"). Even the note Čexov made of the confirmed unjust decision in the case of the stolen pig in Saxalin finds its counterpart in Čapek's work. His "Císař Damoklecián" says that no reasonable statesman interferes unnecessarily in matters of custom.[62] He realizes the injustice, but it satisfies his subjects. Naturally there are some differences in the approach of the two authors to the theme. Čexov presents more cases of miscarried justice and he is more interested in the administered punishment. Čapek, on the other hand, is more concerned with the suitability of the verdict and in absolute justice. These slight deviations do not change the fact that justice and its administration is one of the main issues treated in their respective works.

Truth

The concept of justice is inseparable from that of truth. Therefore both writers also reflect on this notion. Čapek's story "Pilátovo krédo" is an example of a work in which the two themes are brought together. Pilate admits that Christ was innocent, but he reproaches him for preaching a new truth: " . . . když jsem s ním mluvil, viděl jsem, že za nějaký čásek budou jeho žáci křižovat jiné: ve jménu jeho jména, ve jmenu jeho pravdy budou křižovat a mučit všechny jiné, zabíjet jiné pravdy . . . Ten člověk mluvil o pravdě. Co jest pravda? . . . Každý, kdo udělá nějakou pravdu, zapovídá všechny ostatní pravdy."[63] Hence, according to Čapek's protagonist, the crucifixion of Christ is justifiable. He promoted a new truth and for such deeds people always kill one another. Similarly, his followers would kill those who would not accept their truth, because everybody who preaches a truth forbids all the other truths. Joseph of Arimathaea, with whom Pilate is speaking, tries to argue this point of view, and claims that there is only one truth for everybody. This unique and universal truth is the one in which he believes. Naturally Pilate cannot accept such a biased opinion. He believes in a more general truth: "Já věřím, věřím, horoucně věřím, že je pravda a že ji člověk poznává . . . Já věřím, že každý má na ní podíl; i ten, kdo říká ano, i ten, kdo říká ne. Kdyby se ti dva spojili a rozuměli si, vznikla by celá pravda . . . Já věřím. Naprosto nepochybně věřím. Ale co je pravda?" [64] Pilate confesses that he does not know what truth is, but he believes that man is constantly searching to understand the concept; this general truth accomodates all the personal or individual truths.

This contemplation of the Roman procurator is not an isolated attempt at elucidation of truth in Čapek's writings. Václav Černý describes the author of *Boží muka* as a poet on a quest for the truth of life,[65] and he repeats this observation in his analysis of *Trapné povídky*.[66] Ivan Klíma does not limit this quest to the two early collections. According to him, truth is the problem disturbing the writer throughout his life: "Čapka po celý život vzrušovala otázka, jak lze poznat pravdu i člověka. Věčné téma. Věnoval mu část svých *Povídek z jedné kapsy*, svoji trilogii, vracel se k němu ve svých sloupcích i v apokryfech."[67] Furthermore, in his monograph on Čapek, Klíma considers this topic to be one of the fundamental philosophical issues in Čapek's work: "Otázka poznání a pravdy—nikoliv poznatelnosti světa, ale vztahu pravdy a lidské činnosti, pravdy a způsobu její realizace v životě se stává jednou ze stěžejních filosofických otázek Čapkova díla." [68] The author himself confirms this thesis when he rebuts the critics in *Lidové noviny*:

V celé své práci omílám do omrzení dvě zpola morální, zpola noetická themata. První je negativní Pilátovo: Co je pravda? Druhé je pozitivní: Každý má pravdu . . . *Boží muka* mají ten smysl, že hledání pravdy je víc než pravda sama, že největší hodnota pravdy je v jejím tušení a prožití, že, je-li kazdé poznání omezené, je cesta za pravdou sama duchová neomezenost. Této knížce se říkalo, že je abstraktní; zatím to je polemika proti racionalismu. *Trapné povídky* se zase vracejí k thematu: každý má pravdu. Nebot' tady lidé jednají špatně, zbaběle, krutě nebo slabošsky, jedním slovem trapně; a celý vtip je v tom, že nikoho z nich nemůžete odsoudit; po nikom hodit kamenem; podařil-li se mi aspoň trochu tento povídkový cyklus, musel jsem docílit mučivého dojmu, že není koho soudit.[69]

This article was already published in 1922, but Čapek's concern with the theme, as observed above by Klíma, did not diminish. Thus the stories in *Povídky z jedné kapsy* are called noetic and judicial.[70] René Wellek stresses the importance of the theme of truth in *Hordubal, Povětroň,* and *Obyčejný život.* According to him, Čapek's " . . . finest work is the trilogy of novels which centers around problems of truth and reality and constitutes one of the most successful attempts at a philosophical novel in any language.[71] There is ,no doubt about Čapek's interest in the topic. Indeed, his work is permeated with the word truth. The frequency of the word's use does not, however, explain the concept. What is truth? Pilate in the cited excerpt from Čapek's story concludes his deliberation with this question. Boura, the philosopher in "Elegie," lectures at a meeting of the Aristotelian Society. He feels that everything he says is true. Yet, when asked to define truth, Boura refuses to do so. He later explains his attitude to a friend: "Nač odpovídat . . . Nevím co je pravda. Vím, že vše, co jsem říkal, bylo samozřejmé, logické, správné, jak chcete. Ale nebylo to ani samozřejmé ani logické, když mi to prvně přicházelo do hlavy."[72] Boura, who is prepared by his occupation to answer questions of this type, admits that he does not know what truth really is. In order to create a logical system from the notions whirling through his mind, Boura is forced to discard many ideas. Therefore, he feels that the chaotic confusion of thoughts, prior to his organizing them into a system, is closer to the truth than the resulting logical system. Pilate's idea of truth encompassing mutually exclusive concepts recurs here. Čapek's approach to the problem is that of a relativist. There are many truths but, however contradictory they may be, they all should be respected because there are people behind them. The noetic problem becomes an ethical one. People need nothing more than mutual understanding. No one should judge a fellow human being. Instead, he should try to comprehend his truth. Only, as Čapek's Pilate says, everyone who brings about some truth, forbids all other truths. People are not really concerned with truth and justice but with their private interests. This Čapek illustrates in his "Jako za starých časů." But even if they are interested in finding the truth, like the veterans in "Římské legie," it is not possible. These old soldiers reminisce about the memorable military events which they had witnessed. Yet they cannot agree on a single point. The truth eludes them. The protagonists of *Boží muka* search for truth in vain since they seek the general truth which would elucidate the meaning of life for them. The absolute truth cannot be found, but there are personal truths. If an individual acts according to his own concept of righteousness, he cannot be judged for his transgression of societal precepts. Thus Holub in "Milostná píseň: Lída II" says: "Není koho soudit. Není co odpouštět."[73] Similarly, there is no one to be condemned in "Tři" or "Surovec." The relativity of truth comes forth strongly again in *Povídky z jedné kapsy*. The first story in the collection, "Případ Dr. Mejzlíka," is about a police official who has captured a safe-cracker and now deliberates on the reasons which caused him to arrest the criminal. Was it through pure chance, telepathy, or perhaps just the usual police routine? Maybe it was an intuitive or empirical conclusion. Dr. Mejzlík is unable to discern the truth about the case. In "Věštkyně," the Fortune-Teller has her truth, and so does the Magistrate. In "Jasnovidec" a public prosecutor gives a clairvoyant a sample of a murderer's handwriting for analysis. The analyst finds that the writing reveals a cruel character that is evil, dangerous, and of immense strength. Later the prosecutor discovers that by mistake he submitted his own writing for analysis. At first he is upset, but, after contemplating a while, he even enjoys the clairvoyant's description of his character. The next day his colleagues praise him for the speech in which he used the terms suggested by the clairvoyant's description of the criminal nature of the specimen's author. The story "Zločin v chalupě" is based on the idea of two contradictory truths. *Povídky z druhé kapsy* are more concerned with ethical themes, but they too served as a preparation for Čapek's masterpiece. This idea is expressed also in Harkins's book: " . . . [the] writing of these stories had great value for Čapek's development. Seen in retrospect, they constitute a preparation for the trilogy, which also employs oral narration and the element of detection, and which is also concerned with the quest for truth." [74] The three novels of the trilogy are completely distinct in theme and method, but a common conception underlies them all. All retell the very same story from different points of view and thereby stress the variety of meaning, the mysteriousness of ultimate reality. The cognizance of this reality, if possible, is extremely difficult. Miloš Pohorský describes Čapek's aims in his article "Noetické romány Karla Čapka:" "Chtěl . . . ukázat, jak těžko lze pochopit opravdovou lidskou podstatu určitého člověka. Upozorňoval proto na nebezpečí, že se realita jedinečného života ztratí, jakmile ji lidé začnou posuzovat z rozdílné perspektivy."[75] That which is generally accepted as truth or reality does not reach deep enough. This is illustrated in *Hordubal*, where the protagonist's pathetic life is interpreted by other people, who conclude that he is either stupid or deranged. The reader, acquainted with the protagonist's point of view, knows that neither

is true. The novel could conclude with the sentiment expressed in Čapek's
early story "Hora:" "Kdybyste ho jen slyšeli—Ach, jak dobře byste mu
mohli rozumět"[76] In *Povětroň*, the second volume of the trilogy, the author
presents several interpretations of the given facts, and, as he says, many
more interpretations are possible: "Bylo by možno vymyslet ještě bezpočtu
jiných příběhů, ale autor musí mít tolik rozumu, aby s nimi včas přestal.
Všem těm příběhům je společno, že se v nich více méně fantasticky zrcadlí
ten, kdo je vypravuje . . . Vidíme věci různě podle toho, co a jací jsme . . .
Jak ukrutně veliká a složitá, jak prostorná je skutečnost, když v ní je dost
místa pro tolik různých výkladů"[77] A similar idea was already expressed in
the trial report "Co je pravda?" Here too, reality is spacious enough to give
room for a variety of views. The last part of the cycle is *Obyčejný život*, a
curriculum vitae of an unexceptional person. The plurality of truth lies in the
possibilities hidden in this life. The theme is a quest for a self-identity but,
as in the story "O fantazii," Čapek attempts to answer the problem of
knowledge with the idea that in every individual there is more that just the
person himself; everybody else lives a piece of his life and he lives a piece
of everyone else's. This understanding also shows the way out of the prison
of indivual alienation.

Čapek's first collection of stories is entitled *Boží muka*. His character's
quest for truth is therefore described logically as tortuous. In Čexov's
oeuvre there is no such suggestive title, yet Sergej Bulgakov applies the
same term to the quest of the Russian author's characters: "Bol'šinstvo
sravnitel'no krupnyx proizvedenij Čexova, i mnogija melkija, posvjaščeno
izobraženiju duxovnago mira ljudej, oxvačennyx poiskami pravdy žizni
i pereživajuščix muki ètogo iskanija. Ja nazovu "Skučnuju istoriju,"
"Moju žizn'," "Po delam služby," Slučaj iz praktiki," "Palatu No. 6,"
"Duèl'," "Kryžovnik". . . i dr."[78] Bulgokov lists some of Čexov's stories
which deal with the theme of truth and even this incomplete account
supports well Sophie Laffitte's statement that Čexov's 'merciless talent'
was devoted to the expression of truth, in which he saw the joy of life and
happiness.[79] The Russian author is concerned with truth just as much as
his Czech colleague is. The number of Čexov's stories dealing with truth
bears ample evidence of the fact that it is the author who says, through
the mouth of the artist in "Dom z mezoninom," that "Prizvanie vsjakogo
čeloveka v duxovnoj dejatel'nosti—v postojannom iskanii pravdy i smysla
žizni."(IX, 185) Čexov adhered to this idea throughout his creative life,
although his approach to the theme of truth changed. Thus, in "Suščaja

pravda"(1883), it is amusing how an official is unable to communicate the "truth" to his superior. "Xameleon" (1884), with all its humour, already shows the relativity of truth. This theme is also developed in "Zloumyšlennik" (1885) and "Unter Prišibeev" (1885). The story "Imeniny" (1888) brings about further change. Not only is it more complex than any of Čexov's earlier narratives concerned with truth but it is also the first tragic one. There are basically two intertwined themes: social hypocrisy preventing human contact, and late pregnancy, as experienced by a hostess of a nameday party. Not until the baby is stillborn do the protagonists realize what is really important in life, and even then they do not communicate. There is no indication what direction their future social behaviour will take. This story concludes the first period in Čexov's approach to the theme of truth. The stories published before 1889 deal with the problem of communicating truth, the relativity of truth, and social hypocrisy, all of which isolate people. The protagonists of the works appearing after "Imeniny" actually search for truth and the meaning of life. This change of approach is reflected in Thomas Winner's chosing five of the stories from this period, namely "Skučnaja istorija" (1889), "Duèl'" (1891), "Gusev" (1891), "Palata No. 6" (1892) and "Černyj monax" (1893) to discuss them as "a cycle of psycho-philosophical searching stories."[80] The first of them, "Skučnaja istorija," portrays the tragedy of an eminent scientist, who, old and incurably ill, realizes that his life has not been the glorious one he and his admirers had thought it to be. There is something missing, and this void makes his life a failure. The scientist describes it thusly: "V moem pristrastii k nauke, v moem želanii žit' . . . i v stremlenii poznat' samogo sebja, vo vsex mysljax, čuvstvax i ponjatijax, kakie ja sostavljaju obo vsem, net čego-to obščego, čto svjazyvalo by vse èto v odno celoe. . . . daže samyj iskusnyj analytik ne najdet togo, čto nazyvaetsja obščej ideej, ili bogom živogo čeloveka. A koli net ètogo, to, značit, net i ničego."(VII, 307) This lack of a unifying idea changes his entire outlook and it naturally affects his attitude toward people, eventually resulting in his total isolation. The old professor does not identify the object of his quest as truth, but this is obvious from the other "searching" stories where the ultimate goal of the quest is explicitly stated. The longest of these stories, and the only one in which Čexov attempts to resolve the philosophical conflicts within the context of the story, is "Duèl'."

The title itself might refer to the actual duel fought by the main
characters, as well as to the contrariety of their world views. One of
them, Laevskij, is an uncommitted, drifting intellectual who, similar
to the professor in "Skučnaja istorija," considers himself a failure,
while the other one, von Koren, is a zoologist overcommitted to
science, who believes in himself unconditionally. Laevskij and his
mistress have come to the little Caucasian city in which the story is
set, with intentions to "live by the sweat of their face—dig vineyards,
till fields, and all that." They never realize their plans, however, and
lead a life of aimless inactivity. Moreover, Laevskij has ceased to
love his mistress, Nadežda Fedorovna. This changed sentiment, the
opposite of love, is identified with a lie: "Neljubov' Laevskogo k
Nadežde Fedorovne vyražalas' glavnym obrazom v tom, čto vse, čto ona
govorila i delala, kazalos' emu lož'ju ili poxožim na lož' . . . "(VII,
362) The only possibility of negotiating the impasse of his life
Laevskij sees in escaping. This he imagines vividly:

> . . . kak on saditsja na paroxod i potom zavtrakaet, p'et xolodnoe
> pivo, razgovarivaet na palube s damami potom v Sevastopole
> saditsja na poezd i edet. Zdravstvuj svoboda! Stancii mel'kajut
> odna za drugoj, vozdux stanovitsja vse xolodnee i žestče, vot
> berezy i ely, vot Kursk, Moskva . . . V bufetax šči, baranina s
> kašej, osetrina, pivo, odnim slovom, ne aziatčina, a Rossija,
> nastojaščaja Rossija. Passažiry v poezde govorjat o torgovle,
> novyx pevcax, o franko-russkix simpatijax; vsjudu čuvstvuetsja
> živaja, kul'turnaja, intelligentnaja, bodraja žizn' . . . Skorej,
> skorej. Vot, nakonec . . . Kovenskij pereulok, gde on žil kogda-
> to so studentami, vot miloe, seroe nebo, morosjaščij doždik,
> mokrye izvozčiki. . . (VII, 363)

In spite of his present disappointment, Laevskij recognizes the beauty
of life and dreams of its joys. Moreover, he sincerely likes people. Thus, von
Koren tells about him that: "Vo vtorom kurse on vykupil iz publičnogo doma
prostitutku i vozvysil ee do sebja, to est' vzjal v soderžanki, a ona požila s
nim polgoda i ubežala nazad k xozjajke, i èto begstvo pričinilo emu ne malo
duševnyx stradanij."(VII, 371) This episode of Laevskij's life could be
misinterpreted—which von Koren tries to do—were it not for other
demonstrations of his love for humanity. He reproaches himself for not

having done anything for people. Furthermore, he cannot kill a man, however provoked: " . . . daže . . . v minutu sil'noj nenavisti i gneva, on ne smog by vystrelit' v čeloveka. Bojas', čtoby pulja kak-nibud' nevznačaj ne popala v fon Korena, on podnimal pistolet vse vyše i vyše i čuvstvoval, čto èto sliškom pokaznoe velikodušie ne delikatno i ne velikodušno, no inače ne umel i ne mog."(VII, 447) In opposition to Laevskij, von Koren is portrayed as a puritanical fanatic who believes that Darwin's theory of the survival of the fittest justifies the destruction of those who are harmful to society. Laevskij is, according to him, one of the people who should be exterminated. Laevskij describes his adversary in the following manner:

> Obyknovennye smertnye, esli rabotajut na obščuju pol'zu to imejut v vidu svoego bližnego: menja, tebja, odnim slovom čeloveka. Dlja fon Korena že ljudi—ščenki i ničtožestva, sliškom melkie dlja togo, čtoby byt' cel'ju ego žizni. On rabotaet, pojdet v èkspediciju i svernet sebe tam šeju ne vo imja ljubvi k bližnemu, a vo imja takix abstraktov, kak čelovečestvo, buduščie pokolenija, ideal'naja poroda ljudej. On xlopočet ob ulučšenij čelovečeskoj porody, i v ètom otnošenii my dlja nego tol'ko raby, mjaso dlja pušek, v'jučnye životnye; odnix by on uničtožil ili zakonopatil na katorgu, drugix skrutil by disciplinoj, zastavil by, kak Arakčeev, vstavat' i ložit'sja po barabanu, postavil by evnuxov, čtoby stereč' naše celomudrie i nravstvennost', velel by streljat' vsjakogo, kto vyxodit za krug našej uzkoj konservativnoj morali, i vse èto vo imja ulučšenija čelovečeskoj porody . . . (VII, 398-99)

This tirade shows simultaneously von Koren's lack of interest in people and Laevskij's concern for them. Furthermore, the latter approves of Nadežda Fedorovna's criticism of the natural sciences: "Ja ne ponimaju, kak èto možno ser'ezno zanimat'sja bukaškami i kozjavkami, kogda stradaet narod."(VII, 391-92)

It is the love for people which makes Laevskij likable, and the lack of it that makes von Koren disagreeable. Because Laevskij genuinely cares for his fellow man, he can be forgiven all the negative sides of his character; all except one: his falsity cannot be forgiven. Hence, Laevskij's quest actually only begins, when he realizes that lies lead one to another, without solving any problems:

... izredka v golove ego mel'kala mysl', čto ... v otdalennom
buduščem, dlja togo, čtoby razojtis' s Nadeždoj Fedorovnoj i
uplatit' dolgi emu pridetsja pribegnut' k mel'koj lži, on solžet
tol'ko odin raz, i zatem nastupit polnoe obnovlenie. I èto
xorošo: cenoju malen'koj lži on kupit bol'šuju pravdu.
Teper' že, kogda doktor svoim otkazom grubo nameknul emu
na obman, emu stalo ponjatno, čto lož' ponadobitsja emu ne
tol'ko v otdalennom buduščem, no i segodnja, i zavtra, i čerez
mesjac, i, byt' možet, daže do konca žizni. V samom dele,
čtoby uexat', emu nužno budet solgat' Nadežde Fedorovne,
kreditoram i načal'stvu; zatem, čtoby dobyt' v Peterburge
deneg, pridetsja solgat' materi ... Zatem, kogda v Peterburg
priedet Nadežda Fedorovna, nužno budet upotrebit' celyj rjad
melkix i krupnyx obmanov, čtoby razojtis' s nej, i opjat' slezy,
skuka, postylaja žizn', raskajanie i, značit, nikakogo
obnovlenija ne budet. Obman i bol'še ničego. V voobraženii
Laevskogo vyrosla celaja gora lži.(VII, 414)

Having realized that lies would only lead him to another impasse,
Laevskij is well on his way toward the objective of the quest for the meaning
of life. It follows that he also becomes repentant of all the lies in his past:
"Esli by možno bylo vernut' prošlye dni i gody, on lož' v nix zamenil by
pravdoj... I ottogo, čto èto nevozmožno, on prixodil v otčajanie."(VII, 438)
It is only when he is to fight a duel with von Koren, that Laevskij, as he
reassesses his relations with other people (e.g. mother, mistress), is able to
overcome this despair. The happy end of the duel enables him to start a new
life. The newly acquired sincerity gives a great promise for the future. Even
von Koren recognizes Laevskij's achievement, and thus, admitting his
mistake in relations with people, he too makes progress. This uptrend is
limited in his case, however, as he admits a mistake only in this particular
case: "Pravda, kak vižu teper' k velikoj moej radosti, ja ošibsja otnositel'no
vas, no ved' spotykajutsja na rovnoj doroge, i takova už čelovečeskaja
sud'ba: esli ne ošibaeš'sja v glavnom, to budeš' ošibat'sja v častnostjax.
Nikto ne znaet nastojaščej pravdy."(VII, 452-53) Laevskij accepts von
Koren's statement that nobody knows the real truth, but he is more positive
about it. Nobody knows the real truth, but people are on their way toward it:
"V poiskax za pravdoj ljudi delajut dva šaga vpered, šag nazad. Stradanija,
ošibki i skuka žizni brosajut ix nazad, no žažda pravdy i uprjamaja volja

gonjat vpered i vpered. I kto znaet? Byt' možet, doplyvut do nastojaščej pravdy . . ."(VII, 455) The object of the human quest is explicitly stated here. Von Koren's example shows that sincerity itself does not lead to this objective. It had to be complemented by genuine love and understanding for people. The same idea is expressed in the words of Pavel Ivanyč, one of the protagonists in "Gusev:" " . . . ja vsegda govorju v lico pravdu . . . V ètom otnošenii meždu mnoj i vami—raznica gromadnaja. Vy ljudi temnye, slepye, zabityje, ničego vy ne vidite, i čto vidite, togo ne ponimaete . . . Ja uže drugoe delo."(VII, 333) Since he separates himself from other people, sincerity does not help. One has to try to understand his fellow man, not to condemn him. The problem of Ivan Gromov in "Palata No. 6" is similar, although his approach to people is different. As noted by Winner, " . . . Gromov's passionate attachment to life and mankind are in the final analysis attachments to abstractions. In spite of his love for life, Gromov cannot live, and in spite of his love for mankind he cannot love an individual." [81] This brings to mind von Koren's inability to have affection for people, while all his work is meant for humankind. It is the lack of sympathy for an individual that impedes Gromov in his confrontation with the problems of life. He can neither communicate his criticism of social conditions nor live in this society. Hence his confinement to a mental ward is a logical consequence. The administrator in charge of the hospital, Dr. Ragin, is another seeker for the meaning of life. He is as conscious of evil around him as Gromov is, but he withdraws into himself and rationalizes his behavior by quoting various philosophers. According to him no happiness comes to man from without: "Pokoj i dovol'stvo čeloveka ne vne ego, a v nem samom . . . Bol' est' živoe predstavlenie o boli: sdelaj usilie voli, čtob izmenit' èto predstavlenie, otkin' ego, perestan' žalovat'sja, i bol' isčeznet . . . Esli vy počašče budete vdumyvat'sja, to vy pojmete, kak ničtožno vse to vnešnee čto volnuet nas. Nužno stremit'sja k urazumeniju žizni, a v nem—istinnoe blago."(VIII, 100-101) Naturally such a hypocritical point of view, one that requires a man to close his eyes to all the suffering and thereby denying life itself, is not acceptable to Gromov. For him, the essence of life is the ability to react to a stimulus; indifference and life are mutually exclusive concepts. He reproaches Ragin for his disregard for the suffering around him, concluding with the claim: "Molodoj čelovek prosit soveta, čto delat'; kak žit'; prežde čem otvetit', drugoj by zadumalsja, a tut už gotov otvet: stremis' k urazumeniju ili k istinnomu blagu. A čto takoe èto fantastičeskoe istinnoe blago'? Otveta net, konečno."(VIII, 103) Neither of the two protagonists has the answer regarding the meaning of life, but Ragin realizes that he was wrong in his indifference to suffering, when he too becomes a patient in the mental ward. Unfortunately this discovery comes too late. The story brings to mind some of Čexov's earlier work, and not only in the message, which again calls for interest in life and other people. Thus Ragin's lethargy is reminiscent of the sentiments professed by von Sternberg, the student, in "Ogni." The difference is that von Sternberg never regrets his feelings. The young man's inquiry of what to do and how to live brings to mind the same question asked by Katja in "Skučnaja istoria." Also Zinaida Fedorovna in "Rasskaz neizvestnogo čeloveka" propounds this question without obtaining an answer. There are two hints as to the meaning of life. One is given by the narrator who proclaims it to be Christian love: " . . . naznačenie čeloveka ili ni v čem, ili tol'ko v odnom— v samootverženoj ljubvi k bližnemu."(VIII, 207) The other hint is given by Orlov in his statement "Istinno sčastlivyj čelovek tot, kto dumaet ne tol'ko o tom, čto est', no daže o tom čego net."(VIII, 164) The former inference recurs in practically every story, the latter is developed in "Černyj monax." Andrej Kovrin, the protagonist of this work, conceives things not only as they are but also as they are not. His visions of the black monk make him so happy that he becomes scared of his good fortune: "I menja, kak Polikrata, načinaet nemnožko bespokoit' moe sčast'e. Mne kažetsja strannym, čto ot utra do noči ja ispityvaju odnu tol'ko radost' . . ."(VIII, 248) Deprived of his mirage when he is temporarily cured, Kovrin complains "Začem, začem vy menja lečili? . . . Ja sxodil s uma . . . no zato ja byl vesel, bodr i daže sčastliv . . . Kak sčastlivy Budda i Magomet ili Šekspir, čto dobrye rodstvenniki i doktora ne lečili, ix ot èkstaza i vdoxnovenija!" (VIII, 251) The hallucination brought Kovrin contentment but it fails to give him answers regarding the objective of his quest. The black monk tells Kovrin that he is chosen to serve the eternal truth and that he is to lead the human race to the kingdom of eternal truth, but he never explains this notion. Kovrin's question remains unanswered: "Čto ty razumeeš' pod večnoju pravdoj?, Monax ne otvetil.[82] Kovrin vzgljanul na nego i ne razgljadel lica: čerty ego tumanilis' i rasplyvalis'. Zatem u monaxa stali isčezat' golova, ruki . . . i on isčez sovsem."(VIII, 243) The other seeker in the story is the fruit grower Pesockij. He and Kovrin have a common feature of character which impedes their quest. They both feel superior to the people around them. The only difference is that Kovrin feels intellectually and Pesockij professionally transcendent. Neither of them makes any progress before death terminates their search and no trace of their respective life works remain. The protagonist in "Student," on the other hand, does not pretend to superiority, and is strongly afflicted by the living conditions of people around him: " . . . pri Rjurike, i pri Ivane Groznom . . . byla točno takaja že ljutaja bednost', golod, takie, že dyravye solomennye kryši, nevežestvo, toska, takaja, že pustynja krugom, mrak, čuvstvo gneta,—vse èti užasy byli, est' i budut, i ottogo, čto projdet ešče tysjača let, žizn' ne stanet lučše. I emu ne xotelos' domoj."(VIII, 306) His sincerity and compassion is rewarded by his cognition of the most important elements in human life: " . . . pravda i krasota, napravljajuščie čelovečeskuju žizn' . . . vsegda sostavljali glavnoe v čelovečeskoj žizni i voobšče na zemle; i čuvstvo molodosti, zdorov'ja, sily . . . i nevyrazimo sladkoe ožidanie sčast'ja ovladevali im malo-pomalu, i žizn' kazalas' emu vosxititel'noj, čudesnoj i polnoj vysokogo smysla."(VIII, 309) There is happiness in truth, and Čexov's heroes are aspiring to this goal. Unfortunately they do not unite in a communal quest for truth as proposed by the artist in "Dom s mezoninom."(IX, 186) Man is hindered in his search by his lack of interest in his fellow human being and by the ensuing hypocrisy. Furthermore, people err in the direction they take. This idea is again expressed by the artist in "Dom s mezoninom," when he speaks about the proper aims of true art and science: "Nauki i iskusstva, kogda oni nastojaščie, stremjatsja ne k vremennym, ne k častnym celjam, a k večnomu i obščemu,—oni iščut pravdy . . . U učenyx, pisatelej i xudožnikov kipit rabota, po ix milosti udobstva žizni rastut s každym dnem, potrebnosti tela množatsja, meždu tem do pravdy ešče daleko . . ."(IX, 186-87) This statement echoes Laevskij's assertion that no one knows the real truth. The idea itself does not come as a surprise since Čexov believes in the relativity of the notion. As early as 1887 he wrote in a letter to Marija Kiseleva "Vse na ètom svete otnositel'no i približitel'no." [83] Hence it is impossible to deny verity to either view in a controversy (e.g. "Zloumyšlennik"), and even mutually exclusive opinions can be accepted (e.g. "Xameleon"). Olen'ka in "Dušečka" is constantly changing her opinions, yet they can all be accommodated in one truth. The plurality of truth is not, however, the only theme in the story. It also carries *ad absurdum* the idea of an individual living a piece of everyone else's life. The heroine substitutes the life of a person she loves for her own, and in this fashion lives successively four separate lives. Naturally, as she identifies herself with people around her, she cannot suffer from the alienation felt so painfully be other characters of Čexov.

   Although the goal of Čexov's protagonists is specified as truth only

in the stories published after 1890, the theme is present in his *oeuvre* from
the very beginning. The concept is not and cannot be explained, because of
its elusive nature. Truth is relative and volatile. The characters struggle
towards it, but they never attain it.[84] Several protagonists ask for advice on
how to live, without obtaining any answer. Nevertheless, there is a recurrent
hint: Be interested in your fellow beings and try to understand them. Enjoy
life and help others to do the same. The best policy for mutual understanding
is sincerity, the worst is hypocrisy or putting oneself forward. Čexov
stresses human interrelations more consistently than Čapek does, while the
process of cognition of truth is of greater concern for the Czech writer.
Nevertheless, they both are interested in the theme of truth. For both, the
concept is relative and cannot be defined. Perception of reality varies with
perspective, and truth encompasses all the possible views including those
which seem mutually exclusive. Truth is the objective of human quest, and
the protagonists hope to achieve it. The concept, with its contradictory
elements, is, however, too elusive. Man cannot attain his goal, but, by trying
to comprehend the concept and to understand the individual truths of his
fellow human beings, he can find happiness in the proximity of truth.

Lev Šestov does not believe in such a possibility for Čexov's
heroes. He sees them as unable to achieve their aims, and therefore calls
the author "pevec beznadežnosti." [85] They do not have any philosophy to
lean upon, and therefore must succumb in the struggle of life. It is all
because, as Šestov says, Čexov is the "Neprimirimyj vrag vsjakogo roda
filosofii."[86] Sergej Nikolaevič Bulgakov, on the other hand, deduces from
Čexov's work that the solution to the human enigma, if there is one, is
religious.[87] Tolstoj claims the opposite—according to him, Čexov is an
absolute atheist standing outside the religious quest.[88] Winner speaks
about the many relationships of Čexov to the Existentialists,[89] Rayfield
traces the influence of Voltaire,[90] and other scholars find additional
philosophical trends embodied in the *oeuvre* of the Russian writer. A
similar confusion exists in the opinions about Čapek's philosophy. Due to
the fact that Čapek wrote a treatise on pragmatism, however, the argument
centers around the question whether he was or was not a pragmatist.
Alexander Matuška is very reasonable when he says "It is clear that at least
something of what is often ascribed to pragmatism in Čapek's work—and
that something is by no means negligible—has other sources: e.g. in
artistic (though often very philosophical) literature, in Voltaire, Anatole
France, Chesterton; in idealist philosophy."[91] The views regarding the

philosophy of each author are so dispersed that to educe a general philosophy from the writings of either of them will automatically have its opponents. Nevertheless, it is possible, and, as will be shown in the next two chapters, the general philosophies of the two writers are closely related.

Notes

1. K. and J. Čapek, *Krakonošova zahrada—Zářivé hlubiny a jiné prózy—Juvenilie* (Praha: Čs. spisovatel, 1957), pp. 190, 193, and 196. The original quotation is: " . . . what a pity that in life we only get our lessons when they are of no use to us!" from O. Wilde, *Lady Windermere's Fan*, in *The complete Works of Oscar Wilde* (1963; rpt. London: Hamlyn, 1983), p. 32.

2. K. Čapek, A letter to Jiří Říha, dated 14 January 1928, in *Poznámky*, p. 82.

3. _____, *Boží*, p. 24.

4. O. Malevič, *Karel Čapek: Kritiko-biografičeskij očerk* (Moskva: Xudožestvennaja literatura, 1968), p. 42.

5. Ibid., pp. 42-43.

6. Čapek, *Boží*, p. 90.

7. Ibid., p. 93.

8. O. Králík, *První řada v díle Karla Čapka* (Ostrava: Profil, 1972), p. 52.

9. Čapek, *Boží*, p 93.

10. Ibid., pp. 90-91.

11. Ibid., pp. 115-16.

12. Ibid., pp. 105-106.

13. Ibid., p. 79.

14. Králík, *První*, p. 55.

15. Čapek, *Bajky a podpovídky* (Praha: Čs. spisovatel, 1970), p. 121.

16. Ibid., pp. 172-79.

17. Malevič, *Karel*, p. 43.

18. Ibid., p. 44.

19. Čapek, *Bajky*, pp. 208-10.

20. _____, *Povídky*, pp. 157-62.

21. Ibid., p. 13.

22. Winner, *Chekhov*, 95-96.

23. Čapek, *Povětroň* (Praha: F. Borový, 1939), p. 27.

24. Ibid., p. 37.

25. Winner, *Chekhov*, p. 37.

26. Istorija *russkoj literatury XIX veka (vtoraja polovina)*, ed. S. M. Petrov (Moskva: Prosveščenie, 1974), p. 502.

27. D.S. Mirsky, *A History of Russian Literature: From its Beginning to 1900* (New York: Vintage Books, 1958), p. 373.

28. Ibid., p. 377.

29. Ibid., p. 375.

30. A. Hauser, *Sozialgeschichte der Kunst und Literatur* (München: C. H. Beck, 1969), p. 972.

31. Ibid., p. 973.

32. F. Götz, "Karel Čapek (Věci obecnější)," in *Jasní se horizont: Průhledy a podobizny* (Praha: V. Petr, 1926), p. 159.

33. V. Černý, *Karel Čapek* (Praha: F. Borový, 1936), p. 12.

34. Wellek, "Karel Čapek," p. 203.

35. Harkins, *Karel Čapek*, p. 129.

36. Winner, *Chekhov*, p. 91.

37. A.N. Pleščeev, in Čexov (VII, 672-73).

38. A.B. Gol'denvejzer, *Vblizi Tolstogo* (Moskva: GIXL, 1959), p. 98.

39. V.Ja. Lakšin, *Tolstoj i Čexov* (Moskva: Sov. pisatel', 1975), p. 128.

40. H.W. Bruford, *Anton Chekhov* (New Haven: Yale Univ. Press, 1957), p. 16.

41. Winner, *Chekhov*, p. 217.

42. Letter to V.M. Sobolevskij, dated December 4, 1897, No. 2178 (XXV, *Pis'ma*, VII, 112).

43. Letter to F.D. Batjuškov, dated January 23, 1898, No. 2235 (XXV, *Pis'ma*, VII, 157).

44. Letter to A.S. Suvorin, dated February 6, 1898, No. 2248 (XXV, *Pis'ma*, VII, 166-68).

45. Letter to Al.P. Čexov., dated July 30, 1898, No. 2363 (XXV, *Pis'ma*, VII, 247).

46. Čapek, *Povídky*, p. 92.

47. Ibid., p. 95.

48. Ibid., p. 95.

49. Ibid., p. 95.

50. V. Závada, "Hovory s Karlem Čapkem," An interview, in *Rozpravy Aventina*, 7, No. 6 (Oct. 1931), 41-42; rpt. in *Poznámky*, p. 95.

51. Čapek, *Boží*, p. 46.

52. Ibid., p. 54.

53. Čapek, *Povídky*, p. 18.

54. Ibid., p. 22.

55. Čapek, *Kniha apokryfů* (Praha: Čs. spisovatel, 1964), p. 24.

56. _____, *Povídky*, pp. 102-03.

57. Ibid., p. 148.

58. Ibid., p. 127.

59. Ibid., p. 122.

60. R. Hingley, *A New Life of Anton Chekhov* (London, Toronto, Melbourne: Oxford Univ. Press, 1976), p. 128.

61. Letter to A.S. Suvorin, dated March 9, 1890, No. 782 (XXII, *Pis'ma*, IV, 32).

62. Čapek, *Kniha*, pp. 124-25.

63. Ibid., p. 117.

64. Ibid., pp. 121-22.

65. V. Černý, *Karel Čapek* (Praha: F. Borový, 1936), p. 8.

66. Ibid., p. 10.

67. I. Klíma, "Čapkovy apokryfy," in Čapek, *Kniha*, p. 222.

68. _____, *Karel Čapek* (Praha: Čs. spisovatel, 1965), p. 50.

69. Čapek, "Musím dále," in *Lidové noviny*, 11 April 1922, pp. 3-4; rpt. in *Poznámky*, pp. 92-94

70. Závada, p. 95. The term "noetic" refers here to cognizance of truth originating in mind independent of the senses.

71. René Wellek, "Karel Čapek," *Columbia Dictionary of Modern European Literature* ed. H. Smith (New York: Columbia Univ. Press, 1947), p. 139.

72. Čapek, *Boží*, p. 72.

73. Ibid., p. 62.

74. Harkins, p. 182.

75. M. Pohorský "Noetické romány Karla Čapka," *Česká literatura*, 20 (1972), pp. 522-23.

76. Čapek, *Boží*, p. 54.

77. _____, "Co jsem chtěl říci," *Přítomnost*, 9 September 1934, p. 600; rpt. in *Poznámky*, pp. 106-107.

78. S.N. Bulgakov, *Čexov kak myslitel'*, a public lecture, 1904, publ. (Kiev: n.p., 1905), p. 9.

79. S. Laffitte, *Chekhov 1860-1904*, tr. M. Budberg and G. Latta (New York: Ch. scribner's Sons, 1973), p.1.

80. T. Winner, "Čechov and Scientism: Observations on the Searching Stories," in *Anton Čechov 1860-1960*, ed. T. Eekman (Leiden: E.J. Brill, 1960), p. 325.

81. _____, *Chekhov*, p. 108.

82. Note that Pilate asked Jesus a similar question: "What is truth?" His query also remained without an answer. See John xviii.38.

83. Letter to M.V. Kiseleva, dated January 14, 1887, No. 218 (XX, *Pis'ma*, II, 14).

84. The scientists seem to have more difficulties; see Winner, "Čechov and Scientism".

85. L. Šestov, "Tvorčestvo iz ničego: A.P. Čexov," in *Načala i koncy* (S.-Peterburg: M.M. Stasjulevič, 1908), p. 3.

86. Ibid., p. 50.

87. Bulgakov, p. 20.

88. L.N. Tolstoj, as quoted in P. Rossbacher, "Nature and the Quest for Meaning in Chekhov's Stories," *Russian Review*, 24 (1965), 387.

89. Winner, *Chekhov*, p. xvii.

90. D. Rayfield, *Chekhov: The Evolution of his Art* (London: Paul Elek, 1975), p. 187.

91. A. Matuška, *Karel Čapek: An Essay* (London: George Allen & Unwin Ltd., 1964), p. 54.

❦

CHAPTER III

SURVEY OF CRITICAL VIEWS ON THE
PHILOSOPHY OF ČEXOV AND ČAPEK

Čexov is a controversial writer, as confirmed by the disparity of critical views regarding his work. This chapter will illustrate the multiplicity of critics' perceptions and the often diametrically opposed commentaries evoked by his writings. Čapek's works, like Čexov's, tend to provoke polemics and controversy, if to a lesser degree. Whereas Čexov's world view remains implicit, however, Čapek's is expressed more explicitly, this being a reflection of the latter's philosophical training. Therefore, once the affinity between the two writers is established, Čapek's work may help to elucidate Čexov's philosophy. Since their outlook on life is of foremost importance here, the critical commentaries selected for this chapter will be those which have focused on the ideological aspect of their writings.[1] At this point, only an identification of the source will accompany the quotations, as well as a description of the occasion of their utterance. Such a catalogue of selected critical opinions is deemed necessary in order to illustrate the difficulty of defining the philosophical views of these two authors—and particularly those of Čexov—and thereby of proving the claim that a new approach should be attempted. Any critical commentary, personal interpretation, or in-depth analysis will be reserved for the later. The presentation of the critics' perceptions of the two authors, their nature, and the divergent directions discernable in them, represent the sole purpose of this chapter.

On Čexov

The earliest trend in critical approaches to the stories of the young Čexov comes from the populist camp. Russian populists (*narodniki*), whose name was derived from their cult of the people, were the most influential and numerous group of the intelligentsia in Russia from the 1860s to the end of the nineteenth century. It does not mean that populism was a monolithic movement. Nevertheless, all the factions joined forces in their attacks on Čexov. The chief theoretician of the movement was Nikolaj Konstantinovič Mixajlovskij, who emphasized relevance in literature, expecting it to propagate useful ideas and to serve the cause of social progress. Neither he nor his followers found these characteristics in Čexov's writing. Therefore, although Mixajlovskij and the others praised the young writer's talent and abilities,[2] they objected to his detachment from salient contemporary political and social issues, his inability to perceive what is important, his indifference, cold-bloodedness and emphasis on "trifles."

At first, their criticism focused on the young author's literary qualities and possibilities.[3] Čexov's lack of involvement, however, soon became the subject of attacks, as in Mixajlovskij's anonymously published review of Čexov's book *V sumerkax* (1887)[4] or in the following statement by the same critic: "Vysoko cenja bol'šoj talant g. Čexova, ja dumaju, čto esli by on rasstalsja so svoim bezrazličiem i bezučastiem, russkaja literatura imela by v ego lice ne tol'ko bol'šoj talant, a i bol'šogo pisatel'ja."[5] This reproach against the young writer's indifference causes even Roman Aleksandrovič Disterlo—a critic affiliated with *Nedelja* and an avid adversary of Mixajlovskij in his views on the course Russian literature should take—to concur with the latter:

> G. Čexov ničego ne doiskivaetsja ot prirody i žizni, ničego emu ne nužno razrešit', ničto v osobennosti ne zaxvatyvaet ego vnimanija. On prosto vyšel guljat' v žizn'. Vo vremja progulki on vstrečaet inogda interesnye lica, xarakternye scenki, xorošen'kie pejzaži. Togda on ostanovlivaetsja na minutu dostaet karandaš i legkimi štrixami nabrasyvaet svoj risunok. Končen risunok, i on idet dal'še . . . Teper' emu

vstrečaetsja uže drugoj predmet, on tak že legko ego zabyvaet
i ždet novyx vpečatlenij progulki.[6]

The publication of Čexov's "Step'" three months later evoked
substantial critical response, and, for instance, the anonymous attack in
Russkaja mysl', which was, at the time, a moderately liberal journal leaning
toward populism, follows the trend outlined above. The author recognizes
Čexov's literary ability—"nesomennyj i simpatičnyj talant"—but views the
story as " . . . utomitel'nuju, bezplodnuju literaturnuju step'," about which
it is " . . . trudno skazat' daže, radi čego napisana."[7] In an article published
shortly thereafter, Disterlo further elaborates on Čexov's writings, stressing
the lack of a unifying idea:

> Meždu predmetami ego rasskazov net ničego obščego, krome
> togo, čto vse oni—fakty odnogo i togo že mira, vozmožnosti
> odnoj i toj že čelovečeskoj žizni. S *odinokovym* spokojstvem
> i staratel'nost'ju izobražaet on i mečty nesčastnogo,
> tščedušnogo i boleznennogo brodjagi . . . i ljubov' bogatoj
> svetskoj ženščiny k čudaku knjazju . . . i scenu derzkogo
> obmana cerkovnogo storoža . . .[8]

Čexov's new story "Ogni" did not improve the situation. Critics
accused the author of tendentiousness and reproached him for propounding
a problem without solving it. Thus, an unidentified reviewer for the daily
Novosti dnja, who signed his article by the letter "Z," sees "Ogni" as a
"[rasskaz] razbavlennyj s izbytkom tendencioznoj filosofiej"[9] Unfortunately,
according to "Z," the aim of this conducive philosophy remains obfuscated.
The story made an analogous impression on Arsenij Ivanovič Vvedenskij,
an important liberal critic. He concludes that Čexov, wishing to show how
the philosophy of "pessimism" does not bring positive results, tells a sordid
story, the main part of which has nothing to do with pessimism. The story is
not didactic, according to Vvedinskij, and the unpleasant feeling it evokes
in the reader is not that of disgust for vice.[10]

Despite all the negative criticism, Čexov's success as a writer becomes
obvious in 1888. Not only does he begin to publish in the serious literary
reviews, but his third book of short stories *V sumerkax* (1887) is awarded the
coveted Puškin prize, and the second edition almost concurs with the release
of his fifth book entitled *Rasskazy* (1888). This growing popularity entices

many a critic to take up their pens on the issue of the young writer. Thus,
Dmitrij Sergeevič Merežkovskij, a student, who later becomes a quite
celebrated poet, novelist, and leader of one wing of the Symbolist movement,
published a long article on Čexov's writing under the heading "Staryj
vopros po povodu novogo talanta."[11] Merežkovskij finds two main features
in Čexov—the artist, namely, a wide, mystical feeling for nature, and a sober
realism, harmoniously blended. He particularly appreciates Čexov's
humanitarian attitude toward the most common people, and defends him
against reproaches for his supposed lack of social commitment. In the work
of art, veracity and sincerity are more important from a moral point of view.

The attitude of *Russkoe bogatstvo* and its contributors towards
literary criticism is well characterized by the article "Zadači literaturnoj
kritiki" signed N.G.[12] and its supplement "K predyduščej stat'e" written
by Leonid Egorovič Obolenskij, an idealist philosopher and renowned
literary critic.[13] Obolenskij strengthens and further elucidates the ideas
expressed in the original article. He agrees with Merežkovskij in his
disapproval of didacticism in art, or tendentiousness in literature.
According to both the above article and Obolenskij, the objective of art
lies not in the truthful depiction of life but in the evocation of
corresponding emotions, in the formation of altruistic sentiments in
humanity. The rejection of tendentiousness does not prevent Obolenskij
from demanding a moral and political identity (moral'no graždanskaja
ličnost') in the literary work, and he reiterates Disterlo's criticism of
Čexov's writings for their lack of direction. According to him, however,
the dearth of ideals has not been a specifically Čexovian feature, but is
characteristic of all the literary writings of the time: ". . . literatura konca
70-x i načala 80-x godov byla počti soveršenno čužda voprosov obščix
osnovnyx, o celi i smysle žizni voobšče."[14] This led the writers ". . . v
otčajannyj i bezprosvetnyj pessimism, apatiju, beznadežnost'
prostraciju."[15]

The publication of Čexov's collection of short stories, *Xmurye ljud*
(1890), came as if to confirm Obolenskij's insight, and Mixajlovskij in his
article concentrated his criticism on Čexov's attitude towards life:

> G. Čexov i sam ne živet v svoix proizvedenijax, a tak sebe,
> guljaet mimo žizni i, guljajuči, uxvatit to odno, to drugoe.
> Počemu imenno čto, a ne to? počemu to, a ne drugoe?
> Vybor tem g. Čexova poražaet svoeju slučajnost'ju. Vezut

po železnoj doroge bykov v stolicu na uboj. G. Čexov
zainteresovyvaetsja ètim i pišet rasskaz pod nazvaniem
"Xolodnaja krov'," xotja daže ponjat' trudno, pri čem tut
"xolodnaja krov'." . . . Počtu vezut, po doroge tarantas
vstrjaxivaet, počtal'on vyvalivaetsja i serditsja. Èto
rasskaz—"Počta." Začem on mne? . . . I rjadom vdrug
"Spat' xočetsja"—rasskaz o tom, kak trinadcatiletnjaja
devčonka Var'ka, sostojaščaja v njan'kax u sapožnika i ne
imejuščaja ni minuty pokoja, ubivaet poručennogo ej
grudnogo rebenka potomu, čto imenno on mešaet ej spat'.
I rasskazyvaetsja èto tem že tonom, s temi že milymi
kolokol'čikami i bubenčikami, i toju že "xolodnoju
krov'ju," kak i pro bykov ili pro počtu . . .
Net, ne "xmuryx ljudej" nado by postavit' v zaglavie vsego
ètogo sbornika, a vot razve "xolodnuju krov':" g. Čexov s
xolodnuju krov'ju popisyvaet, a čitatel' s xolodnuju krov'ju
počityvaet.[16]

Mixajlovskij sees Čexov as an absolutely apathetic person: " . . . g. Čexovu
vse edino—čto čelovek, čto ego ten', čto kolokol'čik, čto samoubijca."[17]
The young author's unfortunate detachment is augmented by his unexploited
capabilities: " . . . g. Čexov talantliv. On mog by svetit' i gret', esli by ne ta
nesčastnaja 'dejstvitel'nost', v kotoroj suždeno žit'.'"[18] Any unifying idea
is missing:

> . . . vo vsem ètom dejstvitel'no daže samyj iskusnyj analitik ne
> najdet obščej idei. Ni obščej idei, ni čutko nastorožennogo v
> kakuju—nibud' opredelennuju storonu interesa. Pri vsej svoej
> talantlivosti, g. Čexov ne pisatel' samostojatel'no
> razbirajuščijsja v svoem materiale i sortirujuščij ego s točki
> zrenija kakoj—nibud' obščej idei, a kakoj—to počti
> mexaničeskij apparat."[19]

Moreover, Čexov does not even express an interest in ideals, as he
demonstrates when he tries " . . . idealizirovat' otsutstvie idealov . . ."[20] The
only hope Mixajlovskij detects for the author of *Xmurye ljudi* lies in
developing the theme of longing for a unifying idea as presented in the
"Skučnaja istorija:"

Esli on [Čexov] rešitel'no ne možet priznat' svoimi obščie
idei otcov i dedov,—o čem, odnako, sledovalo by podumat'—
i takže ne možet vyrabotat' svoju sobstvennuju ideju,—nad
čem porabotat' vse-taki stoit,—to pust' on budet xot' poètom
toski po obščej idee i mučitel'nogo soznanija ee neobxodimosti.
I v čtom slučae on proživet ne darom i ostavit svoj sled v
literature.[21]

Other populist critics seem to be echoing Mixajlovskij's
judgements. Aleksandr Mixajlovič Skabičevskij, for instance, expresses
his views in these lines: "Proizvedenija Čexova, pri vsej ix fel'etonnoj
skorospelosti, obnaruživajut očen' sil'nyj talant, blestjat
xudožestvennost'ju i jumorom. No v nix odin suščestvennyj nedostatok—
pol'noe otsutstvie kakogo by to ni bylo ob"edinjajuščego idejnogo
načala."[22] Mixail Alekseevič Protopopov dwells upon this and additional
objections. Several pages of his article "žertva bezvremen'ja" are
dedicated to the young writer's inability to find a meaning in life. There
is " . . . pol'noe otsutstvie verxovnoj celi . . . On prosto ne verit v
vozmožnost' plodotvornoj dejatel'nosti, vidit tol'ko iznanku žizni, s ej
meločami i protivorečijami, emu predstavljajutsja frazerstvom vsjakie
tolki ob idealax."[23] The result of this predicament is, according to this
critic, "bezcel'nost' i bezsvjaznost' pisanij g. Čexova . . . indifferentnago
sozercatelja . . . "[24] Protopopov centers on the grief, which he sees as a
major element in Čexov's writings. The story "Step'" is the most typical
one in this regard. According to Protopopov, Čexov

. . . pokryvaet zelenuju i veseluju step' černym flerom svoej
neponjatnoj grusti. Nakonec, stepnyja lamentacii g. Čexova
razrešajutsja čisto pessimističeskim voplem: " . . . mysl' i duša
slivajutsja v soznanie odinočestva. Načinaeš čuvstvovat' sebja
nepopravimo odinokim i vse to, čto sčital ran'še blizkim i
rodnym, stanovitsja bezkoonečno dalekim i ne imejuščim
ceny. Zvezdy gljadjaščija s neba uže tysjači let, samo
neponjatnoe nebo i mgla, ravnodušnaja k korotkoj žizni
čeloveka, kogda ostaeš'sja s nimi s glazu na glaz' i staraeš'sja
postignut' ix smysl, gnetut dušu svoim molčaniem, prixodit na
mysl' to odinočestvo, kotoroe ždet každago iz nas v mogile i
suščnost' žizni predstavljaetsja otčajannoj, užasnoj..."[25]

The gloomy pictures lead to pessimism, and that is what Protopopov finds in Čexov's literary production following the publication of the above story. " . . . [B]or'ba ili, vernee, popytka k bor'be s osazdavšimi Čexova mračnymi obracami [sic] i pessimističeskimi vozzrenijami, i rezul'tatom ètoj bor'by javilas' povest' 'Ogni' . . . "[26] The quality of the story leaves a lot to be desired, according to this critic, but it is important as a psychological document. Čexov in the story rejects the thoughts of the fleeting nature of all things earthly, but his inclinations towards pessimism come through.[27] Protopopov divides Čexov's entire literary production up to this time into three phases: grievous, nihilistic or pessimistic, and the final one, which " . . . sostoit v primirenii s žizn'ju, no ne v vysšem, a v vul'garnom ee značenii,—primirenie s processom, a ne s idealom žizni.'"[28]

Populist views also influenced Petr Petrovič Percov, who in other respects was a propagandist of modernism (symbolism and mysticism). The striking impact of Mixajlovskij is evident in his pronouncements on Čexov. According to him, "Čexovu, kak pisatel'ju, . . . dejstvitel'no, vse ravno— kolokol'čiki-li zvenjat, čeloveka-li ubili, šampanskoe-li p'jut, ili kto-nibud' ni za čto, ni pro čto v tjur'mu popal. Vse èto dlja nego bezrazličnyja i otdel'nyja javlenija . . . [29]In one of his statements, Mixajlovskij compares Čexov to a mechanical apparatus. Percov not only accepts Mixajlovskij's opinions, but even employs the same metaphor:

> G. Čexov ljubit imenno ne tol'ko "razdroblennoj," no i odinakovoj ljubov'ju "i tixij šepot verby," i "vzor miloj devy" . . . Otnošenie g. Čexova k svoemu tvorčestvu napominaet priemy fotografa. S odinakovym bezpristrastiem i uvlečeniem snimaet ètot svoeobraznyj belletrističeskij apparat i prelestnyj pejzaž vesennogo utra ili širokoj stepi, i zadumčivoe lico molodoj devuški, i vz"erošennuju figuru russkogo intelligenta-neudačnika i original'nyj tip odinokogo mečtatelja i tupoumnogo kupca, i bezobraznye obščestvennye porjadki . . . Vse èti snimki vyxodjat živymi i pravdivymi, vse oni bleščut svežest'ju krasok, no v to že vremja izobražaemoe imi javlenie predstavljaetsja otryvočnym i otdel'nym, stojaščim vne cepi pričin i sledstvij, vne svjazi s drugimi, sosednimi faktami.[30]

The inception of the above article expounding populist views coincides with Merežkovskij's preparation of a frontal attack against populist criticism.

Based on two of his public lectures, the essay "O pričinax upadka i o novyx tečenijax sovremennoj russkoj literatury," appeared in print in 1893. In it Merežkovskij proclaims that true literature is the expression of a national idea; its concerns are spiritual, not economic or political. Russian literature is lacking in this regard. One of the resons for its decline is, according to Merežkovskij, the inadequacy of contemporary literary criticism. Protopopov has, for instance, a glib pen, sharp wit, and the political temperament of a born newspaperman. Under other conditions, this would be an asset. In contemporary Russian journalism, however, nothing remains for him, except " . . . sdelat'sja kritikom-publicistom. Mečta takix ljudej—prevratit' literaturu v komfortabel'nuju malen'kuju kafedru dlja gazetno-žurnal'noj propovedi. Kogda živaja original'nost' talanta ne pokorjaetsja im i ne xočet služit' p'edestalom političeskago oratora, g. Protopopov negoduet i kaznit ee."[31] Skabičevskij's criticism, Merežkovskij claims, is less polemically glib and witty, but more sincere and conscientious. He is a great literary historian but his temperament makes him the least suitable person to be a critic of art. "V ego vozzrenijax na iskusstvo est' ta čerta ubijstvennoj banal'nosti, poraboščenija obščepriznannym vkusam tol'py, kotoruju legče otmetit', čem vyrazit' i opredelit'."[32] The ability of an author to move a naive reader to tears, a quality highly praised by Skabičevskij, is, in Merežkovskij's eyes, a symptom of a decline in literary taste. He uses the "Vysočajšee *nravstvennoe* značenie iskusstva vovse ne v trogatel'nyx nravstvennyx tendencijax, a v bezkorystnoj, nepodkupnoj *pravdivosti* xudožnika, v ego bezstrašnoj iskrennosti."[33] Critics like Skabičevskij and Protopopov, unaware of the real issues of art, unwittingly cause a decline of letters by the standards they impose.[34]

    Merežkovskij's commentary on the contemporary Russian literature also includes several pronouncements on Čexov.[35] According to the young philosopher, Čexov loves and understands people. He is also able with the certainty of an artist to render deeply felt, varied impressions of life and nature. For him, nature is the source of all his strength, resolution, and health. The best feature of his writings is, however, the depiction of simple, spontaneous people who think less but feel more. Praiseworthy is also Čexov's ability to eliminate everything superfluous, such as all the narrative padding so popular among the critics; this renders his stories as compact as a lyric. Moreover, his curiosity for new impressions and artistic sensitivity allow him to react to the slightest quiver of life, and represent it in a manner reminiscent of music as it embraces the human soul. Merežkovskij concludes his analysis of Čexov by stating that he is an impressionist oriented towards the new budding idealism: "Čexov odin iz vernyx posledovatelej velikago učitelja Turgeneva na puti k novomu grjaduščemu idealizmu, on tak že, kak Turgenev, *impressionist*."[36]

This view of Čexov gains in value when the main points of Merežkovskij's essay are considered. He demands that art be liberated from non-aesthetic considerations, insists that it be recognized as man's highest metaphysical activity, and argues that great art is, and has always been, the product of religious faith. The essay closes by offering symbolist art as a theurgy, a means to higher truths and a basis for the spiritual revival of Russia through literature.

One of the critics attacked in Merežkovskij's article, Skabičevskij, later (1895) modifies his views on Čexov, as shown by the article he publishes in *Novosti* under the heading "Est'-li u g. A. Čexova idealy?"[37] The renowned critic's reassesment of Čexov admits the presence of some, albeit concealed, ideals in his work:

> U g. Čexova najdete vy svoi fal'šivyja stranicy, kakovy naprimer koncy ego proizvedenij "Duèl'" i "žena," no èti koncy stradajut vovse ne xudožestvennym indifferentizmom i *ne otsutstviem idealov* [italics mine, P.Z.S.], a, naprotiv togo, tem krajnim idealizmom, kotoryj polagaet, čto vera i ljubov' v bukval'nom smysle dvigajut gorami, i čto samomu otpetomu negodjaju ničego ne stoit pod ix vlijaniem obratit'sja v rycarja bez straxa i upreka . . .
> . . . g. Čexov nikogda ne formuliruet svoix idealov teoretičeski; voploščat' že ix v živye obrazy emu ne prixoditsja . . . emu prixoditsja ponevole skryvat' svoi idealy, podrazumevat' ix, vystavljaja javlenija, stojaščija v pol'nom protivorečii s nimi.[38]

Skabičevskij's dissent, coming from the midst of the populist camp, perhaps resulting from the writer's widespread acclaim, passed virtually unnoticed in the by then firmly entrenched trend of criticism.

The general consensus in critical views was disrupted by the publication of "Mužiki" (1897), which led to a vigorous press controversy. Čexov's mercilessly truthful depiction of village life was a heavy blow to the traditional populist concept of the post-reform village and social potentiality of Russian peasants. The opponents of populism lost no time in utilizing this fact. Petr Berngardovič Struve, a leader of the liberal movement,

was a Marxist in his youth, and it was he who began the polemics between
the Marxist *Novoe slovo* and populist *Russkoe bogatstvo* based on Čexov's
story. His article, published under the pseudonym "Novus,"[39] praises Čexov
as the best representative of that generation of Russian writers who, after the
abolition of serfdom were not inspired by any social ideal. The only possible
progression from this state of literature is the "sosredotočennoe izobraženie
žizni" of which "Mužiki" is a great example. The significance of this work,
according to Struve, is not in the depiction of the horrible conditions in
which the peasants live, but in the difference between their lives and those
of the city dwellers. Educational efforts and speeches regarding the debt of
the intelligentsia to the peasant are not sufficient. The recognition of the
individual, and his rights, is necessary. Angel Ivanovič Bogdanovič, another
Marxist, stresses the importance of the development of the city's cultural
influence, directly attacking the populist credo that the city destroys, while
the village saves.[40]

Mixajlovskij responded for the populists. His article corroborates the
general esteem of Čexov's talent. Some unidentified obstacles, however,
prevent the full development of this talent. As Mixajlovskij states, Čexov is
a " . . . sil'nyj talant, kotoryj možet, konečno, promaxnut'sja i slaboj vešč'ju,
no kotoromu, glavnoe, kakija to obstojatel'stva mešajut rozvernut'sja vo
vsju meru svoej sily."[41] Furthermore, he cannot understand the lavish praise
critics pour upon "Mužiki." According to him, this story is far from Čexov's
best, and he claims that it will fail just as completely as *Ivanov* has. If all
Čexov's writings are taken into consideration, it becomes clear that there is
no connection between them. Mixajlovskij recalls "Skučnaja istorija,"[42]
where the hero complains that

> . . . vo vsex mysljax, čuvstvax i ponjatijax, kakie ja sostavljaju
> obo vsem, net čego-to obščego, čto svjazyvalo by vse èto v
> odno celoe. Každoe čuvstvo i každaja mysl' živut vo mne
> osobnjakom, i vo vsex moix suždenijax o nauke, teatre,
> literature, učenikax i vo vsex kartinax, kotorye risuet moe
> voobraženie, daže samyj iskusnyj analitik ne najdet togo, čto
> nazyvaetsja obščej ideej, ili Bogom živogo čeloveka.
>
> A koli net ètogo, to, značit, net i ničego.(VII, 307)

The same, according to Mixajlovskij, is true of the author. Moreover, " . . .
g. Čexov daže rovno ničego ne xotel pokazat', a prosto pisal, kak pisalos'

. . . Dlja menja lično nikakie obščie vyvody ne sleduet iz napisannoj im kartiny, v kotoroj stol'ko skučajnago, èkzempljarnago, neproporcial'nago i nedogovorennago, nesmotrja na gromkoe i kak by sumprujuščee zaglavie 'Mužiki.'"[43] The polemics continues with another article by "Novus,"[44] a response by Mixajlovskij,[45] and the last contribution by "Novus" in the December issue of *Novoe slovo*, [46]shortly before this publication was banned. A reverberation of this polemics passes into the 1898 article commenting on contemporary Russian literature.[47] The author, Petr Filipovič Jakubovič, another populist of *Russkoe bogatstvo*, singles out Čexov as a good representative of the generation of gifted literati overflowing with lugubrious skepticism and cold despair.[48]

This reproach for despondency as a salient feature in Čexov's stories gains in importance when Bogdanovič, who so praised the "Mužiki," and who closely followed Čexov's literary production thereafter, detects a new trend in his prose, namely, the involvement of the author. Čexov, renowned for his objectivity, even criticized for indifference, according to this critic, cannot now refrain from occasionally expressing his ideas and views through the mouths of his protagonists.[49] Hence, Bogdanovič's criticism of the general outlook expressed in Čexov's more recent writings runs deeper, and he even subtitles his article on Čexov's new stories "Pessimizm avtora." His analysis then begins: "Est' čto-to v poslednix proizvedenijax g. Čexova, čto uglubljaet ix soderžanie, byt' možet, pomimo voli samogo avtora, pridaet im kakuju-to terpkost' i ostrotu, volnuet i pričinjaet ostruju bol' čitatelju."[50] Pessimism becomes the critics' major objection to Čexov's work in 1898. Skabičevskij, to give yet another example, although still concerned with the absence of ideals in Čexov's writings, claims now that their highest merit lies in the lack of ideals, not in the works, naturally, but in the life depicted by the writer,[51] and sees in the stories a pessimistic attitude and "bezysxodnyj mrak."[52]

Dmitrij Nikolaevič Ovsjaniko-Kulikovskij, an adherent of the psychological trend in literary criticism, seeks the roots of Čexov's pessimism. It is based, according to him, on the " . . . unyloe i bezotradnoe čuvstvo, vyzyvaemoe v xudožnike sozercaniem vsego, čto est' v nature čelovečeskoj zaurjadnago, pošlago, rutinnago "[53] Commonplaces, stereotypes, routines evoke a feeling of dejection, but not hopelessness. On the contrary, Čexov's pessimism, according to Ovsjaniko-Kulikovskij, " . . . osnovyvaetsja na glubokoj vere v vozmožnost' bezgraničnago progressa čelovečestva na ubeždenii, čto on vovse ne idet nazad, . . . i glavnym prepjatstviem, zaderživajuščim nastuplenie lučšago buduščago, javljaetsja *normal'nyj* čelovek, kotoryj . . . ne opuskaetsja niže normy, no i ne sposoben xot' čutočku podnjat'sja vyše eja.[54]

At the time, however, Čexov gained a strong supporter in Aleksej Maksimovič Peškov, better known under his pen-name of Maksim Gor'kij, who was the current literary sensation. In 1900 Gor'kij published an article entitled "Po povodu novogo rasskaza A.P. Čexova 'V ovrage,'" in which he defended Čexov against all the objections raised by the critics. He insists, for instance, that " . . . každyj novyj rasskaz Čexova vse usilivaet odnu gluboko cennuju i nužnuju dlja nas notu—notu bodrosti i ljubvi k žizni."[55] Hence, Gor'kij directly contradicts all the accusations of pessimism made against Čexov. Moreover, he defends Čexov's general attitude, thus challenging the criticisms he suffered over his supposed lack of ideals:

> U Čexova est' nečto bol'še, čem mirosozercanie—on ovladel svoim predstavleniem žizni i takim obrazom stal vyše ee. On osveščaet ee skuku, ee neleposti, ee stremlenija, ves' ee xaos s vyššej točki zrenija. I xotja èta točka zrenija neulovima, ne poddaetsja opredeleniju—byt' možet potomu, čto vysoka,— no ona vsegda čuvstvovalas' v ego rasskazax i vse jarče probivaetsja v nix. Vse čašče slyšitsja v ego rasskazax grustnyj, no tjaželyj i metkij uprek ljudjam za ix neumen'e žit' vse krasivee svetit v nix sostradanie k ljudjam i—èto glavnoe!— zvučit čto-to prostoe, sil'noe, primirjajuščee vsex i vsja.[56]

The publication of the first volume of Čexov's collected works, *Sobranie sočinenij: rasskazy*, by Adol'f Fedorovič Marks preceeded the story "V ovrage" by one month. Hence the critical reaction to the story coincided with the appearance of more general assessments motivated by the *Sobranie sočinenij*. One example is Mixajlovskij'a article "Koe-čto o g. Čexove."[57] Here, the critic recapitulates his views on Čexov's writings, but he recognizes a change in Čexov's outlook:

> . . . g. Čexov nastojaščij, bol'šoj talant, i neudivitel'no poètomu, čto on ne ostalsja pri bezrazličnom otnošenii k svetu i mraku . . . "Idealy otcov i dedov nad nami bezsil'ny,"—govorili teoretiki "panteističeskago" mirosozercanija.. . . [Čexov]

zatoskoval, ponjal, čto "panteizm," kotoromu on poslužil bez
bor'by, bez dumy rokovoj," ateizm, i zatoskoval, ili po krajnej
mere, prevosxodno izobrazil ètu tosku.[58]

"Skučnaja istorija" illustrates the longing for a unifying idea, but the actual
break in the writer's attitude to reality comes with the "Palata No. 6" and
"Černyj monax."[59] The former story shows two possible attitudes to reality.
One of the protagonists, Ragin, is, according to Mixajlovskij, a " . . .
'panteist,' esli pozvolitel'no razumet' pod panteizmom primirenie s
dejstvitel'nost'ju, kakova-by ona ni byla . . . "[60] The other protagonist,
Gromov, disagrees with such a "rehabilitation of reality." He believes that
God created man with warm blood and with nerves so that he should respond
to any stimulus."[61] Čexov's new approach to reality leads to "Mužiki."
Here, Mixajlovskij repeats his earlier pronouncements, but notes that the
author did not get carried away by the lavish praise given the story, and
responded with "Moja žizn'." Mixajlovskij sees the latter story as
contradicting the former one with regard to the superiority of city life over
village life. No fashionable trend could claim Čexov as one of its adherents;
he stood only for himself. The change in his writings cannot be attributed to
anything but a transformation in the author's concerns. It is not just triteness
(pošlost') that, according to Mixajlovskij, interests Čexov in the late 1890s.
The anecdotes of his early works disappear. No longer do the stories inspire
happy laughter but rather gloomy reflections. The story "O ljubvi" contains
a statement about the necessity to consider each case individually without
any attempt to generalize.(X, 66) These words seem to express, according to
Mixajlovskij, a theoretical justification for Čexov's entire literary
production.[62] Moreover, the hero of the story "O ljubvi," Alexin, comes to
the conclusion that one's tender sentiments have to be considered on a
higher plane: "Ja ponjal, čto kogda ljubiš, to v svoix rassuždenijax ob ètoj
ljubvi nužno isxodit' ot vysšego, ot bolee važnogo, čem sčast'e ili nesčast'e,
grex ili dobrodetel' v ix xodjačem smysle, ili ne nužno rassuždat' vovse."(X,
74) This loftier, more significant point, from the height of which happiness
and misfortune become equally acceptable, intrigues Mixajlovskij, for
whom Alexin's attitude indicates a new direction in Čexov's writings:

> . . . jasno kažetsja, kak doroga stala g. Čexovu vertikal'naja
> linija k nebesam, to tret'e izmerenie, kotoroe podnimaet ljudej
> nad ploskoj dejstvitel'nost'ju, kak daleko ušel on ot

"panteističeskago" (čitaj: ateističeskago) mirosozercanija, vse prinimajuščago, kak dolžnoe i razve tol'ko kak smešnoe...[63]

In further analysis, the critic questions the blind workings of chance in Čexov's stories, the mechanisms of which are recognized rather late. Both the author and his protagonists contemplate bitterly the senseless reality which it is wise to "rehabilitate." The question remains, however, why such abuse and agony had to occur. At this point, Mixajlovskij philosophizes:

> ... tol'ko sami ljudi, vtorgajas' v pričinnuju svjaz' javlenij so svoimi celjami, berut na sebja otvetstvennost', svjazannuju s voprosom: "začem?" Strašnaja èto byvaet otvetstvennost', i vse zdes' zavisit ot dostoinstva celej, radi kotoryx delaetsja tot ili drugoj šag.[64]

There is a definite change in Čexov's writings, Mixajlovskij concludes: the old theme of common triteness abides, but it loses its comical qualities, becoming dreadful and odious in the process.

Another general work on Čexov published in 1900 is Akim L'vovič Flekser's "Anton Čexov."[65] Flekser, an art and literary critic, the chief collaborator of *Severnyj vestnik*, writing under the pseudonym of A. Volynskij, gained recognition by his attacks on the materialistic positivism of contemporary radical writers, and advocated a rather vague and mystical idealism. Čexov's stories serve him as material for abstract ethical and philosophical statements.(X, 388) The small trilogy, "Čelovek v futljare," "Kryžovnik," and "O ljubvi," reveals, according to Flekser, the inner needs of the human soul, and the inner suffering of people.[66] In the *Précis* he states that " . . . vse èti očerki v gorazdo bol'šej stepeni prinadležat sovremennoj volne idejnyx nastroenij, čem raznye tendencioznye pisanija s namereniem priobščit'sja k ètoj volne.[67] Flekser's attitude comes forth again in his criticism of Čexov's "Slučaj iz praktiki." He objects to the artistic qualities of the story, but values its idea of the approaching spiritual revival, as opposed to the terrifying nightmare of contemporary real life. In his own words: "Možno skazat', čto ves' rasskaz . . . proniknut skrytoju mečtoju o kakom-to voskresnom utre, o kakom-to novom vozroždenii ili, vernee skazat' o duxovnom pereroždenii ljudej . . .. Voskresnoe utro—kakoj živoj simvol, vylivšijsja iz vstrevožennoj duši čutkago sovremennago čeloveka."[68]

Virtually the same interpretation is repeated in all Flekser's commentaries on Čexov's stories.

During the last years of his life Čexov concentrated his efforts on dramatic production,[69] which correspondingly forms the focus of critical response. The few general criticisms appearing during this time seem to echo earlier judgements. Thus, for instance, Nikolaj Sergeevič Rusanov, a lesser critic using the pseudonym of V.G. Podarskij, viciously attacks Čexov for his lack of principles: "G. Čexov—pisatel' gluboko amoral'nyj: on živet s svoimi sozdanijami dejstvitel'no po tu storonu dobra i zla . . . "[70]

On the other hand, Anatolij Vasil'evič Lunačarskij, a Marxist philosopher, critic, dramatist, and later Soviet Minister of Culture, admires Čexov unconditionally. As he writes,

> Mjagkij i nepoddel'nyj jumor, ruka impressionista pozvoljajuščaja dvumja štrixami karandaša dat' žizn', kotoroj drugoj ne ulovit v tščatel'no vypolnenoj kartine, glubina ponimanija čelovečeskoj duši, ogromnyj krugozor ot geroev "Ovraga" do izjaščnyx "Trex sester." Dovol'no davno uže ètot isključitel'nyj, očarovatel'nyj, milyj talant posvjatil sebja opisaniju samoj seroj, samoj tuskloj žizni. S strašnoj pravdoj vystupala žiznennaja pošlost' v "Trex godax," "Bab'em carstve," v udivitel'noj "Moej žizni." No nakonec... nakonec stalo kak-to strašno na duše. A.P. Čexov tak ob"ektiven, tak ob"ektiven![71]

Lunačarskij's only complaint is that Čexov does not show any possible way out from the impasse of the gloomy, sombre life he depicts. He believes that Čexovians must be told that the "Svetlaja, prekrasnaja žizn' suščestvuet, no ee usloviem javljaetsja bor'ba! Gotovnost' riskovat', borot'sja, rešimost' — vot ključ . . ."[72] Hence, even Lunačarskij, who is later to serve in the Soviet government as a Commissar, does not read into Čexov's works any call for or prediction of the revolution. Such claims, incidentally, were not made prior to the writer's premature death in 1904.

After Čexov succumbed to the disease that plagued many years of his life, a new approach in the criticism of his literary production is evident. Now that his *oeuvre* is complete, critics and philosophers of various denominations are able to claim Čexov for their cause without fear of a forthcoming work which would deny their assertion. For the same reason, the importance of chronological order in the criticisms diminishes; henceforth they will be categorized according to their spiritual affinity rather than their historical placement.

One of the critical trends, a prominent representative of which is Sergej Nikolaevič Bulgakov, a leading religious philosopher, claims that Čexov too is a religious thinker. Bulgakov's 1904 lecture "Čexov kak myslitel'" is very typical of this orientation in criticism. Because of the importance of the arguments he presents, an extensive recapitulation is necessary. Initially, he acknowledges the controversy among the interpreters of Čexov's writings,[73] and then proceeds to analyze it. At the outset of his literary career Čexov was, according to him, criticized for lack of direction, but later it was conceded that a trend nevertheless exists in his writing. Thus, Čexov's work is usually divided into two periods: " ... pervyj xarakterizuetsja otsutstviem u nego civičeskix dobrodetelej, a vtoroj pojavleniem."[74] Bulgakov refutes this division, basing his claim on the author's own indifference to the chronology of his works. He concludes that "I nam dejstvitel'no ona [literaturnaja dejstvitel'nost' Čexova] predstavljaetsja edinym celym, proniknutym odnim obščim mirovozzreniem ... "[75] Moreover, according to Bulgakov, Čexov is a philosophical writer:

> ... on [Čexov] javljaetsja pisatelem naibol'šago filosofskago značenija.
> "Prizvanie vsjakago čeloveka,—govorit Čexov ustami xudožnika v 'Domike s mezoninom,'—v duxovnoj dejatel'nosti, v postojannom iskanii pravdy i smysla žizni... udovletvorit' ego mogut tol'ko religija, nauki, iskusstva... Nauki i iskusstva, kogda oni nastojaščija, stremjatsja ne k vremennym, ne k častnym celjam, a k večnomu i obščemu,— oni iščut pravdy, smysla žizni, iščut Boga, dušu." V ètix slovax opredeljaetsja i obščee soderžanie tvorčestva i samogo Čexova, i ono v čem on videl zadaču istinnoj nauki i iskusstva: iskaniju pravdy Boga, duši, smysla žizni.[76]

The majority of Čexov's larger works, according to Bulgakov, and many of his minor ones, are dedicated to the depiction of the spiritual world of people in search for the truth of life. Among these works are: "Skučnaja istorija," "Moja žizn'," "Po delam služby," "Slučaj iz praktiki," "Razskaz neizvestnago čeloveka," "Palata No. 6," "Duèl'," and "Kryžovnik." Bulgakov analyzes these stories, and comes to the conclusion that of all philosophical problems, Čexov is most concerned with that of lack of moral strength: " . . . obščečelovečeskij, a po tomu samomu i filosofskij vopros, dajuščij glavnoe soderžanie tvorčestvu Čexova, est' vopros o nravstvennoj slabosti, bezsilii dobra v duše srednjago čeloveka, blagodarja kotoromu on svalivaetsja bez bor'by . . .[77] This, however, is only one of the leitmotives of Čexov's writings. In addition to the people who lack strength and who have lost their God, the gallery of Čexovian characters contains a number of " . . . 'seryx' ljudej, kotorye pošly, daže zly, . . . u kotoryx v duše net otčetlivago soznanija dobra i zla . . . . . Čexov v polnom ob"eme xudožestvenno postavil problemu posredstvennosti, umstvennosti i nravstvennoj organičennosti [sic], duxovnago meščanstva, kotoroe obezvkušivaet ee skučnoj i postyloj."[78] Therefore, Bulgakov rejects the term "Čexovian hero." He says that the total lack of anything heroic is the most characteristic feature of Čexov's protagonists. Aleksandr Aleksandrovič Fadeev, a renowned Soviet novelist, criticizes Čexov on precisely this point. He finds extensive reading of Čexov tedious for the writer does not depict "the titanic figures of Russian revolutionaries, scientists, the giants of literature, painting, and the theater — all this went unnoticed by Čexov the writer. Not a single outstanding peasant, or worker, or intellectual!"[79]

According to Bulgakov, the most negative quality of Čexov's protagonists is indifference. "S užasom i unyniem Čexov postojanno vnov' i vnov' vozvraščaetsja k ètomu skotskomu rovnodušiju srednjago obyvatelja, k ego bezsmyslennoj zlobnosti, tupomu ègoizmu, k vse obvolakivajuščej pošlosti."[80] The analysis of Čexov's work leads Bulgakov to the eduction of the qualities stipulated by the writer as necessary for mankind:

Čeloveka oblagoraživaet, delaet čelovekom v nastojaščem smysle slova ne čto strannoe obožanie natural'nago, zoologičeskago sverxčeloveka, "belokuroj bestii" Nicše, no vera v dejstvitel'no sverxčelovečeskuju i vsemoguščuju silu dobra, sposobnuju pererodit' povреždennago i podderžat' slabago čeloveka. Tol'ko verja v nee, možem my verit' v sebja i v svoix brat'ev—čelovečestvo. Takov vyvod, kotoryj, dumaetsja nam, neosporimo vytekaet iz vsego tvorčestva Čexova. Zagadka o čeloveke v Čexovskoj postanovke možet polučit' ili religioznoe razrešenie ili... nikakogo. V pervom slučae ona prjamo privodit k samomu central'nomu dogmatu

xristianskoj religii, vo vtorom k samomu užasajuščemu i
beznadežnomu pessimizmu . . .[81]

Thus Bulgakov narrows the controversy around Čexov to a choice
between Čexov the Christian and Čexov the disconsolate pessimist. The
latter possibility, however, is contradicted by all the positive and conciliatory
motives present in his writing. This leads the critic to a general conclusion
that "Voobšče govorja, vsja literaturnaja dejatel'nost' Čexova proniknuta
ves'ma svoeobraznym i trudno poddajuščimsja opredeleniju na jazyke
škol'noj filosofii idealizmom i nad vseju neju gospodstvuet odna obščaja
ideja, tot bog, kotorago ne našel v sebe v kritičeskuju minutu staryj professor
iz 'Skučnoj istorii' i kotorago dolgo ne umeli raspoznat' u Čexova ego
kritiki."[82] Bulgakov also claims that throughout Čexov's literary work are
scattered diffident remarks reflecting a steadily growing religious belief
undoubtedly carrying a hint of Christianity. Without such a belief, Čexov's
writings would be, in effect, an unsolvable riddle for the reader, and stories
like "Student" would be psychological and logical nonsense.[83] Religious
belief is the one thing that gives Čexov his unfailing faith in man. One
exception exists, however, to his love of humanity. As Bulgakov says, "K
odnomu Čexov otnosilsja dejstvitel'no s neprimirimoj i neskryvaemoj
vraždoj,—k uproščennym geometričeskim formulam, v kotoryja
prjamolinejnye ljudi pytajutsja uložit' i žizn' i buduščee . . .. Počti
karikaturnyj obraz prjamolinejnago doktrinera Čexov dal v lice učenago
zoologa fon-Korena (v 'Dueli'), kotoryj, po vole avtora, ustupaet v ponimanii
žizni nemudrjaščemu sel'skomu d'jakonu."[84]

   This refusal to accept any strict classification of people according to
preconceived formulas apparently eluded Boris Julianovič Poplavskij, one
of the finest poets of the Russian emigration, the author of brilliant surrealist
and, at times, mystical poems. In 1929 he wrote in his personal journal that
Čexov is the most (Russian) Orthodox of Russian writers or, more correctly,
the only Orthodox Russian writer.[85] He bases this statement on the claim
that Russian Orthodoxy is nothing if not absolute forgiveness, absolute
refusal to condemn. Similar to this is the perception of Čexov's works by
Mixail Grigor'ev Kurdjumov, who nevertheless arrives at a somewhat
different conclusion.[86] According to this critic, Čexov never condemns
anyone. His protagonists are pitiable, not condemnable.[87] He loves man
compassionately, but " . . . ljubov' k ljudjam est' tol'ko *vtoraja* zapoved'
Božija, neispolnimaja do konca i počti bezsmyslennaja bez *pervoj.* 'Vozljubi

Gospoda Boga Tvoego vsem serdcem tvoim...'"[88] Thus Kurdjumov feels that the discontent and melancholy of Čexov's protagonists has one common root: "V rjade složnyx individual'nyx pričin, neudovletvorennosti i toski u vsex dejstvujuščix lic Čexova vystupaet odna obščaja pričina: otsutstvie osnovnago duxovnago dvigatelja každoj čelovečeskoj žizni i vsex žiznej vmeste, otsutstvie *vysšago opravdanija i vysšix celej bytija.*[89] In other words, Čexov created a picture of the spiritual crisis of his epoch, or even, as Kurdjumov describes it, Čexov's work is an " . . . opredelennyj protest protiv bezreligioznago progressa i very v nego."[90] According to Kurdjumov, the entirety of Čexov's literary production epitomizes the idea that love is the single most important element in human life and that the ability to love one's fellow man is rooted in religion. Thus Kurdjumov speaks of the " . . . ègocentrism Čexovskix geroev, vytekajuščij iz podsoznatel'no-religioznoj trevogi . . ."[91] Father Jakov in "Košmar," on the other hand, exemplifies that " . . . sčast'e i sila čeloveka v soveršennoj vere i soveršennoj ljubvi k Bogu i k ljudjam."[92] Religion and its direct corollary, love for humanity, bring strength and happiness, or, at least, resigned contentment. Faith gives meaning to life and prevents the pessimism which victimizes so many of Čexov's characters.[93] Moreover, religion liberates man from the fear of death, while, on the other hand, the "Geroi Čexova, kak i on sam, ne rešajas' do konca stat' religiozno verujuščimi, uverovat' v bezsmertie, v suščnosti ob ètom bezsmertii bol'še vsego i toskujut. Mysl' o konce otravljaet im žizn' . . ."[94]

Science is not the answer to the quest of so many of Čexov's protagonists. Kurdjumov also considers this possibility. As he writes, the professor in "Skučnaja istorija" admits, in his last breath, the superiority of love over science.[95] The same is implied in the story "V ovrage:" "One [Lipa i Praskov'ja] nikogda o nauke ne slyxali, no one, esli ne znajut soznaniem, to oščuščajut serdcem, čto v žizni samoe važnoe, samoe pervostepennoe est' pravda."[96] In fact, such ignorance may be a blessing. Čexov himself suffered, according to Kurdjumov, precisely because he was versed in science: "Čexov skryval tu složnuju i zaputannuju oblast' svoej duši, gde podsoznatel'noe oščuščenie blizosti Boga i Božestvennogo Promysla v mire mučitel'no borolis' s samoljubivym soznaniem 'naučno mysljaščago' i potomu neverujuščago čeloveka."[97] This is a formidable quandary for Čexov's protagonists. Two of the examples Kurdjumov uses to illustrate this claim are Laevskij in "Duèl'" and Anisim in "V ovrage." For the former God is the only measure, without Him, there is no truth or meaning in life.[98]

The latter believes that there cannot be any conscience if one doubts God's existence.[99] On the other hand, even an agnostic can find relief in religion. Mixail Aver'anyč in "Palata No. 6" observes that even a person who does not believe in God, feels better after a prayer.[100] Kurdjumov gathers many examples of Čexov's protagonists before he seeks and finds parallels between them and the author. Eventually, he argues that Čexov's turning back to childhood and compassion shows emotional confusion, or indicates that he is not a confirmed atheist.[101] He finds the fact that the God-seeking Tolstoj would write *Voskresenie*, and that the unbelieving Čexov would pen stories such as "Arxierej" or "Svatoju noč'ju" remarkable.[102] He reaches the conclusion that Čexov stood all his life on a threshold which his heart wished to cross. Therein lies the explanation for his understanding of those who hesitated or suffered from a lack of faith.[103] Moreover, Kurdjumov identifies Čexov's feelings towards people as Christian love.[104] Such feelings do not offer a suitable basis for revolutionary activity. The main protagonist in "Rasskaz neizvestnogo čeloveka" is supposed to kill a man but ceases to be a revolutionary rather than take the gift of life. This explains why Čexov, as Kurdjumov says, " . . . nikogda, daže namekom, ne govoril o 'želannoj revoljucii,' o kotoroj mečtala dobraja polovina russkoj intelligencii."[105] The revolution does not give meaning to life, and according to Kurdjumov, Čexov sought, above all, the highest meaning of human existence,[106] "My znaem, on obronil odnaždy frazu, čto 'obrazovannyj čelovek ne možet verovat' v Boga.'"[107] Nonetheless, as indicated in "Pari," Čexov expresses the view that everything passes, death equalizes all the differences, only God endures.[108] Kurdjumov's book provides a solid basis for his statement that "On [Čexov] žil v postojannom kolebanii duši, uverennyj v tom, čto 'nikto ne znaet nastojaščej pravdy'."[109] The final conclusion is, however, that Čexov, whether he knew it or not, was a believer in the teaching of the Russian Orthodox Church.

This idea is shared by Boris Konstantinovič Zajcev, one of the leading writers of the Russian emigration in post-revolutionary years. In fact, Zajcev is more definite in his claims about Čexov's Christianity. One should mention that Zajcev's biography of Čexov is, according to the American Slavist Simon Karlinsky, probably the least satisfactory book on Čexov ever written.[110] Gennadij Andreevič Andreev, a renowned émigré literary journalist, maintains, however, that this impression is incorrect, and that Zajcev's study offers deeper insight in Čexov's writings than, for instance, Bunin's better written work *O Čexove*.[111] Furthermore, he writes that Zajcev's views are well argued in the book.[112] One may add that this work is a good illustration of the émigré approach to Čexov. Where Soviet commentators stress "Nevesta," as Čexov's ultimate statement on life and politics, Zajcev dismisses it in a single sentence: "On [Čexov] napisal ešče blednuju 'Nevestu' ..."[113] The discussion of "Arxierej," however, in which Zajcev sees proof of Čexov's religiousness, spans a whole chapter. The conclusion to his analysis of "Skučnaja istorija" progresses in a similar fashion. For Zajcev this story is the end of Čexov's materialism: "Pisatel' sovsem, sobstvenno, molodoj ... vzjal uxodjaščego professora, pereodelsja čast'ju v nego, napisal pronzitel'nuju vešč' i ne soznavaja togo, poxoronil materializm, o kotorom vsegda otzyvalsja s velikim uvaženiem. Xudožnik i čelovek Čexov ubil doktora Čexova."[114] Naturally, according to Zajcev, Marxism is a strange world for Čexov. He stresses Čexov's distance from the Marxists using the story "V ovrage" to substantiate his claim,[115] and reaches conclusions identical to those of Kurdjumov.

The above seems to indicate that the views on Čexov expressed by the émigré critics are uniform. Such an impression is, however, misleading. Lev Isaakovič Schwarzmann, for instance, one of the foremost idealist philosophers of the twentieth century, writing under the pseudonym of Lev Šestov, expressed contrary views in his extensive essay on Čexov published under the title "Tvorčestvo iz ničego."[116] He too believes that a certain tendency exists in Čexov's writings, thus opposing the claims that direction is lacking in his works. He does not, however, identify it as religion. According to Šestov, Čexov is a poet of hopelessness:

> U Čexova bylo svoe delo, xotja nekotorye kritiki i govorili o
> tom, čto on byl služitelem čistago iskusstva i daže sravnivali
> ego s bezzabotno porxajuščej ptičkoj. Čtoby v dvux slovax
> opredelit' ego tendenciju, ja skažu: Čexov byl pevcom
> beznadežnosti. Uporno, unylo, odnoobrazno v tečenie vsej
> svoej počti 25-letnej literaturnoj dejatel'nosti Čexov tol'ko
> odno i delal: temi ili inymi sposobami ubival čelovečeskie
> naděždy. V ètom, na moj vzgljad, suščnost' ego tvorčestva.[117]

The assessment of Čexov as a killer of human hopes has been readily accepted by other critics. Thus, Ivan (Alekseevič) Bunin, for instance, writing half a century later, values Šestov's essay as one of the best articles on Čexov.[118] Yet as already noticed by Andreev,[119] Bunin's understanding of the phrase "Tvorčestvo iz ničego" differs from that of Šestov. The last author mentioned speaks of Čexov's independence, about his rejection of the ideas and traditions accepted by contemporary society. This, according to Šestov, is an abnormal attitude: "... Čexov nadorvavšijsja, nenormal'nyj čelovek ... Čexovskie že geroi, ljudi nenormal'nye *par excellence*, postavleny v protivoestestvennuju, a potomu strašnuju, neobxodimost' tvorit' iz ničego. Pred nimi vsegda beznadežnost', bezysxodnost', absoljutnaja nevozmožnost' kakogo by to ni bylo dela. A mež tem oni živut, ne umirajut...[120] Šestov does not accept such a philosophical outlook. Millennia have passed, he writes, and humanity has a store of experiences. Čexovian heroes, however, cannot draw on this store, and must create everything for themselves.[121]

> Verojatno, otsjuda to neskryvaemoe prezrenie, s kotorym oni otnosjatsja k naibolee cennym produktam obyknovennago čelovečeskago tvorčestva. O čem by vy ni zagovorili s Čexovskim geroem, u nego na vse odin otvet: *menja nikto ne možet ničemu naučit'*. Vy predlagajte emu novoe mirovozzrenie, no on s pervyx slov vašix uže čuvstvuet, čto vse ono svoditsja k popytke na novyj maner pereložit' starye kerpiči i kamni, i neterpelivo, často grubo, otvoračivaetsja ot vas. ... [K]akuju neskryvaemuju brezglivost' projavljaet on [Čexov] k prijatym idejam i mirovozzrenijam.[122]

Bunin accompanies his commentary on Šestov's essay with a quotation from *Samopoznanie* by a leading twentieth-century religious philosopher, Nikolaj Aleksandrovič Berdjaev. Through this juxtaposition, he introduces a new concept of "creation from nothing." Berdjaev identifies this "nothing" as freedom necessary for any artistic creativity. As he writes,

> [p]roblema tvorčestva byla dlja menja [Berdjaeva] svjazana s problemoj svobody. ... Tvorčestvo vozmožno liš' pri dopuščenii svobody, ne determinirovannoj bytiem, *ne vyvodimoj* iz bytija. Svoboda vkorenena ne v bytii, a v "ničto," svoboda bezosnovna, ničem ne opredeljaema, naxoditsja vne kauzal'nyx otnošenij kotorym podčineno bytie i bez kotoryx nelzja myslit' bytija. ... [V] *Smysle tvorčestva* [1915] ja uže vyrazil osnovnuju dlja menja mysl', čto tvorčestvo est' tvorčestvo iz ničego, t. e. iz svobody. Kritiki pripisyvali mne

nelepuju mysl', čto tvorčestvo čeloveka ne nuždaetsja v materii, v materialax mira. No ničego podobnogo ja nikogda ne utverždal. Tvorčeskij akt čeloveka nuždaetsja v materii, on ne možet obojtis' bez mirovoj real'nosti, on soveršaetsja ne v bezvozdušnom prostranstve. No tvorčeskij akt čeloveka ne možet celikom opredeljat'sja materialom, kotoryj daet mir, v nem est' novizna, ne determinirovannaja izvne mirom. Èto i est' tot èlement svobody, kotoryj privxodit vo vsjakij podlinnyj tvorčeskij akt. V ètom tajna tvorčestva. V ètom smysle tvorčestvo est' tvorčestvo iz ničego. Èto liš' značit, čto ono ne opredeljaetsja celikom iz mira, ono est' takže èmanacija svobody, ne opredeljaemoj ničem izvne. Bez ètogo, tvorčestvo bylo by liš' pereraspredeleniem èlementov dannogo mira i vozniknovenie novizny bylo by prizračnym.[123]

Such freedom is apparently not acceptable to Šestov, who is at a loss when trying to establish a philosophical system to which Čexov subscribes. A dearth of ideas and lack of connection between the events of life strike him as the most significant and original features of the writer's creative work.

Daže u Tolstogo, tože ne sliškom cenivšego filosofskie sistemy, vy ne vstrečaete takogo rezko vyražennago otvraščenija ko vsjakago roda mirovozzrenijam i idejam, kak u Čexova. On xorošo znaet, čto mirovozzrenija polagaetsja čtit' i uvažat', svoju nesposobnost' preklonjatsja pred tem, čto sčitaetsja obrazovannymi ljud'mi svjatynej, on sčitaet svoim nedostatkom, s kotorym nužno vsemi silami borot'sja. On daže i borotsja s nim vsemi silami, no bezuspešno. Bor'ba ne tol'ko ni k čemu ne privodit, no naoborot, čem dol'še živet Čexov, tem bol'še oslabevaet nad nim vlast' vysokix slov — vopreki sobstvennomu razumu i soznatel'noj vole. Pod konec on soveršenno èmancipiruetsja ot vsjakago roda idej i daže terjaet predstavlenie o svjazi žiznennyx sobytij. V ètom samaja značitel'naja i original'naja čerta ego tvorčestva.[124]

Only once, according to Šestov, did Čexov join the host of Russian writers and began to glorify the "idea." In "Palata No. 6," he renounces philosophical indifference and nonresistance. "On [Čexov] počuvstvoval

nevynosimost' beznadežnosti, nevozmožnost' tvorčestva iz ničego.
Kolotit'sja golovoj o kamni èto tak užasno, čto lučše uže vernut'sja k
idealizmu."[125] To Šestov's disappointment, however, "Palata No.
6" was followed by "Duèl'," and he sees its conclusion as seemingly idealistic, but
only seemingly. Herein lies the basis for Šestov's concern:

> Čexov neprimirimyj vrag vsjakago roda filosofii. Ni odno iz
> dejstvujuščix lic v ego proizvedenijax ne filosofstvuet, a esli
> filosofstvuet, to obyknovenno neudačno, smešno, slabo,
> neubeditel'no. Isključenie predstavljaet fon-Koren, tipičeskij
> predstavitel' pozitivno-materialističeskago napravlenija. . . .
> V razskazax Čexova mnogo geroev materialistov, no s ottenkom
> skrytago idealizma, po vyrabotannomu v 60-x godax šablonu.
> Takix Čexov deržit v černom tele i vysmeivaet. Idealizm vo
> vsex vidax, javnyj i tajnyj, vyzyvaet v Čexove čuvstvo
> nevynosimoj goreči. Emu legče bylo vyslušivat' bezpoščadnyja
> ugrozy prjamolinejnago materializma, čem prinimat'
> xudosočnyja utešenija gumanizirujuščago idealizma.[126]

The above passage contains the message Šestov draws from Čexov's
writings. He finds it objectionable, and re-iterates in the following
statement: "Edinstvennaja filosofija, s kotoroj ser'ezno sčitalsja i potomu
ser'ezno borolsja Čexov—byl pozitivističeskij materializm. Imenno
pozitivističeskij t.-e. ograničennyj, ne pretendujuščij na teoretičeskuju
zakončennost.'[127]

Andreev explains Šestov's attitude through historical circumstances:

> Stat'ju Šestova nevozmožno ponjat' ne pomnja o
> gospodstvujuščix togda vozzrenijax, kotorymi žilo obščestvo,
> naxodivšeesja počti bezrazdel'no vo vlasti racionalizma i
> pozitivizma. I Čexov otdaval im nemaluju dan'—no tvorčestvo
> ego ostavalos' ot ix gruza svobodnym (Šestov, Bunin, drugie
> pisateli otmečali udivitel'nuju svobodu Čexovskogo
> tvorčestva) i podčinjalos' ne idejam i nastroenijam vremeni, a
> čemu-to drugomu, vysšemu. Odnako uvidet' ètogo togda bylo
> sliškom trudno, mešala v"evšajasja v dušu "progressivnaja"
> zloba dnja,—verojatno poètomu Šestov v svoej stat'e mnogo
> vnimanija udelil "Skučnoj istorii," "Palate No. 6" i prošel

mimo "Duèli," "Studenta," "Mužikov," "V ovrage," "Arxiereja."[128]

Further, Andreev notes that Bunin, who valued Šestov's essay so highly, suddenly breaks off his commentary and begins to discuss Kurdjumov's views.[129]

Less subtle is Bunin's reaction to the critics who claim that Čexov is a budding revolutionary. Thus, Vikentij Vikent'evič Smidovič, a radical novelist who published under the pseudonym of Veresaev, writes in his memoirs of Čexov that " . . . revoljucionnoe èlektričestvo, kotorym v to vremja [1903] byl perezarjažen vozdux, vstrjaxnulo v dušu Čexova. Glaza ego razgoralis' surovym negodovaniem, kogda on govoril o neistovstvax Pleve, o žestokosti i gluposti Nikolaja II."[130] Bunin comments on the preceeding with a single word "brexnja,"[131] and then derides Veresaev's conclusion in which the author turns to Čexov's story "Nevesta:" " . . . pod konec žizni Čexov sdelal popytku,—puskaj neudačnuju, ot kotoroj sam potom otkazalsja,—no vse-taki popytku vyvesti xorošuju russkuju devušku na revoljucionnuju dorogu."[132]

Vladimir Vladimirovič Ermilov, an orthodox Stalinist Soviet critic, does not fare better in Bunin's eyes when he claims "Nevesta" to be a " . . . čudesnyj obraz russkoj devuški, vstupivšej na put' bor'by za to, čtoby *perevernut' žizn'*, prevratit' vsju rodinu v cvetuščij sad."[133] Bunin's reaction is a simple repetition of Ermilov's assertion: "Perevernuli! Prevratili!"[134]

The vision of Čexov as a prophet of revolution is not limited to the two critics Bunin derides. Vaclav Vaclavovič Vorovskij, a Bolshevik activist, Marxist journalist and literary critic is, for instance, quite explicit in this regard. According to him, Čexov " . . . svoim tonkim xudožestvennym čut'em . . . predvidel nadvigajuščeesja novoe." [135]Vorovskij perceives Čexov's heroes as "lišnie ljudi," who were once popular in Russian literature but who were at this time disappearing as a social group, and he distinguishes three possibilities for these protagonists. Some of them turn away from social ideals and social service to aesthetic ideals and "pure" art. Others free themselves through productive work. Labour in its most literal and physical sense is an ideal, a panacea for all ills. Neither of these two possibilities seems realistic to Vorovskij, and he turns to the last method for breaking away from the "lišnie ljudi" that he detects in Čexov. He finds this to be the correct, although the most difficult alternative. It requires a storm to sweep away the old and establish a new life.[136] The connotation of Vorovskij's "Lišnie ljudi" can be reduced to the author's statement cited earlier that Čexov sensed the coming of a new epoch. Čexov has not, however, held this idea for long. According to Vorovskij, he evolved, and only in Čexov's last works does the critic find a pronounced expectation of an impetuous change.[137]

The concept of development in Čexov's *oeuvre* towards the expressed need for a reformation of the standing order and towards the belief in a better future is central to the modern Čexovian interpretation in the Soviet Union. One of the leading Soviet experts on Čexov is the Academician Georgij Petrovič Berdnikov, the erstwhile Director of the Gorkij Institute of World Literature. In his major work on Čexov,[138] Berdnikov presents a study of Čexov's entire literary career. Because his approach is representative of Soviet Čexovian scholarship, a recapitulation is justified.

According to Berdnikov, Čexov's literary career begins during a time of crisis in the populist movement, and one of his major themes becomes the struggle against embellishment of life. His sensitivity and growing compassion forces him to turn to the ever more complex and acute problems of the time. He criticizes, however, the narrowness and dogmatism of the liberal populists, and the commonplaceness of the democrats. His struggle to remain outside the current political trends led to accusations of indifference. Yet, Berdnikov does not hesitate regarding Čexov's philosophical outlook. As he says, "[s]voi materialističeskie vzgljady Čexov ubeditel'no prodemonstriroval v spore s A.S. Suvorinym po povodu knigi Burže [Paul Bourget (1852-1935)] Učennik."[139]

Pessimism, Berdnikov observes further, is a widely spread complex social phenomena of the time. The theme is attractive to Čexov who, striving for objectivity, is unable to form his own world view. He realizes this, and is aware of the resultant limitation on his creative possibilities and aesthetic judgements. He, however, does not consider pessimism on the political, or even social level, but purely on the philosophical one.[140] This fact does not mean that Čexov is detached from life. He always tries to apply philosophy to real life. Thus, he is, for a time, greatly influenced by Tolstoj's idea of universal love as supposedly the best, if not the only way of resolving all social problems. Fifteen stories later, however, he takes a dispassionate look at Tolstojan moral philosophy, rejecting it in favour of understanding, justice, and work. Čexov, Berdnikov maintains, rejects passivity, but, at the same time, he is skeptical about the contemporary political trends, " . . . buduči v èto vremja [1889] tverdo

ubežden, čto revoljucii v Rossii nikogda ne budet . . . "[141] According to
Berdnikov, strict objectivity and a flat rejection of illusory ideas enabled
Čexov to deepen his ideas of justice and invest them with concrete
historical and social content. Čexov shows that the prevailing social
system is alien and hostile, not only to the exploited people, but to
everyone. A thin line, however, separates objectivity from passivity,
which Čexov refutes in his stories. Thus the writer's approach changes in
the early 1890s. Berdnikov describes it in the following:

> Borjas' s passivnost'ju i prisposoblenčestvom, vystupaja protiv
> vsjačeskix popytok opravdat' drjablost', bezvolie, bezrazličie
> i otstupničestvo, Čexov vse nastrojčivee i uverennee
> protivopostavljaet vsemu ètomu ideju bor'by. "Rasskaz
> neizvestnogo čeloveka" i v ètom smysle javljaetsja novym
> šagom vpered v tvorčeskom razvitii pisatelja.
> Čto smysl žizni—v bor'be so zlom, govorit ne tol'ko Zinaida
> Fedorovna. Ob ètom svidetelstvuet tragičeskaja istorija
> Neizvestnogo čeloveka, žizn' kotorogo, kak okazyvaetsja imela
> smysl, soderžanie i cennost' liš' do tex por, poka on byl
> borcom.[142]

Berdnikov observes in Čexov's writings, during this time, a gradually
strengthening idea of protest and struggle. The entire life of Misail Poloznev
in "Moja žizn'," for example, is built on a sharp conflict with the existing
social order, and Berdnikov also quotes another protagonist in this story,
Maša Dolžikova, commenting on contemporary life: "Odno nesomenno . . .
nado ustraivat' sebe žizn' kak-nibud' po-inomu...,"[143] and her later, more
explicit exclamation " . . . čto smirjat'sja s dejstvitel'nost'ju nevozmožno,
čto ždat' nel'zja i čto sleduet iskat' dlja pereustrojstva žizni kakie-to drugie
sposoby bor'by, sil'nye, smelye, skorye!"[144]

    Berdnikov regrets that Čexov's only information about Marxism
came from the opponents of the movement, who purposely distorted Marxist
thought.[145] This, in turn, was an impediment to the writer's quest for a
means of changing an unacceptable reality. Nevertheless, in the second half
of the 1890s Čexov progresses from narrating the opression and suffering of
the working people to revealing the social psychology of the poor. Eventually,
he turns away from analyzing general philosophical and moral problems
towards concrete social investigation. Čexov, according to Berdnikov,

criticizes the lack of freedom in the present system and the false equation of happiness with material satisfaction. He rejects personal happiness, calling for struggle against bourgeois satisfaction which operates at the expense of human feelings. Čexov's criticism of the social system culminates in "Nevesta," where the heroine not only comes to the conclusion that to live in this manner is impossible, but she also finds the strength to realize the old dream of Čexov's protagonists; she breaks off the old life to start a new one. Berdnikov illustrates this with a quote from the story: " . . . vperedi e risovalas' žizn' novaja, širokaja, prostornaja, i èta žizn', ešče nejasnaja pol'naja tajn, uvlekla i manila ee."[146] Hence Berdnikov's conclusion that "Čexov vse uverennee i vzvolnovannee govoril, čto buduščee radostno veličestvenno . . . "[147]

These sentiments are repeated in Berdnikov's opening article in the 1980 issue of *Sovetskaja literatura* dedicated to the 120th anniversary of Čexov's birth. A part of the article concerns, however, the critical imbroglio around Čexov's writings. Bearing Berdnikov's ideological background in mind, it does not come as a surprise that the view of Čexov as a pessimist and a relativist is refuted just as strongly as the claim that he is the forerunner of modernism. The strong bias in favour of social content is reflected in the other articles compiled in the anniversary issue. The critical survey "Chekhov through the Eyes of the World," for instance avoids statements like Galsworthy's " . . . Tchechov, more modern than the moderns,"[148] and selects from the essay only a sentence, where the English writer says that Čexov " . . . reveals to us the very soul of a great people, and that with a minimum of parade or pretence."[149] Three authors figure prominently among the sixteen selected for this survey, namely William Saroyan, Faiz Ahmed Faiz, and Thomas Mann. The choice is not surprising when political views of these writers are taken into account. Faiz, a Pakistani Marxist poet and journalist, who stands in high esteem in the Soviet Union, speaks of Čexov's optimism, and defines his basic theme as "the twilight of a social order in decay, the malaise that precedes great social changes . . . "[150]

Similarly, there is no doubt about the political orientation of Saroyan a man who refused the Pulitzer Prize as a form of bourgeois patronizing and who wrote his contribution to this survey in the form of a letter of thanks for his trip to Moscow provided by the Soviet authorities, a dubious honour, refused by such writers as William Faulkner. The most interesting is the excerpt of Mann's 1954 essay "Versuch über Tschechow," which was so successful that it was translated and published in the Soviet Union within a year of its original publication.[151] The quality Berdnikov values most in Mann's article is its emphasis on the social significance. As he says, "Thomas Mann saw Chekhov as a writer deeply concerned with social problems who dreamed of a just social order."[152] In order to comprehend Mann's approach to Čexov, one must recall the German writer's vision of the artist as a man, whose vital energy declined simultaneously with an almost pathological refinement of nerves and senses, thus restricting his participation in life and forcing him to note its riches with a feeling of incessant and vain nostalgia. Mann recognized that Čexov, like himself, was troubled by serious doubts concerning the meaning and value of his literary work. He, however, follows this line of thinking to the extent that he parallels his and Čexov's ethical concept; he identifies Čexov's psychological profile with that of his protagonists. Based on several Čexovian characters and selected letters, Mann pronounces his judgements. Hence, Čexov is a positivist who expresses " . . . das Verlangen nach einer besseren Wahrheit, schöneren, edleren, Leben, eine dem Geiste wohlgefälligeren menschlichen Gesellschaft . . . "[153] At the same time, however, Mann refers to Čexov's remarkably accute eye for noting the dubious nature of human progress. He speaks of the change the Russian writer underwent during his career, and which resulted in

> . . . der Zunahme moralisch-zeitkritischer Reizbarkeit, das heißt: dem immer sich verstärkenden Gefühl für das gesellschaftlich Verurteilte und Dahinsinkende und für das, was da kommen soll . . . [Daraus erklärt] sich auch Tschechows ungemeine Schätzung der Arbeit überhaupt, seine Verurteilung alles nicht arbeitenden Drohnen- und Schmarotzertums . . . , seine immer klarere Verwerfung eines Lebens, das, wie er sagte, "auf Sklaverei aufgebaut ist."
> Das ist ein hartes Urteil über die bürgerlich-kapitalistische Gesellschaft, die sich ihrer Humanität doch rühmt und von Sklaverei nichts hören will. Aber unser Geschichtenerzähler bekundet einen auffallenden Scharfblick für die Fragwürdigkeit des Fortschritts in Humanen und der sozial-moralischen Verhältnisse nach der Bauernbefreiung in seinem heimatischen Rußland . . .[154]

The basis for this argument is an oration in "Moja žizn'" by Misail Poloznev, one of the protagonists Mann identifies with Čexov. Another example of this fallacy is his matching of Čexov's ideas with those expressed by the old professor in "Skučnaja istorija." Helene Auzinger comments on the latter instance when she finds in Čexov

> . . . die Schwierigkeit in der Erfassung des 'Nicht-zu-Ende-gesprochenen,' das jedem Leser die Möglichkeit freier Auslegung überläßt. Nicht immer stimmt diese mit den Absichten des Dichters überein, wie Čechovs briefliche Äußerungen über die 'Langweilige Geschichte' beweisen. Thomas Mann kannte sie wahrscheinlich nicht, sonst hätte er sich wohl mit ihnen auseinandergesetzt."[155]

Nonetheless, the parallelism between Čexov and his heroes substantiates the German writer's emphasis on such statements as "Die Hauptsache ist, das Leben umzugestalten; alles übrige ist unnütz."[156] The message Mann discerns from Čexov's *oeuvre* is condensed in his observation that the Russian knew for certain only, " . . . daß Müßiggang das Schlechteste ist und daß man arbeiten muß, weil nämlich Müßiggang Arbeitenlassen, Ausbeutung und Unterdrückung bedeutet."[157] This labour leads to the bright future envisioned in "Nevesta" by Saša, who is also identified with the author: " . . . riesige, wunderschöne Häuser . . . , herrliche Gärten mit Fontänen, und bemerkenswerte Menschen werden hier leben . . . "[158] The result of Mann's approach to Čexov's work is his belief that the popularity of the Russian author rests on his ability to find " . . . Laute sozialen Grames, die seinem Volk ans Herz griffen . . . "[159] Moreover, he believes it appropriate to quote an unnamed journal which labelled Anton Pavlovič as one of the "Sturmvogeln der Revolution."[160]

The view of Čexov as a stormy petrel of the Revolution is unacceptable to many scholars. Karlinsky, for instance, refers to "Nevesta," the story employed by Veresaev, Ermilov, and Mann in their respective arguments. According to Karlinsky,

> [t]his story has become the traditional prize exhibit of orthodox Soviet critics, who are out to prove that at the end of his life Chekhov was moving toward espousing the cause of violent revolution. Although the text of the story does not state the

exact future path that the heroine of "The Bride," Nadya, will follow, it is invariably assumed by the commentators in Soviet editions of Chekhov that in Nadya he has portrayed an upper-class girl who is about to become a revolutionary . . . [161]

But to reduce "The Bride" to the clichés and platitudes that are compulsory in Soviet criticism is to deprive a unique and remarkable story of its particular meaning.

The central idea of "Nevesta," Karlinsky maintains, is that of a purely personal liberation. As a matter of fact, he describes the heroine's sentiments at the close of the story in these words: "A revolution based on the promise of material affluence and on humanity reduced to a standardized common denominator rather than on freedom of thought and universal equality now holds as little attraction for Nadya as it did for Chekhov himself."[162] Moreover, according to the American scholar, Čexov dismissed any division of human beings into social groups in favour of individual action. He rejects any stereotypes, and therefore, as Karlinsky observes, "[i]n the Soviet Union, where the labeling and compartmentalizing of groups of people is the basis of an entire culture, this aspect of Chekhov would be explosive indeed if anyone dared to bring it into the open."[163] Karlinsky strengthens his point when he speaks of Čexov's aversion to political fanaticism, and refers to Kornej Čukovskij, whom he describes as "a perceptive and knowledgeable Soviet critic, [who] pretended to be puzzled why the do-gooder Chekhov depicted Lida, [the socially and politically active young girl in 'Dom s mezoninom,'] so harshly and her idle younger sister with so much kindness and sympathy."[164]

Pod gipnozom čexovskogo masterstva-koldovstva vsja Rossija poètičeski vljubilas' v ètu besxarakternuju, slabuju, devušku i zaprezirala ee staršuju sestru za te samye dela i postupki , kotorye *ne v literature, a v žizni* byli tak dorogi Čexovu. Tot Čexov, kakim my znaem ego po besčislennym memuaram i pis'mam — zemskij vrač, popečitel' bibliotek, osnovatel' učilišč, vstret'sja on s Lidoj ne v literature, a v žizni, nesomenno, stal by ee vernym sojuznikom, a v literature on — ee obličitel' i vrag.[165]

Karlinsky is impressed by this observation, for, as he says:

> In a book published in the Soviet Union, this is as far as
> Chukovsky could go in making his point, but the story itself
> tells us more. Yes, there is no doubt that Lida's social-
> improvement program parallels Chekhov's own. But this
> outwardly civilized partisan of civil rights is in her private life
> an authoritarian who keeps her mother and sister in fear and
> subjugation. She is also a political fanatic. When her political
> convictions are brought into question . . . she strikes out at her
> opponent with every ethical and unethical means she can
> muster. In this story, political fanaticism is as inhuman and as
> destructive as religious fanaticism was in "Peasant Women"
> and "The Murder."[166]

Èdgard Leopol'dovič Brojde, an émigré Russian Čexovian scholar, is
more forceful in his pronouncements. He speaks about the catastrophe of
October 1917,[167] thus identifying the Revolution as a catastrophe. Čexov,
according to him, was warning about such perdition. Čexov is topical today
precisely because of his philosophy. Brojde sees Čexov as a

> . . . xudožnik-myslitel', [kotoryj] rešal problemy, vo mnogom
> blizkie i našej èpoxe: osvoboždenie iskusstva ot
> ideologičeskogo davlenija, pereocenku cennostej, preodolenie
> dogmatizma "partijnogo myšlenija," ego futljarnoj
> zamknutosti. Svoimi proizvedenijami Čexov preduprezždaet
> vozmožnoj Katastrofe, o gibeli Kul'tury.[168]

The author argues in this vein throughout his book. He maintains that
Čexov " . . . otvergal ljubuju 'futljarnost',' partijščinu, dogmu,—
nazyval pričiny vozmožnoj Katastrofy, zval k soveršenstvovaniju
Kul'tury."[169] Čexov also anticipated the sad turn that events were to
take, but was not understood: "Ne doždavšis' ot Čexova 'jasnyx
ukazanij' o celjax i sredstvax bor'by, pisatelju pripisyvali filosofiju
pessimizma, xotja on liš' *preduprezždal* . . ."[170] Furthermore, according
to Brojde, "Čexov pokazal, čto prirodnuju glupost' i neznanie žizni
ljudi čašče vsego maskirujut ideologiej—rasprostranennym stereotipom
myšlenija, stadnoj, massovoj ideej. Na ètom baziruetsja totalitarizm vo

vsex ego raznovidnostjax, nacional'nyx i social'nyx."[171] Utilization of
this phenomenon is very simple, and Brojde finds in "Rasskaz
neizvestnogo čeloveka" an instance, where "Čexov *obvinjaet* ideologov
v èkspluatacii naivnosti neposvjaščennyx . . . "[172] The next step is the
ideological fanaticism of which Karlinsky has already spoken in an
earlier quotation. Brojde discerns a message regarding this eventuality
in Čexov's "Na puti:" "Ideologičeskij fanatizm, kak obyčno, v korne
iskažaet vse žiznennye, estestvennye processy . . . "[173] Naturally, any
anticipation of ruination is accompanied by intense interest in future
revival. Brojde observes that "Čexova interesovali slučai duxovnogo
vozroždenija: èto simvolizirovalo sposobnost' Rossii preodolet'
grjaduščuju Katastrofu.[174] Moreover, Brojde refutes the criticism
claiming that Čexov did not know the way to a better future. According
to him,

> [n]el'zja soglasit'sja s mneniem, podderžannym kazennoj
> naukoj, čto Čexov jakoby "ne znaet puti" ili "... ešče ne znal."
> Čexov-myslitel' znal,—kuda idti; doroga èta, kak i nyne,
> zavalena glybami partijnyx "učenij," da i vse čelovečestvo
> možet byt' pogrebeno pod nim *okončatel'no*. Čexov obladal
> isključitel'noj trezvost'ju vzgljada, filosofskim realizmom,—
> ne izgotovljal skoropelyx receptov, predpočital ne oblačat'sja
> v mantiju učitelja. On zval na drevnij *izvestnyj* put'
> obščečelovečeskoj Kul'tury.[175]

Nor does Brojde accept the accusation of nihilism levied against Čexov:
"Antidogmatizm Čexova ne označal nigilističeskogo otricanija nadobnosti
mirovozzrenija, kak stalo modno utverždat' segodnja. Čexov tverdo znal
različie meždu dobrom i zlom, ego simpatii i antipatii *javny* i logičny.
Drugoe delo, čto on nisprovergal *šablony* i stereotipy."[176] Brojde elaborates
on this idea when he compares a dog's feelings to an ideology:

> Ideologija nizvedena Čexovym s početnogo p'edestala na
> uroven' *životnyx* instinktov; Partija, vooružennaja "učeniem,"
> sumela ispol'zovat' *stadnoe*: nenavist', zavist', koryst', strax,
> "veru," edinomyslie, "nacional'nye tradicii," idiotizm: "...
> Vse čelovečestvo Kaštanka delila na *dve* očen' neravnye časti:
> na *xozjaev* i na zakazčikov... [italics are Brojde's] [177]

The quotation from "Kaštanka," and the animal "ideology," is paralleled by the cobbler's muttering in "Sapožnik i nečistaja sila," where his division of the world corresponds to that of Kaštanka.[178] Moreover, he considers the dearth of political orientation more important than all the good qualities of his wife.(VII, 224) He is, however, given the opportunity to learn how wrong such a philosophy is.

Brojde is even more specific with regard to Čexov's view of communism. He believes that the destructive apparition produced by a nineteenth-century professor of philosophy in "Černyj monax" has an affinity with the spectre haunting Europe in the first sentence of the *Communist Manifesto*.[179] No ideology knows the real truth,[180] and no single, all-encompassing program for the establishment of a better future can exist. Čexov's strategy, as detected by Brojde for instance in his analysis of "Palata No. 6," is based on individual action: "Duxovnaja *aktivnost'*-glavnoe uslovie preodolenija zla. Dlja Čexova ne suščestvenna 'partijnaja programma' togo ili inogo personaža,—avtor soznatel'no 'smešal karty.' Likvidacija Palaty trebuet usilij *vsex* ljudej."[181] If we all work for a better morrow, if we join forces in the struggle, a new life will commence. Čexov's dream of a moral renascence[182] may be the basis for the interpretation of his writings as a prophecy of a revolution.

The philosophical outlooks of Brojde and other critics examined to this point are reflected in their respective approaches to Čexov's writing. Other commentaries, however, are less prescriptively conditioned. Representative of such criticism are Karl Kramer's *The Chameleon and the Dream*, and Vladimir Kataev's *Proza Čexova*. The author of the former work, an American scholar, elaborates on the dual perspective of the heroes and the ambiguity of Čexov's stories in general. One method of presenting a multiplicity of views on reality consists, according to the critic, of " . . . a sudden about-face on the part of one of the characters. An apparently trivial detail suddenly causes the character to change his behaviour in such a complete and unexpected manner that it is difficult to recognize him as the same person."[183] From these stories, Kramer discerns a notion that man lacks a sense of personal identity, which implies " . . . a correlate absence of any clear-cut notion about the nature of reality. Finally, a world whose nature is indefinable because it is constantly changing must forsake any sense of moral value."[184]

No change in any of the character's feeling occurs in stories like

"Toska," or "Panixida." Yet, the double vision of the world is obvious when
the critic refers to the latter story in which the protagonist recollects " . . .
a walk that he and his daughter had taken during their last meeting. She had
reflected on the beauty of the landscape, while Andrej condemned the land
as bad for farming."[185] According to Kramer, 1886—the year in which
"Panixida" is published—marks a new trend in Čexov's writing. He becomes
preoccupied with the device of the distorted point of view. As Kramer
observes: "Of course, every artist strives to illuminate for us the tangled
muddle of actual living. What distinguishes Čexov's effort is the double
perspective—an ironic one if you will—whereby ordinary reality and the
distorted vision of it are seen in conflict."[186]

This dual view is exemplified by such stories as "Doma," where a
seven-year-old boy draws a soldier taller than the house next to which he
stands. When his father objects, the boy insists that if the man were smaller
his eyes would not be visible.[187] "Poceluj" is a more complex story. The
protagonist's imagination creates for him a new reality, or, as the critic
describes the situation, in the hero's " . . . private world he [Čexov] has
established a special kind of relationship with the real one—a relationship
which is denied to all the others."[188]

Another form of duality is the distinction between the private and the
public world. The first story in which Kramer observes the conflict between
the characters' external and internal identities is "Neprijatnost,'"[189] the
best known is "Skučnaja istorija." The critic supports his thesis by a
reference to the original title of the story "Moe imja i ja."[190] His analysis of
the work confirms the implication carried by this title: "There is, indeed, a
feeling that the person who goes by the name of Nikolaj Stepanovič is
someone entirely different from the old professor's own conception of
himself.[191]

The double perspective leads to ambiguity. This term does not satisfy
the American scholar because it implies two or more co-existing
interpretations, while, with regard to Čexov, the two or more meanings of a
given story are ordinarily opposed to each other. Hence, he prefers to
classify the type of ambiguity in Čexov's stories as "unresolved paradox."[192]
Having defined the phenomenon, Kramer elaborates: "Čexov's ambiguity
frequently emerges from the reader's perception of contradictions in parallel
passages throughout a given story."[193] He feels, for instance, that in
"Nevesta" the ambiguity is deliberately planted. The point of the ambiguity
is, according to the critic, " . . . to highlight the precarious relationship

between actuality and one's consciousness of it."[194] He illustrates this by referring to the story "Černyj nomax," where " . . . the writer is studying the hero's distorted relationship to actuality."[195] "Slučaj z praktiki" is an example interesting for its setting and its implications. The reader is shown the miserable conditions of the workers in a factory as well as the unhappiness of its owners, or the absurdity of the entire system. The story ends with an assurance that the present is a very difficult time and that within a generation or two the problems which face those living now will have resolved themselves.[196] Kramer finds this reassurance about the problems of the present, which cannot even be understood, unconvincing. His explanation is " . . . that in a hopeless situation and one that is absurd, the only source of hope for the future is at least no more irrational than the hopelessness of the present."[197] This, according to the critic, might be Čexov's answer to Lev Šestov: "to ignore logical processes does not necessarily mean to kill hopes."[198]

Kramer concludes that:

> Ambiguity is a concomitant of Čexov's impressionism; whenever our focus shifts from what is to what it seems to us to be, we have opened the floodgates to a deluge of possibilities, none of which can ever be certainties. . . . His splintering of meaning within a character's perception of the external world forms a bridge between the realist's single-plane view of actuality and the symbolist conception of heterogeneous levels of actuality encompassed by a single image. "The Bishop" ["Arxierej"] is an appropriate story with which to end an account of Čexov's studies in the tenuous and uncertain nature of man's existence in a world whose exact proportions he is incapable of ascertaining, and where all truths are relative. Although this vision of life was not a consciously thought out and formulated philosophic conception, nevertheless it is a fundamental theme, which both in its presence and in the attempt at its denial, runs from the very earliest through the final stories that Čexov wrote.[199]

Vladimr Kataev's *Proza Čexova: problemy interpretacii*, referred to previously as evidencing reduced tendentiousness, begins with the author's introduction. Kataev, a Soviet scholar, emphasizes the necessity of exposing the writer's intent, his view of the world, rather than reading in the critic's own ideology. He does not at first mention the double perspective, but rather defines the "rasskaz otkrytija" in Čexov's work. The protagonist, an ordinary man set off by an unimportant detail, suddenly gains a new perspective of life. He rejects his former attitude in view of the newly acquired understanding of reality. This discovery is not a new philosophical outlook or religion, but simply a new perspective.[200] This implies, as the Soviet critic observes, the importance for Čexov of the gnoseological theme. Kataev gives numerous examples of stories based on the double composition of "it seemed—it turned out." The main subject in these stories of discovery is man's orientation in the surrounding world, his cognition of life.

> I èta sfera dejstvitel'nosti, ugol zrenija na nee stanut opredeljajuščimi v dal'nejšem tvorčestve pisatelja.
> Nazovem ètot ugol zrenija na dejstvitel'nost' gnoseologičeskim. Ibo v 'rasskazax otkrytija' nametilsja takoj podxod k izobraženiju žizni, pri kotorom osnovnoj interes avtora sosredotočen ne stol'ko na javlenijax samix po sebe, skol'ko na predstavlenijax o nix, na vozmožnosti raznyx predstavlenij ob odnix i tex že javlenijax, na putjax formirovanija ètix predstavlenij, na prirode, illjuzii, zabluždenija, ložnogo mnenija.[201]

Kataev emphasizes the difference between knowledge based on facts and personal observation. He also mentions other artists concerned with the shift between actual events and the report of them. One of the three to whom he actually refers by name is Karel Čapek and he mentions the novels *Hordubal* and *Povětroň*. [202]Čexov is definitely interested in the cognitive processes and the forms of this cognition but this, according to Kataev, does not mean that he is a philosopher. His interest in gnoseology takes a purely artistic form. As an artist, Čexov depicts contemporary life, and this phenomenon is the philosophical conceptual basis of his artistic world.[203] He was criticized for dearth of a general idea, but Čexov merely rejects any dogmatism. He cannot be placed within the framework of any philosophical school or trend.[204] He does not pretend to have discovered eternal secrets. According to Kataev, "[v] proizvedenijax Čexova pered nami vsegda živaja i cel'naja kartina dejstvitel'nosti. A tot avtorskij ugol zrenija, kotoryj my opredeljem kak interes k problemam poznanija čelovekom mira, orientirovanija v nem, prisutstvuet v glubine ètoj kartiny."[205]

A number of Čexov's stories have at their core a controversy between the protagonists. One of the Kataev's examples is "Ogni." His detailed analysis of the story yields observations like: "nevozmožno prijti k edinym i obščeznačimym vyvodam iz odnix i tex že faktov..."[206] Čexovian protagonists strive for some understanding of life, but cannot achieve this goal. Not solutions but the accurate presentation of problems is the writer's concern. Hence, as stated by Kataev, "[a]vtorskaja pozicija . . . ne svoditsja k utverždeniju sobstvennogo, zaranee sformulirovannogo znanija o žizni. No ona objazatel'no predpologaet ocenku čužix znanij, mnenij, 'pravd,' issledovanie priznakov, uslovij istiny."[207]

Even Čexov's humour relates to the gnoseological theme. The comicality is based on different conceptions of the world. Thus, it is perfectly natural for Van'ka Žukov in "Van'ka" to address a letter to the grandfather in the village, which is absurd from the postman's point of view.[208] The opposite of this situation, when a single hero operates with several conceptual systems, occurs, for instance, in "Vory." When asked whether devils exist, the hero responds conditionally. If one ponders the question scientifically, the answer is no, that would be a superstition. Taking a plain man's view, however, devils do exist.[209] The confusion of different semiotic systems, however, does not only provide a basis for comical situations. The dearth of mutual understanding is also caused by separation of individual conceptions of the world. Everybody is totally absorbed in his own definite outlook, and does not allow for divergent opinions.[210] Hence, as observed by Kataev, Čexov " . . . otricaet kak obščepriznannye tak i obščeobjazatel'nye rešenija, princip generalizacii kak takovoj. Obščie kategorii vstupajut v protivorečie s konkretnymi javlenijami, obščepriznannye položenija na dele okazyvajutsja ložnymi, net toj istiny, kotoraja byla by ubeditel'na dlja vsex . . . "[211] At another point, the Soviet scholar elaborates on this idea: "Čexov vidit v každom čeloveke ne material dlja podtverždenija toj ili inoj ideologemy, a edinečnyj mir, kotoryj vsegda trebuet svoego nepriložimogo k ostal'nym rešenija žiznennyx protivorečij."[212]

According to Kataev, scientific principles save Čexov at the time of disillusionment with unsound "general ideas."[213] The scholar echoes the sentiments expressed more than half a century ago by the renowned Formalist critic Leonid Petrovič Grossman, who says: "Škola Darvina i Klod Bernara v metodologii literaturnoj raboty Čexova vyrabotala strogo materialističeskie principy. . . . Strogo pozitivnye metody svoej medicinskoj

školy on vnosil i v pervuju stadiju svoego literaturnogo tvorčestva."[214]
Kataev, however, does not agree entirely. According to him, Čexov who
never forgot his original profession of physician, closely follows the
development in medicine, which in the 1880s concentrates, in psychology,
on the problems of cognitive processes. The critic further notes that

> Idei pozitivizma, provozglasivšego zadaču očistit' ves'
> mexanizm čelovečeskogo poznanija i privesti ego v točnoe
> sootvetstvie s principami estestvennonaučnogo obraza
> myšlenija, ne mogli ne pokazat' sil'nogo vozdejstvija na
> estestvoispitatelej vsego mira. No Čexovu, razdeljavšemu
> pafos nisproverženija "fal'šivyx doktrin" i izučenija faktov
> vmesto konstruirovanija metafizičeskix vydumok okazalis' v
> to že vremja čuždy krajnosti pozitivizma.[215]

Kataev repeatedly emphasizes the writer's aversion to generalizations
of any kind and his avid interest in human cognitive activity.[216] Naturally,
Čexov individualizes each instance of man's orientation in the world he
observes. Kataev discovers that generalizations exist also in Čexov's,
namely, in his negation:

> Neizmenny v Čexovskom mire otnositel'nost', obuslovlennost'
> idej i mnenij, stereotipov myšlenija i žiznennogo povedenija,
> otkaz ot absoljutizacii ljubogo individual'nogo rešenija,
> neosnovatel'nost' raznoobraznyx pretenzij na obladanie
> "nastojaščej pravdy." . . .
> Vystupaja protiv absoljutizacii zavedomo neokončatel'nyx,
> individual'nyx, častičnyx "pravd," Čexov otnjud' ne sčital
> absurdnym stremlenie k polučeniju konečnyx produktov
> myslitel'noj i—šire—orientirovočnoj, poznavatel'noj
> dejatel'nosti . . . "Nastojaščaja pravda" nevedoma ili
> ponimaetsja ložno i po-raznomu, no imenno stremlenie k
> nej okazyvaetsja ustojčivym priznakom samyx različnyx
> geroev . . .[217]

Truth in Čexov's world is above all a synonym of complexity, and his heroes
most often do not know the entire truth.[218]

Stories like "Arxierej" lead to a discussion of religious elements in Čexov's works. Kataev categorically rejects any notion of Čexov as a religious man. He does, however, quote from an article by an American scholar, Richard Marshall, Jr., who says of Čexov that "[h]is humanistic philosophy was to a large extent a secular version of the traditional Judaeo-Christian ethic... The coincidence of his values with those of clergy was great."[219] Aleksej Nikolaevič Tolstoj, a popular Soviet writer, criticizes Čexov precisely for this *raznočinnyj* humanitarianism, and specifically for its ineffectuality.[220] George Ivask, another American scholar, also comments on the uncertainty in Čexov's world view: "The many critics who have affirmed that Čechov believed neither God nor future life may be right; but the matter is more complicated than most of the supposed. Čexov's scepticism deterred him from all absolute statements.[221] He supports his statement with a quote from one of Čexov's notebooks, where the writer says: "Meždu 'est' bog' i 'net boga' ležit celoe gromadnoe pole . . . "(XVII, 224) According to Ivask, Čexov prefers to stay in that field. The position taken by the above American scholars is not as clear-cut as Kataev's denial, but fits well with the Soviet scholar's conclusion to his study: "Absoljutizm v čexovskom xudožestvennom mire javljaetsja, takim obrazom, liš' otnositel'nost' vsex izvestnyx častnyx 'pravd' v sopostavlenii s 'nastojaščej pravdoj,' stremlenie k nej, neizmennye poiski ljud'mi 'nastojaščej pravdy,' vse usložnjajuščeesja o nej predstavlenie."[222]

This survey of critical views on Čexov's philosophy cannot possibly claim to be complete. A single volume of *Chekhov: The Critical Heritage*, for instance, contains over 200 articles by English and American critics in the period from 1891 to 1945 alone.[223] It does, however, represent all the major trends in the interpretation of Čexov's philosophy.[224] Mention should, perhaps, also be made of Čexov's relation to science as observed by the critics. Three evaluative patterns exist with regard to this relationship. Boris Mixajlovič Èjxenbaum, the renowned Russian formalist, for example, refers to Čexov's statements concerning his relation to science, and concludes that Čexov needed science as an aid in the preservation of his objectivity.[225] Èjxenbaum finds that Čexov has an interest in scientific methods, but not necessarily any admiration for the scientist. A study of a different type is Viktor Trofimovič Romanenko's *Čexov i nauka*.[226] The relevant parts of this book, however, are covered in the earlier discussion on recent Soviet Čexovian scholarship. The last form of approach, and the most interesting one, is that of the American Slavist, Thomas Winner. This scholar speaks about the theme of the search for a guiding idea in Čexov's writings, and stresses " . . . the problem of man's dedication to science, to the scientific point of view and thus the relationship of science to man. This was a problem of focal significance in the age of scientific optimism of the late nineteenth century, with its spirit of empiricism and positivism.[227] Winner observes that

> Čexov's scientific positivism, and his admiration for Darwin,
> were among the compelling reasons for his lack of enthusiasm
> for Tolstoj's religious views . . . Nevertheless, it would be a
> gross exaggeration to consider the scientist and the scientific
> way of life in Čexov's works as unqualifiedly identical with
> the ideal.[228]

He diagnoses the problem encountered by the writer as that of " . . . the reification of science and thus already emerging conflict between the new science and traditional humanistic values."[229] Over-dedication to science, or an artificial intellectualism separate man from his fellow beings, and as Winner concludes, " . . . the individual personality, in its total complexity, is the ultimate reality for Čexov; and no intellectual system, no matter how enticing, can subjugate the intricacies of human action to its ordered reality.[230]

The preceding text shows the great variety in the critics' evaluation of Čexov's *Weltanschauung*. Perusing the critical literature, the reader learns to appreciate a refreshing view like that of Il'ja Èrenburg who claims: "Nastavlenija Čexova ne v nastavlenijax a v ego iskusstve."[231] The reader of these lines will also appreciate that the critical literature on Čapek is much less voluminous, perhaps due to his writing in a minor language.

On Čapek

František Xaver Šalda, the greatest figure in the history of Czech literary criticism, and the father of its modern development, was well-established at the time when Čapek entered the literary world. Unfortunately for the young writer, their first encounter was not amicable. Čapek began his literary career by co-authoring several short stories with his brother, in addition to separately publishing poems and theoretical treatises, all within a short period. It was the last of these genres that brought about the first encounter of the two literati. Čapek's review of Krejčí's novel *Červenec*[232] resulted in an extensive polemic, in the course of which Šalda claims that Čapek is the theoretical speaker for youth in literature, who " . . . napsal jednu novelu novoromantickou, jednu novoklasickou a jest dnes u něčeho jako 'unanimismus,' aby byl zítra — kde?"[233] He finds the same superficiality in the young writer's criticism: "Pan Karel Čapek ve svých kritických statích jest jen manekýnem poslední módy, poslední theoretické knihy, již právě přečetl."[234] The controversy over their literary views gradually became more personal, and it had not been resolved when, in 1917, Čapek published his first independent book, the collection of short stories *Boží muka*. Šalda reviewed the book in his article "Karel a Josef Čapkové" and, as could be expected, his review was not favourable. He refers to the earlier joint effort of both brothers *Zářivé hlubiny*, as

> . . . nejen kniha průpravná, nýbrž přímo kniha školních úkolů a příprav: kniha okreslovaných vzorků literárních. Jsou v ní zastoupeny všecky ne směry, nýbrž přímo *formule*, které dotkly se znepokojeného ducha mladých literátů českých v posledních sedmi letech.[235]

Only after this preamble does Šalda approach *Boží muka* itself. The criticism then is similar to that which has often been directed at Čexov, namely, the author prefers a heavy atmosphere and lacks sympathy for his characters. As Šalda says:

> Na první pohled jest patrné, že nejsou to ani povídky ani novely, ač je pan autor tak pokřtívá: schází jim všechna *melodie fabulistická*, všecko lehké odhmotňující kouzlo duchové hry. Jsou to *procesy*, těžké, úmorné, podrobné a závažné procesy duševní, jimiž chtějí si osoby Čapkovy něco rozřešiti, nebo něčeho se dobrati, na čem visí jejich spása.[236]

He further argues that "Karla Čapka nezajímá duše lidská a její svět, jak vtělily se v určitý karakter lidský, nýbrž dějství životné *samo o sobě*, mechanika a logika událostí, deduktivnost a dialektika životného dění. Nezajímá jej člověk . . . "[237] Šalda also finds that all Čapek's protagonists have read Bergson, and concludes, that " . . . to co chce vysloviti K. Čapek dalo by se trvám nejednou vysloviti celeji a naléhavěji essayí nebo studií filosofickou."[238]

Miroslav Rutte, a pragmatically-oriented critic of Čapek's own generation, discerns the same elements in Čapek's prose, but he sees them more positively. Thus in *Krakonošova zahrada* and *Zářivé hlubiny* the subject matter is everything that both external and internal life have to offer. The leitmotif is the realization that, while an idea may be manageable and predictable in theory, it is often unmanageable and unpredictable in practice.[239] Rutte explains this theme:

> V oblasti myšlenek jsou pouze možnosti a pravděpodobnosti: v oblasti lidských srdcí jsou však osudnosti, v nichž relativnost mění se v absolutno."[240]

When assessing *Boží muka*, Rutte stresses the motif of expected liberation, but how it will come about remains a question. "Čapkova kniha nechce ničeho vyřešiti, nedává určité odpovědi ani útěchy . . . "[241]

The critic also attempts to explain the atmosphere of the stories through references to the general situation in contemporary literature: "Vyčítavý stesk , pessimism a nechut' ke skutečnu jež stoupají z literatury na sklonku XIX. stol. mohli bychom pojati jako *praktickou krisi idealismu*."[242] According to him, modern philosophy managed to satisfy the needs of the intellect, but not those of the heart, and poetry is, above all, a need of the heart. Poets suffered with the realization that life cannot be changed to correspond to philosophy. Rutte sees solution in a new philosophical concept, the philosophy of pragmatism. He calls it "the struggle for faith in life," and claims that

> *Pragmatism dovedl svým teleologickým a vývojovým stanoviskem ulomiti skepticismu jeho nihilistický hrot*: nepokouší se uvésti lidského ducha v rovnováhu sladkým zapomněním a nevěděním; ponechává mu všechnu svobodu— i svobodu sebetrýzně a nedůvěry; ale proměňuje i skepsi v hybnou páku života . . . "[243]

One by one, the essays in Rutte's book deal with various aspects of pragmatism. These components are then, according to him, integral to Čapek's writings.

The observations are the same, although the conclusions differ, in the work of František Götz, a keen literary analyst and ideologue, who was very influential with the post-war generation. In the *Anarchie v nejmladší české poesii* he writes about Czech literary cubism as evidenced in Čapek's stories. He contends that it is derived from the general European mood which he calls an absolute nihilism. Götz quotes the German philosopher of history Spengler, who claims that the destruction of traditional values resulted in an absolute skepticism, materialism, and relativism. Hence, as Götz observes,

> Evropský nihilismus je vědomí nesmyslnosti a bezúčelnosti života ve vesmíru, všeho, co tu jest. Duše lidská, jíž jest nezbytností míti nějaký cíl, aby mohla prostě býti, stojí v bezúčelném světě bezradně a zmateně. Kubistická naše povídka je obrazem této duše, zbavené představy cíle života . . .[244]

Lack of direction, skepticism, and nihilism are once again terms employed in the criticism of Čexov's literary production.

Contemporary Czech literature is also reviewed in an article by Arne Novák, a renowned literary historian and critic. This scholar too sees Čapek as a skeptic, but denies his nihilism: "He is a sceptic, but a very indulgent and kind-hearted sceptic. You would do him an injustice if you regarded him as a nihilist. On the contrary. He believes in the goodness of the human heart."[245]

Šalda is not that discriminating when he combines Götz's and Rutte's observations in his commentary:

> . . . předválečná generace kubisticko-futuristická jest celým svým rázem *pragmatická*. To znamená: subjektivistická po výtce, poslední výběžek romantismu; konec konců nová směs ironie a sentimentality, nová jen v jejich dosírování... Přiznávám, že nejmladší nejsou ještě dost orientováni a že přejímají mnoho z tohoto dědictví otců; ale že pragmatism svým relativismem a konec konců indiferentismem jen pobuřuje . . . , jest znamení, že chtějí jít k objektivismu pravého poznání.[246]

The idea of affinity between the 1890s generation, the pragmatist generation (grouped around the 1914 almanac of *Přehled*), and romanticism, is further developed in Šalda's contribution to the current literary polemics, "Spory literární." Here, however, he does not explain indifferentism as an attempt at objectivism, but rather attacks the pragmatist method:

> Nevíme nic o Bohu, nemáme nijakého náboženství, ale tvařme se *jako by byl, jako bychom* v něj věřili. Neznáme nic ze světa a života našeho bližního . . ., ale říkejme a jednejme *jako by byl* dobrý a *jako bychom* ho znali a milovali. Dělejme *gesta víry a lásky*: snad se dostaví později víra i láska . . .[247]

The works of the brothers Čapek, and of Karel in particular typify this method. However, as Šalda writes, " . . . zapomíná se, že Čapkové nejsou vynálezci pragmatismu, ani jediní pragmatisté v české literatuře. Nové badání [sic] ukázalo řadu pragmatiků před pragmatismem (na příklad náboženská filosofie Rousseauova jest zcela patrně pragmatická).[248] Despite his questioning of the originality of pragmatism, Šalda admits that the Čapeks were the first to develop literary pragmatism into a system.[249]

In 1926, at the time of publication of Götz's *Jasnící se horizont*, the denotation of Čapek's generation as that of pragmatism is firmly established. The connotation of the term is, however, still under discussion. Götz expresses his view in the book:

> Generaci Čapkově říká se *pragmatická*—ale její pragmatism to není jenom instrumentální teorie pravdy, jež vyvozuje poznání z ideologických základů lidského jedince—to není jenom humanistický relativismus, jemuž každá hodnota je hodnotou pro člověka—tento pragmatism je prostě samotná metoda nazírání, vidění a žití složité moderní reality tak, aby právě její *mnohohlasost* byla plně vychutnána. . . . Karel Čapek nestačí ani vykládat jak jsou mu *odporné* generalisace a systémy, nebot' v nich vidí nepřátele života a světa jako takových. Ale ovšem tato základní skepse, jež je přímo typickým rysem generace, chce být skepsí tvořivou, je to skepse k fikcím lidského mozku a k velkým slovům—není to však pessimistická skepse, popírající realitu.[250]

The same text contains an analytical sketch of Karel Čapek and his writing to date. Götz begins with references to Čapek's 1924 article "Proč nejsem

komunistou?" which, he believes, leads to the very centre of his artistic world
view. Čapek is not a communist because the last word of communism is not
to save but to rule, not help but exercise power. "Čapek věří, že problém
chudých je úkolem *dnešního* dne, ne teprve zítřků; věří, že 'důležitější je kus
chleba a teplo v kamnech, nežli revoluce za dvacet let'."[251] Communism is,
according to Götz, too hateful for Čapek. His humanism is based on a
conviction that man is of immense value and is therefore the measure of all
things.[252] The rest of the essay is dedicated to the illustration of Götz's
theory, that Čapek's humanism developed from the surmounting of post-war
nihilism, a process which is evidenced, for instance, in *Trapné povídky*.[253]

Šalda also mentions the essay "Proč nejsem komunistou?" He does
this, however, six years later, when the article appeared in a collection
entitled *O věcech obecných čili Zóon politikon*. True to his approach
hitherto, Šalda ridicules Čapek for what he terms protecting the poor from
communism, and he discerns a message that everything would fall into
order, were it not for the communist instigators who plant hatred, vengeance,
wrath, and despair in the hearts of the indigent. "Karel Čapek stojí příkře
proti dnešnímu boji sociálnímu, třídní nenávisti, sociální revoluci. Myslí, že
jsou zbytečné; svět nestane se rájem po revoluci."[254] He proceeds to quote
a line form the essay, where Čapek proclaims: "Myslím, že by se s trochou
obyčejné lásky a srdečnosti daly ještě delat zázraky."[255] To Šalda, this
statement is merely a pose, since Čapek did not even attempt to arrange for
an entente based on such love and cordiality. Moreover, as the critic
concludes:

> Literátští a revoluční pozéři jsou mu [Čapkovi] lenoši, kteří
> sedí za pecí a krasořeční na ní. Kritisují do vzduchu a dělají
> revoluční nebo reformační návrhy a plány do vzduchu—vesměs
> povidlí žvanilů, tlachalů, historiónů. Demokratický člověk
> má prý si vyhrnout rukávy, dát se do práce a neustat, pokud ho
> smrt k zemi nesrazí.[256]

Such a disposition, according to Šalda, boomerangs, because Čapek is also
a poseur. The entire book is reviewed in this vein. In spite of the sarcasm,
however, the reader is presented with Čapek's basic postulates. He speaks
of love, loyalty, and sincerity. Generalization is, according to him, a great
evil, and a great misfortune for humanity. Going against the spirit of
Christianity, he identifies with the practical Martha, rejecting the theoretical

Mary. Skepticism, then, is an art of finding some truth in every statement, or a road to knowledge. All this is just a pose according to Šalda; yet, he admits that some consider the author to be the greatest contemporary Czech writer.[257]

Ferdinand Peroutka, a liberal journalist of pragmatist orientation, devotes a long treatise to Čapek and his generation in which he analyzes their philosophy and attitude towards life.[258] The situation after the war is, Peroutka maintains, chaotic. Social structure cedes to the pressure; raging side is pitted against raging side; single-minded philosophy takes up arms against single-minded philosophy; one extreme idea is set against another; every allegation finds its denial. The world loses all ability to reach any sort of agreement. This antagonism results in a negativism which drowns the positive mood, and in a philosophy of resignation which claims that nothing can be done except to wait. The reaction of Čapek's generation is different; based on a feeling of responsibility, they want to reduce this chaos. As individuals they develop a sense of positive values, of human understanding, and also a belief in the stability of the establishment. They teach not to be ashamed of building, and that other things exist besides protests and destruction. Their moderation has its source in love of life, in an endeavour to pass into the future with the fewest possible sacrifices. Peroutka not only demonstrates all these features in Karel Čapek, but he also stresses the writer's positiveness, and his ability to stop and observe. Since any certainty was lacking in the accumulation of contradictory ideas, Čapek takes recourse to the realism of small things, the existence of which offers at least some certainty.

Peroutka divides humanity into two types, romantic and classic. The former endeavours to avoid participating in reality, while the latter, that of Čapek and his contemporaries, advocates common sense, a modicum of coolness, sternness, calmness, restraint, and a portion of anticipatory prudence. They are people with their feet planted firmly and with pleasure on the ground. Čapek's patient observation of small things is, according to Peroutka, a demonstration of classicality. Peroutka's classification of humanity is philosophically based on the differences between monism and dualism. The monistic type is characterized by Peroutka as a man who is convinced that the entire world runs according to a single principle. Herein, one finds pantheism, which means nature's invasion into religion, Rousseauism, which is nature's invasion into science about society, and anarchism, which represents invasion of naturalness into the realm of the good and the moral. Dualism is, according to Peroutka, more truthful, although more difficult. It rejects the claim that man and nature are one, and distinguishes clearly between the two orders. If man does not want to be just a part of the jungle, he has to control nature including that within him. Hence, we find evidence of the restraint for which Čapek is criticized. Moreover, the measure of propriety is the immediate empirical experience, and intellectuals should contemplate and write as to provide a basis for an imminent action. Their fascination with reality results in the refusal of any changes.

Precisely this is one of the complaints Šalda brings against Čapek. He agrees with the writer that nothing is cheaper than negation for the sake of negation, but maintains that an indiscriminate defense of standing order is just as cheap as mere negation.[259]

Stanislav Kostka Neumann, poet, essayist, and enthusiastic supporter of the communist revolution, also complains about Čapek's failure to advocate positive action, and even reproaches him for denying the need for tumultuous change:

> Karel Čapek . . . zaměřil veškero své úsilí na export, nikoli na světové umění. K tomu mu chybí . . . citová a intelektuální velikost, nesmlouvavá povaha, *mužný poměr k pravé skutečnosti, který chce svět nejen poznati, nýbrž také změniti*; vášnivý poměr k životním otázkám doby, který opovrhuje uměníčkem, které chce býti pouhou hrou.[260]

Similarily, when speaking about the latest Čapek novel, *Povětroň*, Neumann criticizes the author's attitude toward reality:

> [Čapek] s chladnou virtuositou literárního všeumělce vytvoří z pouhé fantasie vymyšlenou konstrukci, bravurní hříčku plnou erudice, kde se dokonce pochlubí i tím, že i on dovede zahráti na struny vášnivé erotiky. *To je ovšem literatura čistě samoúčelná*, a může být jistě spor o to zda emoce, které může poskytnouti nenáležejí k tomu nejnižšímu, co dává umění."[261]

Čapek responded to these accustations in the same journal. At this point, the reply becomes relevant even in a survey devoted to critical views. His response is so very Čexovian that—precisely in light of it—the original criticism acquires a new dimension in the discussion of the affinity between the two writers: *"Básnictví nic neřeší, nýbrž nalézá, objevuje, odhaluje skutečnost a její konflikty.* Nejhlubší a nejintensivnější vztah ke skutečnosti je poznat ji . . ."[262] Aesthetician and renowned structuralist scholar, Jan Mukařovský's understanding of this, is revealed in his article on Čapek's fiction. Here, he observes that all independent narrative prose by Karel Čapek is dedicated to solving a certain problem which can be defined as both artistic and philosophical. Literary history introduces realistic objectivity as the next evolutionary step after romantic subjectivity. In this situation, the highest possible measure of objectivity becomes the ideal. Not the essential truth, but rather the impression of verity is important. The development eventually leads to the ever more strongly expressed requirement that the narration of an event must be distinguished from the event itself. A trend to free the story from undue dependence on the mere chronological sequence of facts without any trace of a unifying sense corresponding to it in "reality," and to stress the method of relation, i.e. the linguistic expression, becomes evident. The brothers Čapek, according to Mukařovský, aim at a renascence of pure epicality. Karel Čapek, in his independent writings, attempts to separate the semantic element of the narration from the facts. Mukařovský speaks about the stressed " . . . rozpětí mezi událostí jako 'skutečností' a vypravováním jako zprávou o ní.[263] He also notes that, in Čapek's stories, the most important component of the event is placed somewhere behind the scenes.[264] Again, this observation can also be applied to Čexov. Furthermore, as Mukařovský stresses in his conclusion, with Čapek, this element of creative work is based on conscious effort.[265] An expanded version of this article becomes an introduction to the 1934 anthology of Čapek's prose.[266] Mukařovský further develops his idea of two separate levels in Čapek's narrations, and classifies different methods whereby the author achieves this duality. Already mentioned is the span contrived between the actual event and its narration. Another variant is the introduction of a discrepancy in the interpretation of an incident. The opposition produced in Čapek's writings by evaluation of an occurrence as a private affair of the protagonists on the one side, and as a conventional understanding on the other, is never resolved. The cognitive ability is one of Čapek's major concerns. In Mukařovský's words: "Autor [Čapek] stále provádí kritiku poznávacích schopností člověka: se zálibou ukazuje často, že táž událost, blížíme-li se k ní různymi poznávacími metodami a s různých stanovisk, může se jevit v různých podobách."[267] Čapek is not interested in

exposition but in interpretational possibilities. Thus, Mukařovský quotes a
detective from Čapek's story "Smrt barona Gandery," whose sentiments
bring to mind Čexov's "Švedskaja spička:"

> Pane kolego, vy máte jiný styl než já; vám by z toho vyšlo něco
> docela jiného nežli mně. To se nedá míchat. Co já bych si
> počal s vašimi špióny, hráči, paničkami a takovou tou honorací?
> Kamaráde, to není nic pro mne. Mám-li to zpracovat já, tak z
> toho vyjde takový ten můj všední a špinavý případ... Každý
> dělá co umí.[268]

The *Povětroň*, published at the same time as Mukařovský's article, strengthens
his allegations by its multitude of interpretations. Seeing two-level approach
as a part of the contemporary antirealistic trend, Mukařovský turns to a
comparison of Čapek and Jan Neruda, who, incidentally, has also been
compared with Čexov.[269]

Václav Černý, a literary scholar with a Western orientation, and
presently a dissident critic and historian, published a monograph on Karel
Čapek in 1936, with a discussion of his writings up to the *Obyčejný život*.
Already in *Boží muka*, Černý, like Mukařovský, observes that everything in
the stories points to something undefined beyond their scope. The critic sees
Čapek in *Boží muka* as a poet depicting a tormented quest for the truth of
life.[270] *Trapné povídky* develops the theme in such a way as to allow the
protagonists a glimpse of this truth, but only by means of pain, which they
all undergo, " ... a čekají od sebe čin, něco nového, něco jakkoliv vedoucího
ze slepé uličky . ... Ale všichni náhle ochabnou, ... a vrátí se do starého
otroctví zvyku a pokoření ... "[271] Naturally, such endings lead to accusations
of pessimism, which Čapek, on several occasions, felt the need to dispute.
Černý supports his defense, claiming that it really is just a label wrongly
inspired by the poet's objectivity.[272] Once more the affinity with Čexov is
obvious. In the following text Černý repeats and strengthens the already-
mentioned issues, with the sole exception of Čapek's trilogy. Again like
Mukařovský, the critic is partial to the pluralism he discerns in all three
novels. Thus, *Hordubal* " ... demonstruje nutnost skreslování lidské duše,
jakmile jest promítána v rovinu t.zv. poznání objektivního.[273] In *Povětroň*
the multiplicity grows. Four possible views and, as Černý observes, " ...je
opravdu ohromivé v jaké horké, naléhavé konkretnosti dovede Čapek vybásnit
čtverou, v daném případě stejně možnou empirii životní . . . "[274] Does it

mean, asks Černý, that when truth is not tied to a person, but generally human and valid, it will inevitably escape us? Our view can never duplicate another's life and soul.[275] *Obyčejný život*, then, with its idea that a single life is a cluster of possibilities, completes the trilogy. Černý views the work as a poetically blessed discovery of a road out of pluralism: "Čapek se dostává od lidské jednotliviny k celku, od mnohosti názorů k jedné pravdě. Interpolací obdiv vzbuzující dobyl z plurality věcí skrytu jejich jednotu . . ."[276] Man is a being of countless possibilities—this optimistic conclusion implies human freedom, and in turn, the disparity between finite limitation and infinite freedom. This disparity indicates that any man's spirit contains more than merely the history of one human individual. Our freedom gives us, according to Černý, the possibility of becoming, at least temporarily, any one of our human fellows, or of, perhaps, identifying with him forever. In other words, the principle of our freedom implies a principle of human fraternity, unity, and equality of people as people.[277]

Černý in his treatise also refutes Čapek's, at the time, generally accepted pragmatism. He claims that the writer's involvement with that philosophy was a political statement at the time of World War I, but is a thing of the past.

Na rozdíl od obecně přijímaného názoru si Čapek odnesl leccos z Jamesovské filosofie mravnosti a nepříliš mnoho z pragmatické noetiky. Po této poslední stránce stanovisko Čapkovo je asi toto: svět není jen místem pro řešení teoretických problémů, ale i polem pro tvoření dobra a vůbec pro činnost; hledíte-li zlepšit svůj život, nemůžete na této cestě trvale ztratit pravdu a zabřísti navždy do omylů. Tot' zajisté něco jiného než pragmatická instrumentální teorie noetická, podle níž pravdivost myšlenky tkví v její schopnosti vykonati jistou užitečnou práci. Důraznější je v Čapkovi vliv pragmatismu etického: pro Čapka hodnota člověka nepochází ze žádného apriorního, nadlidského světa, místem mravnosti jest jen život empirický, v němž samém leží jeho neodvoditelná cena; jen jednající osobnost je morální a v denní práci a všedním hájení života máme žít svůj mravní život . . . "[278]

Čapek's philosophy is not a major concern in the book reviews by the literary critic and leading Czech poet, Josef Hora. Yet, already in 1924, he compares Čapek's *Krakatit* with the works of Il'ja Èrenburg and H.G. Wells, concluding that the Czech writer is an optimist, because for him destruction is merely something to be undone.[279] Five years later, when reviewing *Povídky z jedné kapsy*, Hora speaks of Čapek's duality. On the one hand, he is perhaps the greatest skeptic of Czech literature, a poet of the cold philosophical void, and on the other, a neighbourly optimist, and seeker of reason in the human animal.[280] In the conclusion to this review, Hora proclaims that these stories contain just as much philosophy as Čapek's plays. The same themes which are used by others to depict the horror and boundlessness of life, are to Čapek a proof for the existence of a great equilibrium. Every fault is already punished in this world, and on the whole we can be contented.[281] The review of *Válka s mloky*, while it repeats Hora's earlier sentiments, is still of considerable interest because of the simile he used. Nineteen years after Šalda's complaint that Čapek's works are formulae for all literary movements in the recent past, Hora views him as one " . . . z těch významných autorů, jichž neuchopíte jedinou formulí."[282] The critic also comments on the use of a utopian symbol which, as he says, gives Čapek space for a philosophical satire not only on the current state of humanity, civilization, social and political derangements, but most importantly, it affords him the opportunity to do so without engaging in direct criticism which, despite the greatest struggle for objectivity, might lead to injustice.[283]

"Bajky o válce občanské," Čapek's aphoristic caricatures of the Spanish insurgent generals, resulted in attacks against the author for his unhealthy writings which lack manliness. At this time, the leftist critics rose to Čapek's defense.[284] The remarkable reversal of their views is well illustrated in articles by Zdeněk Nejedlý, an ideological critic, and later, a minister of culture for the communist government. The scholar in question already voices his dissatisfaction with Čapek in the 1920s. About *Ze života hmyzu*, for instance, he says that its popularity cannot be explained either on the grounds of wit or effectiveness, both of which it lacks. On the contrary, the audience looks on dispassionately.[285] Moreover, no central concept worth mentioning emerges. Even when reviewing Šalda's theatrical piece, Nejedlý refers to works by the brothers Čapek in negative terms. The artistic form of Šalda's play is far superior; " . . . to však není dáno tím, že Šaldova technika je zralejší než např. Čapků, nýbrž daleko spíše tím, že se v tom projevuje mátožnost světového názoru u Čapků na jedné a pevnost tohoto názoru u Šaldy na druhé straně."[286] In other words, Nejedlý detects a feeble world view in the Čapeks' writings. In addition, he discerns from Karel

Čapek's article "Proč nejsem komunistou?" that literati feel uneasy about their peculiar position of not being in the forefront of current intellectual development.[287] He mitigates the criticism, however, after Čapek's death in 1938. In an article in *Učitelské noviny*, Nejedlý speaks of Čapek's unquestionable qualities, and acknowledges him as one of the best of those who led Czech literature in the past quarter century.[288] Furthermore, he explains the attacks against Čapek shortly before his death by the author's identification with the recently dissolved democratic system in Czechoslovakia. Herein also lies his great popularity. Nejedlý praises Čapek for his love of common people and his only objection to the author, at this time, is that after World War I he wanted only peace which, to this critic is not satisfactory.[289]

A comprehensive picture of Karel Čapek as seen by the leftist critics is exemplified by Marxist sociologist and literary scholar, Bedřich Václavek, in his survey of modern Czech literature.[290] Like Götz or Peroutka, he sees Čapek as a member of the 1914 generation which attempts to overcome the nihilism ensuing from the crisis of the individualist life style. They turn to American pragmatism, which does not realistically seek absolute truths, but rather adopts expediency in life as the criterion of truth. This leads to a new humanism which leans favourably towards man and reality in life, meliorist humanism, even optimistic, democratic civilism, and love for quotidian experience.[291] A difference exists, however, between Czech pragmatism and its American counterpart. Václavek maintains that it does not have the same immediacy, thus indicating that the change is rather forced and can be understood as an attempt to hide thus far unreconciled conflicts rooted in individualism. Václavek describes the Czech pragmatist

> Přiklánějíce se k člověku jakožto základní jistotě, nerozuměli pod ním lidského kolektiva, nýbrž samostatnou solipsistní jednotku, jedinečnou individualitu. V teorii poznání zdůrazňovali osobní zrod pravdy. Hledajíce jedinečnost životního dění, negovali vlastně ve svém relativismu jakýkoliv lidský řád nadosobní a dospěli posléze k relativisaci všech lidských hodnot . . .[292]

Karel Čapek is, according to Václavek, very typical of his generation. He believes that the writer's entire production is basically contained in his first book co-authored with his brother Josef. In *Krakonošova zahrada*, the

Čapeks are fascinated by the world of technological civilization which, however, at the same time, horrifies their traditional sensibility. The world of capitalist civilization is for them a world of romantic possibilities, but it is also a strait jacket restraining personality, and it always implies an inevitable fate.[293]

Analyzing *Boží muka*, Václavek concludes that Čapek in this work is much more a philosopher than a poet. Searching for that which is individual and which distinguishes one man from another, he, naturally, arrives at irrationality and relativism denying any kind of order, he makes even the most universal image, God, to be relative, necessarily resulting in romantic pain caused by free decision and absolute passivity of will. Taking such a stand, Čapek, according to Václavek, had to reach absolute human pessimism and disbelief in man.[294] Čapek's *oeuvre* evidences the author's negative attitude to his times, but having often shown the impasse of the capitalist civilization through sharp criticism, he is unable to find a positive solution. Václavek describes Čapek's philosophy as follows:

> Když byl spekulující rozum Čapkův popřel *všecky* klady v životě, zachraňuje se násilným skokem k jakémusi primitivnínu před- nebo mimocivilisačnímu stadiu lidského života, aniž nás ovšem tento útěk k jadrným, ale prostoduchým lidovým figurkám může přesvědčiti. V těchto násilných zlomech jeho románů i her jeví se jednak neorganičnost a výhrady, se kterými Čapek přejal pragmatismus, jednak nemožnost vyrovnati se s tohoto hlediska se složitostí současného života osobního a zejména společenského.[295]

Of Čapek's later writings, Václavek singles out *Povídky z jedné a druhé kapsy* and the trilogy. In the former, he sees the author as a professed eulogist of present social order even in its police form. The only purpose of the latter is, he claims, to present a part of Čapek's philosophy. These novels are to convince the reader of the polymorphism, depth, complexity, and richness of life. They philosophize, however, about diverse modes facilitating comprehension and explanation of the same reality in a variety of ways instead of taking the appropriate poetic action to present this polymorphous reality directly. Čapek is prevented from taking such a course by his relativism, and he leaves the reader to orientate himself in this relativistic chaos, advising him to take the subjective stance.[296] This Václavek sees as a lack of certainty which the author should give to the reader, thus also damaging the artistic effect of the work.

A number of articles appeared during the years following Čapek's untimely death, and most of them agree on his accomplishments, and his love for and interest in the common man. One exception to this trend is an extensive study by Miroslav Rutte. His treatise interprets Čapek's *oeuvre* in the spirit of the approach already advanced in Rutte's *Nový svět*, namely, in an exegesis of pragmatism. After the preamble about the Čapeks' beginnings which he had already examined in his earlier work, Rutte opens the discussion of Karel Čapek's work with the claim that the author's progression towards an understanding of truth and man cristallizes in the pragmatist philosophy, which he introduced to Czechoslavakia through his popular book *Pragmatismus čili filosofie praktického života.*[297]

> Američtí filosofové, kteří se pokusili osvoboditi člověka z bludiště nepoznatelna naukou, že živým znakem pravdy není její absolutní platnost, nýbrž *mravní a životní účelnost,* určili hlavní směrnici i Čapkově noetice a jeho moralismu. Přijal Deweyovy zásady, že "vědecké soudy mají byt asimilovány soudy mravními" a že hlavním úkolem filosofie je "ideál největší starosti o účinné účasti na životě." Vyznává spolu s F.C.S. Schillerem, že "objektivní svět je tím v co se vyvíjí," a že naše ideály jsou skutečným součinitelem v jeho vznikání. A věří s melioristou Williamem Jamesem, že "každý můžeme přispěti svou vlastní činností ke spáse světa," jehož stavba není dokončena, protože Bůh ponechal i člověku účast na jeho tvorbě.[298]

In his analysis of individual works, Rutte, like Mukařovský, finds that the double perspective so typical of Karel Čapek's mind-searching method has its roots in his first stories.[299] *Boží muka* consists, according to this critic, of a number of noetic adventures which, starting from relativism, make a simultaneous attempt to overcome relativity and reach certainty. Although based on reason as the most powerful support against the unknown, they cut at the same time its very roots, thus showing reason's powerlessness. Čapek uses logic in order to discover illogicality at its basis, to demonstrate the dubious nature of even our certainties.[300] Although the stories collected in *Trapné povídky* seem realistically simple, Rutte believes that in them Čapek asserts the law of double perspective by showing man both the way he is and the way he appears to others. The double image of every protagonist is, according to Rutte, a subconscious anticipation of the pluralism reached by Čapek years later in *Povětroň and Obyčejný život*. Therein also lies the reason for not solving the conflict between extrinsic and intrinsic truth, but rather allowing for the equal validity of both to show that every man has more than one set of appearance and character traits. His reality consists only in the totality of the good and the evil, the negative and the positive.[301] Thus, although Čapek stresses in *Povídky z jedné a druhé kapsy* the importance of the capability for sensitive observation, he also demonstrates how instinct or inspiration can be wrong, and unveils the baseness of human nature. This leaves him one step short of the question posed in *Hordubal*, namely, whether justice, reconstructing the case from external data alone, can penetrate the actual core of the matter and recognize human action in its entire vital, and sentimental sphere, in its true essence.[302] The relativity of knowledge and the duplicity of perspective is further developed in *Povětroň* and *Obyčejný život*. Rutte views the entire trilogy as a new phase in Čapek's noetic method: "Čapek dospívá v ní od relativismu k *perspektivismu* a od individualismu k *pluralismu*. Člověk poznává sice i nyní jen dle sebe sama, ale nezná už pouze jediný úsek pravdy, jenž se mu podobá, nýbrž *celou řadu různých úseků*, protože sám v sobě má nespočetně možností a podob.[303]

Čapek's utopian works also provide Rutte with an opportunity to support his allegation of the author's adherence to the programatic philosophy:

> Pragmatismus, k němuž se Čapek hlásí od svych počátků a jenž klade filosofii jako nejvyšší postulát činnou účast na životě, projevuje se i v jeho utopiích: nejde v nich pouze o samoúčelnou hru vědecké obraznosti, nýbrž vždy o cosi více: *o filosofické podobenství, o mravní kritiku společenského vývoje, o varovný výkřik k lidskému svědomí.* . . . Čapek staví se v nich na obranu člověka proti "ideovému lidožroutství" a hájí v nich přirozený životní řád proti titanské i revoluční zvůli.[304]

Rutte illustrates this claim with a quotation from *Krakatit*, where the inventor of a destructive explosive who resists the temptation to relinquish it to humanity, is told: "Nespasíš svět ani jej nerozbiješ. Chtěl jsi dělat příliš veliké věci, a budeš dělat věci malé. Tak je to dobře. Kdo myslí na nejvyšší, odvrátil se od lidí. Za to jim budeš sloužit."[305] The critic finds this statement, which he describes as a capitulation of reason before the divine order, to be typical of Čapek. Moreover, it is one of Rutte's examples for what he calls a typical happy ending by a pessimist who is hiding his fear for man and of man beneath abstract concepts.[306] Although Čapek is a meliorist, he does not have exceeding trust in either the good will or the nobility of people. Thus, according to Rutte, even Leibnizian optimism is actually a profound pessimism, since it proves that man is, in his heart, unalterably evil and selfish, and that his deeds contribute to damnation rather than to the salvation of the world. Therefore, Čapek mistrusts all big words and great passions, for he is convinced that they often mean vast desolation. He prefers honest labour, informal conviviality, and healthy human animality to heroism and titanism, both of which may even lead to death.[307]

This sentiment is also reflected in Mukařovský's last critical writing which otherwise deals with the linguistic features of Čapek's literary production. This scholar speaks about the possibilities for philosophical analysis present in the writer's emphasis on the individuality of people and things, although his highest praise is reserved for that which they have in common. The point of departure for Čapek's approach to the world is, indeed, an individual seen exclusively through the eyes of others, determined and limited by the relations between them. A person presented in this manner is the direct opposite of the "I" observing the world from its centre and considering its own likes and dislikes to be the laws of the Universe. Čapek is hostile to such an "I," thus qualifying, according to Mukařovský, as an adversary of romantic titanism.[308] Čapek's admiration and love for diversity in individuals is matched by his sentiments for the polymorphism of other forms of reality. This leads one to inquire whether Čapek's ontology is monistic or pluralistic, whether it reduces reality to a single principle or sees its multiplicity and diversity as transcendent, existing independently of man and his attitude to things. According to Mukařovský, evidence can be found in Čapek's work to interpret the differences the author so passionately stresses, as either existing in reality itself, or as imparted to reality by man. The critic accepts this apparent contradiction in Čapek's *Weltanschauung* since such "polyphony" can

mark any philosophical system. The consistent practice of a certain principle
cannot, therefore, act as a criterion for evaluating Čapek's world view.
The role of poetry is not to fit everything into a system, but always to
reveal a new reality in man.[309]

Professor Černý who, in his 1936 monograph, contended that Čapek's
major concern is human and poetical veracity, and denied accusations of
pessimism brought against the writer, now, four years later, finds a single
principle exercised in Čapek's writing. This critic accepts the theory advanced
by Rutte, and views pessimism as the driving force in the writer's creativity.
As presented in Černý's review of Čapek's collection of short articles *O
lidech*, pessimism is even the basis for his love for and faith in man. Thus the
critic also explains Čapek's conservativism—he was against any reformation
since he feared change for the worse.[310]

During the German occupation Čapek's works are banned not only
because of the antifascist themes in some of them, but also because they
represented the period of Czech history which the new rulers wish to
eradicate. The end of World War II does not bring a reinstatement of Čapek
to his former rank. Only two weeks after the re-establishement of the
Czechoslovak republic, Václav Kopecký—at that time the communist
Minister of Information—calls a large meeting at which he proclaims that
Čapek's period in literature is irrevocably past recall.[311]

After the communists' assumption of power in Czechoslovakia in
1948, works by the author of the essay "Proč nejsem komunistou?" become an
even more sensitive issue for the authorities. His books are removed from
public libraries. Young literary critics, seeking approval from the authorities,
begin their careers with attacks on Čapek.[312] Writings by an author of
Čapek's magnitude could not, however, be entirely suppressed. In addition,
the popularity he attains in the Soviet Union with his antifascist works,
augmented by the social criticism contained in his writings which the Soviet
scholars intepret as an exposure of capitalist society, does not diminish after
the war. Indeed, the first impulse for a revaluation of Čapek's literary heritage
comes from the Soviet Union in the form of a publication of Čapek's selected
works, supplemented by an essay on the author by the Soviet scholar Sergej
Vasil'evič Nikol'skij.[313] The importance of this event as a turning point in the
assessment of Čapek's *oeuvre* is attested to by the rapid translation of
Nikol'skij's treatise into Czech.[314] Václav Černý confirms this fact in his
recently published memoirs. Reminiscing on the spring of 1954, he says: " .
. . Karel Čapek, v Československu zakázaný a vyřazený z knihoven, se k nám

už zase pomalu vracel, zaštítěn sovětskou slávou 'pokrokového' autora . . .
"[315] In another reference, Černý is even more explicit:

> Čapky totiž stalinský režim původně zuřivě negoval. Ale pak
> přišel ze Sovětů pokyn ke změně, objevili tam Čapka *Bílé
> nemoci a Matky*, Čapka nejslabšího sic, ale polemika s
> nacistickým totalitarismem, a tedy adaptovaného,
> anektovatelného, a sovětská milost, založená na posunuté
> interpretaci Čapka napůl zamlčeného, byla u nás rozkazem,
> Čapek počíná znovu vycházet, a znovu v obrovitých
> nákladech.[316]

Peroutka, who returns to the theme of Čapek's reception again in
1959, views the writer's rehabilitation as a mixed blessing. Since Čapek
has not been silenced, it is a victory, but the limitations imposed on the
author represent a defeat. Peroutka summarizes the situation stating that
the Nazis ban all Čapek's books without exception. The communists
initially ban them, too, but later permit publication after a careful process
of selection, in which parts are occassionally omitted, and, sometimes,
entire works are rewritten.[317] Moreover, this critic explains the need for
alteration to Čapek's writings. His work grows from experiences of
everyday life, while, according to Peroutka, "Komunističtí kritikové
nepřestávali vyzývat Čapka, aby se pokusil být něčím jiným než je a aby
také se stal agitátorem. Dráždilo je, že se odvažuje popisovat malé věci a
obyčejné lidi . . . "[318]

The ideas expressed by these dissidents do not substantially deviate
from the officially accepted view. For example, Inna Abramovna Bernštejn,
a Soviet Bohemist, speaks about Čapek's literary rehabilitation for which,
as often admitted even by Czech writers, the credit largely belongs to Soviet
scholars. She provides the example of Ivan Klíma who describes the
situation as follows:

> České poválečné kritiky se daly často zaslepit při hodnocení
> Čapkova díla Čapkovým společenským postavením. Viděli v
> jeho díle jen jeho oficiálnost a ideovou slabost... Sovětská
> kritika neopomíjí tyto nedostatky; na druhé straně však u
> vědomí toho, že je naší povinností z literárního odkazu
> měšťáckého umění vzít vše, co v něm bylo kladného, vše co

kriticky zobrazovalo nedostatky předešlých řádů, vidí klady
Čapkových děl, cení si v nich míst, která ostře poukazují na
nedostatky současného řádu.[319]

This statement epitomizes the new approach to Čapek. Thus, *O
věcech obecných* and *Hovory s T.G. Masarykem* disappear from the list of
Čapek's works, and, for example, in the 1953 edition of *Válka s mloky* the
editor removes references to the Communist International, and the
proclamation by comrade Molokov.[320] The direction of Čapek criticism,
under such circumstances, is predictable. Hence, readers encounter comments
like those made by Jiří Hájek, a confirmed communist critic, in his "afterword"
to the 1955 edition of *Povídky z jedné a z druhé kapsy*. He finds that from
these stories, as well as from a number of observations and critical lashes
elsewhere, the criminal essence of the capitalist order, of class proprietary
morals, and of the bourgeois justice transpires.[321] Unfortunately, according
to this critic, narrative excellence is not sufficient for the creation of a
masterpiece. For a writer, a definitely formed world view is a key to an
understanding of the meaning of life, all life's phenomena, and their
continuity. A dearth of such a scientifically founded world view reduces an
author to a toy of naive soporific illusionism and crippling skepticism.[322]

A very specific source for essays of this type is offered in a commentary
by Czech émigré literary theoretician and historian, Milada Součková.
According to her, at the time of Čapek's rehabilitation, the Soviets were
preparing a major work on the history of Czech literature.

Its publication (1963) gave Čapek a space reserved for the
foremost authors. The essay on Čapek in *Ocherki istorii
cheshskoi literatury XIX-XX vekov* was written by S.V.
Nikol'skii, the Russian specialist on him. . . . No Communist
critic, whether he is Russian or Czech, will dissent from this
official model criticism.[323]

Since the scholar mentioned by Součková is the author of the essay on
Čapek referred to earlier, which apparently began to re-establish the writer
as a major figure in Czech literature, and since the same critic has been
singled out for his contribution in this regard by Inna Bernštejn,[324] this
comprehensive work provides a good illustration of the "new approach" to
Čapek's literary production. Nikol'skij's treatise opens with criticism of

the writer for his lack of revolutionary enthusiasm: "Mirovozzrenie i tvorčestvo Čapeka otražajut osobennosti duxovnogo mira toj časti čexoslovackoj intelligencii 20-30-x godov, kotoraja, oščuščaja neblagopolučie kapitalističeskogo stroja, v to že vremja ne našla puti k revoljucionnym idealam . . ."[325] The cause of this shortcoming in Čapek's writings is the author's lack of a historical perspective which, in spite of his artistic ability and social sensitivity, comes out clearly. Nikol'skij phrases his observations as follows:

> S bol'šoj xudožestvennoj siloj vyjavljaja v svoem tvorčestve mnogie poroki buržuaznogo mira, vystupaja protiv vojn i fašizma, ispytyvaja bol' za neustroennost' čeloveka v sovremennom obščestve, Čapek v to že vremja ne videl istoričeskoj perspektivy. Pisatel' byl zaražen neveriem v radikal'noe, revoljucionnoe izmenenie žizni. On pytalsja iskat' vyxod v oslablenii i primirenii obščestvennyx protivorečij na baze samoj buržuaznoj dejstvitel'nosti, naivno vozlagaja vse nadeždy na èvoljucionnyj progress, na razvitie i uglublenie buržuaznoj demokracii.[326]

These naive views which render Čapek powerless in the face of social evils are a result of the undue influence of the then Czechoslovak president Tomáš Garrigue Masaryk's evolutionary socialism. In Nikol'skij's eyes, Masaryk " . . . svoim lžesocializmom i psevdogumanizmom . . . " leads Čapek astray.[327] *Hovory s T.G. Masarykem*, a three-volume work presenting a story of the president's life and his credo on religion, ethics, and politics as told by Masaryk himself, plays, according to the Russian critic, a reactionary role in the ideological struggle of the time.[328] Nevertheless, Čapek remains a " . . . krupnyj predstavitel' kritičeskogo realizma XX v. . . . "[329] His work is divided by Nikol'skij into four periods: the groping of his early writings which contain some social criticism; from 1920 to the mid 1920s he reflects on the conflicts and problems of the time; 1925-1934 are the years of Čapek's "officialdom" and his relationship with T.G. Masaryk; and finally come the critical years eloquent of the writer's antifascist stand.[330] When describing the first phase in Čapek's evolution, Nikol'skij refers to the picture of a pre-war youth Čapek drew in his article "O čapkovské generaci."[331] The Austrian monarchy's governmental system becomes too narrow, ossified, and incapable of development, in the

opinion of this young man, and he loses all interest in political skirmishes
of the time. The laxity in this regard is, to a certain extent, compensated
for by increased attention to social matters. Should a revolution with a
slogan of new world order begin, this pre-war youth would join with
conviction and enthusiasm.[332] This protest, however, eventually becomes
merely an opposition to the contemporary tastes, manners, and literary
standards.

The war-time impressions, Nikol'skij finds, play an immense role in
the formation of Čapek's views. The young writer, according to him, begins
to contemplate philosophical problems and strives to discover the sources of
life's contradictions.

> On naprjaženno iščet kriterij istiny 'pervopričinu' vsego
> proisxodjaščego v žizni . . . . mučitel'nye razdum'ja pisatelja
> sovpali s izučeniem im filosofii pragmatizma i reljativizma
> . . . kotoroj on ničego ne možet protivopostavit', nevol'no
> prinimaja ee i starajas' najti v nej racional'noe zerno."[333]

Nikol'skij categorically rejects any claim that, in Čapek, the pragmatist
philosophy stimulated an optimistic view of life, or his critical temperament
as has been claimed by contemporary bourgeois literary scholars.[334]

> Meždu tem, [govorit Nikol'skij,] idealističeskie koncepcii,
> otricavščie ob"ektivnuju istinu, po suščestvu svoemu ne
> mogli imet' takogo vozdejstvija. Soznanie togo, čto vsjakaja
> istina sub"ektivna, čto nadežnye kriterii dobra i zla
> otsutstvujut, pritupljalo, a ne obostrjalo kritičeskoe
> otnošenie k dejstvitel'nosti, paralizovalo volju xudožnika,
> velo k kompromissnosti v ocenkax životnyx javlenij. Éto
> dolgo, vplot' do 30-x godov, skazyvalos' v tvorčestve
> pisatelja.
> Vsled za traktatom o pragmatizme Čapek ne slučajno pišet
> samye pessimističeskie svoi proizvedenija . . . [335]

Further, the Soviet scholar states that after 1918 many Czech writers find
the meaning of life and struggle in the ideas of scientific socialism. Čapek,
however, " . . . byl duxovno razoružen vlijaniem reljativizma, teorijami o
tom, čto radikal'naja likvidacija protivorečij obščestvennogo bytija i

izmenenie žizni čelovečestva k lučšemu voobšče nevozmožny."[336] In the eyes of this writer, social suffering becomes a necessary companion of human civilization, and man, its creator, is powerless in the face of it. This leads to abstract humanism. "Čapek iščet puti preodolenija ili, po krajnej mere, oslablenija obščestvennyx protivorečij v moral'no-ètičeskoj oblasti, vystupaja protiv inyx, v tom čisle revoljucionnyx, form bor'by."[337]

Although Nikol'skij does not explicitly mention the duration of Čapek's relativism, he discusses it, as observed earlier, in the pre-war Čapek, and again in his analysis of the 1934 trilogy, thus implying that it is an inseparable part of Čapek's writings for over two decades. Only in 1934, according to Nikol'skij, does the Czech author manage to overcome relativism: "V trilogii dajut sebja znat' otgoloski reljativizma. Odnako v celom ona illjustriruet process izbavlenija pisatelja ot reljativistskix predstavlenij."[338] The mechanistic pluralism which leads to mutual understanding is a positive development. The most reliable sign of Čapek's spiritual evolution is, however, the awakening in him of an interest in the Russian people, their new ways and goals.[339] In addition, Nikol'skij cites Čapek's commentary on the draft of the new Soviet Constitution to illustrate how little the Czech writer knows about the Soviet Union before this time.[340] The remainder of the article predominantly consists of lavish praise for Čapek's opposition to fascism.

The last issues discussed become *topoi* of the Soviet approach to the Czech writer.[341] Milada Součková, however, is not convinced by Čapek's expressed approval of the USSR and its policies. As she says, "In the past, Čapek had been known for his reluctance to sign leftist proclamations. In 1936, however, in his growing anxiety about the future of Czechoslovakia, he was ready to lend his name to political propaganda. He was looking for an ally in the political danger closing around his country."[342] Whatever the writer's reasons, the outcome is that the last period of Čapek's life and work receive unanimous and sincere accolades from both Russians and Czechs.

On the other hand, Čapek's relativism is, according to Soviet critics, the weak point of his *oeuvre*. Nikol'skij, as demonstrated earlier, refutes any possibility of a positive contribution resulting from such a philosophy. Inna Bernštejn in her book inadvertently denies Nikol'skij's basic premise. For Nikol'skij, the dearth of an objective truth renders any optimism, or critical temperament in Čapek's work impossible.[343] Bernštejn, when analyzing *Hordubal*, finds that " . . . suščestvuet istina, xotja do nee i trudno dobrat'sja, tak kak ona roždaetsja iz soprikosnovenija mnogix pravd."[344] Nevertheless, both scholars concur in their criticism of Harkins. Bernštejn minimizes the philosophical component in Čapek's trilogy. According to her, the writer is now, as in his utopian novels, concerned with global social problems. His negative attitude toward a revolutionary solution does not change, hence he turns to the possibilities inherent within human personality. Therein, he seeks a source of mutual understanding and solidarity. Therefore, the gnoseological problems are of utmost importance.[345] Later, she quotes Harkins,[346] who perceives the work as a philosophical one, and who speaks of its tripartite division:

> The conflict in *Hordubal* is that of subjective and objective points of view; in *Meteor* it is between different objective views. In *An Ordinary Life* the final possibility is considered: a conflict of different subjective views. [This] . . . suggests the triad formula of dialectic: thesis, antithesis, and synthesis. The three novels of the triology stand in this relation.
> *Hordubal* is the thesis: all men are separate and distinct, and no man can know the truth of another's life. *Meteor* is the antithesis: all men are related in the common essence, and each man has the potentiality of knowing another through his knowledge of himself. The synthesis is given in *An Ordinary Life*: there is both unity and plurality in human nature, both within the individual and in the society of man without. But it is unity within plurality; the plurality of persons within us makes possible a link with other men.[347]

Bernštejn cannot accept this scheme. Rather than separating the individual volumes, she sees the trilogy as one coherent unit with three complementary parts. She also categorically rejects Harkins's proposal of its possible relation to the perspectivism of Ortega y Gasset or that of Karl Mannheim, claiming that Čapek uses such an artistic approach before he becomes acquainted with their philosophical works. In fact, she interprets the writer's perspectivism as a result of an artistic rather than a philosophical quest: "Voobšče priem sopostavlenija različnyx toček zrenija nado . . . rassmatryvat' ne tol'ko v specifičeski filosofskom aspekte, no v plane xudožestvennyx iskanij v oblasti romana, kotorye pereklikajutsja so mnogimi javlenijami v razvitii ètogo žanra v naše vremja.[348] Bernštejn repeatedly stresses that philosophy is not Čapek's only concern, that he is also interested in human characters, relations, and life in general with its material riches. Yet, the important factor is his acknowledgement of an objective truth: " . . . trilogiju otličaet ot mnogix sxodnyx s nej po vnešnim primetam proizvedenij zapadnyx pisatelej priznanie suščestvovanija ob"ektivnoj istiny ob"ektivnyx moral'nyx cennostej, i v častnosti čelovečeskoj solidarnosti vmeste s ogromnym uvaženiem k čelovečeskoj ličnosti . . . "349

The accord of Soviet critics in their rejection of Harkins's interpretation of Čapek's writings, in spite of the disparity in their reasoning, indicates the need to examine the American Slavist's work. Nikol'skij's reference is to a 1958 general article on "Čapek's generation," while Bernštejn selects a passage from Harkins's monograph on Čapek published four years later. The former investigates the reflection of pragmatist philosophy in Czech *belles-lettres*. To this purpose, the author identifies the major philosophical themes in pragmatism:

> (1) All thought is individual and purposive; "pure" thought as an abstract ion does not exist. Hence a logic from which considerations of personal interest are entirely excluded is false; (2) Truth becomes a value, rather like the beautiful and the good; (3) Truth is to be measured by its consequences in human action; some consequences of action even become the criterion of truth . . . . (4) Pragmatism provides a foundation for religious belief, since it makes the consequences of such belief for individual life the ultimate test; (5) Pragmatism encourages optimism and a belief in progress, particularily in progress through and by the individual.350

According to Harkins, these last two points, which apply particularly to James's thought, had the strongest influence on the Czech "pragmatist generation." Further, the American scholar speaks of Čapek's treatise *Pragmatismus čili filosofie praktického života*, which is, as he says, a largely expository work, and only in its second edition (1925) does the author add a strong comment of personal approval.351 Čapek accepts the label of "pragmatist generation," but stipulates those attitudes which he believes their pragmatism should consist in:

> (1) a dislike of purely verbal solutions; (2) a return to reality;

(3) an end to "neurotic subjectivism"; (4) individualism, but an "objective" indvidualism; (5) freedom of spirit; (6) all facts to be considered "philosophic," including crude, vulgar or negative ones; and (7) all questions of thought to be conceived essentially as questions of our behaviour in relation to our experience.[352]

Harkins infers that these propositions leave little doubt of the essentially pragmatist character of Čapek's position.

He never identified his philosophy as purely pragmatist, . . . and . . . he diverged more and more from a simple pragmatism as he grew older. Relativism and pluralism, in a sense philosophical correlatives of pragmatism, were more fundamental parts of his philosophical position, though, later he abandoned an unmodified relativism for a more subtle "perspectivism."[353]

The main attraction of pragmatism for Čapek does not lie in a specific set of ideas but rather in its new way of thinking. As Harkins notes " . . . it is the ethical emphasis, the optimism, the stress on the nature and role of the individual, the constructiveness of pragmatist ideas which please Čapek."[354]

As a matter of fact, no common system of ideas or universal truth exists for the Czech "pragmatists." This suggests to Harkins that they were more influenced by James than by the other pragmatists.[355] The same naturally applies to their art. According to the American scholar, " . . . the members of the Czech pragmatist generation did not produce a more systematic pragmatist theory of art. They were not systematic philosophers. And they found no specific source for their esthetic theories in the pragmatist philosophers themselves."[356] Moreover, no consistent attempt is evident on the part of these writers to aply a pragmatist philosophy in literature.[357]

In Čapek's early writing, Harkins notes nostalgia for an absolute truth beyond human attainment, and relativism which later helps to pave the way for the writer's acceptance of pragmatism, since pragmatist epistemology is essentially relativist.[358] Still in *Boží muka* the reader is confronted with " . . . the conflict between man's striving for an absolute and the desirability for him to content himself with the relative. The nostalgia for a lost absolute pervades most of these tales . . . with a sombre mood rare in Čapek's work."[359] Next, Harkins discusses the collection of *causeries* on inflated, meaningless words and phrases, *Kritika slov.* According to him, this work is " . . . in the pragmatist spirit, perhaps the highpoint of Čapek's 'pragmatism.' For Čapek truth resides in facts and people, not in words: philosophy must go beyond words and phrases if it is to discover truth."[360] In addition, Harkins quotes the protagonist of *Krakatit*, who declares: "Já znám ... jen fakta; *já je dělám*, jsou to *má* fakta, rozumíte? A přece ... já ... já za nimi cítím nějakou pravdu; ohromnou obecnou pravdu . . . Ale ta velká pravda ... je za fakty a ne za slovy. A proto, proto musíš za fakty!"[361] Hereon the scholar bases his idea of the critical temperament in Čapek's work as a contribution made by a pragmatist type of thought, which Nikol'skij denies.[362] *Továrna na absolutno* represents to Harkins a retreat from pragmatism. In it, he observes that Čapek

> . . . defends the relativism which had earlier been associated with his pragmatism, and applies a scathing satire to every form of absolutism, metaphysical or ethical . . . . [I]t is "practical," not "pragmatic:" man's aspirations for spiritual progress are rejected. In compensation for his loss of faith in spiritual progress, Čapek develops a pluralistic humanism: human life, though devoid of abstract spiritual values, is enriched by the unending variety of nature and life.[363]

Harkins observes this attitude in Čapek's literary production of the 1920s, which is marked by the comparative absence of human beings:

> If men appear it is usually in the guise of amiable eccentrics whose whole life is devoted to a single hobby. Critics speak of Čapek's optimism (životní optimismus) in this period, but what appears as optimism is in fact an enthusiasm, chiefly esthetic, for the natural order. It can hardly be said that Čapek has found a faith in man. This he achieved only with the 1930s and his trilogy.[364]

Povídky z jedné a z druhé kapsy show, according to the American critic, a new hesitation to accept a pragmatist epistemology.[365] He concludes that:

In truth for Čapek relativism and pluralism, the correlatives of
a pragmatist metaphysics, were always more important than
pragmatism itself. And in the end it is only pluralism which he
accepts: relativism terrifies him. Hence in the 1930s the main
direction of his philosophical activity is turned towards the
discovery of more stable and more nearly absolute ethical and
political ideas.[366]

Harkins's interpretation of Čapek's trilogy, rejected by Bernštejn,
has already been outlined here. Noteworthy is, however, that Bernštejn
slights the philosophical aspect of the work while emphasizing the plurality
of points of view as an artistic device, but she never mentions that Harkins
sees cubism as the strongest influence on Čapek's esthetics.[367] According
to the American scholar, it was cubist theory which provided Čapek with an
artistic formula for expressing his relativist attitude towards truth.[368]

Oleg Malevič, another Soviet Bohemist, admits Čapek's philosophical
orientation, but stresses the social content of his work. This critic cites Marx
and Lenin to prepare ground for his claim that Čapek's interest in new
philosophical trends is rooted in the belief that the world can be improved.[369]
The writer rejects pragmatism, however, as a theory of knowledge; its
definition of truth as one species of good defies, Malevič observes, the
fundamental rules of science.[370] Like pragmatists, Čapek believes that in
cognition of reality man can follow only his personal experience, not
trusting any theories or generalizations. Developing his idea further, the
critic states that

Priznav nepreložnym princip otnositel'nosti i social'noj
obuslovennosti vsjakogo znanija, pisatel', podobno
pragmatistam ne vidit v otnositel'nyx istinax krupic absoljutnoj
istiny. Odnako deljačeskij, utilitarnyj dux pragmatizma emu
gluboko čužd. Počtomu on zamenjaet pragmatičeskij kriterij
individual'noj pol'zy obščečelovečeskoj . . . "[371]

Malevič understands the common benefit as a basis for social criticism, and
he stresses this element in Čapek's writings. Hence, although he recognizes
the trilogy to be a philosophical work, he emphasizes its hidden message in
observations like " . . . Amerika—èto i nečelovečeskij trud i organizovannyj
grabež . . . , i lokauty i bezrabotica,"[372] which he finds in *Hordubal*, or

. . . pisatel' raskryvaet obščestvennyj smysl èkonomičeskix processov.

V džungljax oxvačennogo krizisom kapitalističeskogo mira Èkonomičeskie Zakony predstavljajutsja pisatelju . . . božestvom,

ot . . . kotorogo zavisit sud'ba rjadovogo čeloveka,"[373]

taken from *Povĕtroň*.

The Czech variants on the Russian criticism of Čapek are many. Milada Součková selected from the large number of introductions and afterwords to the new editions of his works, articles, and books, three representative monographs for discussion: Ivan Klíma's *Karel Čapek*, Josef Branžovský's *Karel Čapek, světový názor a umění*, and Alexander Matuška's *Človek proti skaze*.[374] Since the publication of her book (1970) two more monographs worthy of discussion appeared in print, namely, Oldřich Králík's *První řada v díle Karla Čapka* and František Buriánek's *Karel Čapek*. The first work discussed by Součková, that by the now blacklisted novelist Ivan Klíma, according to her, is the most conformist. She says that its author " . . . approximates Nikol'skij, though without the latter's poise of authority. Klíma formulates anew what had already been said or what one expects to be said, on the subject."[375] Even so, the monograph " . . . provoked violent reaction in its attempt to rehabilitate [Čapek]."[376] The reviewers attacked Klíma for being "excessively understanding in his justification of all Čapek's ideological errors," for his attempt to correct the negative attitude of the socialist critics in view of the readers' continuing interest in Čapek's works, and for the misinterpretation of some of them.[377] Neither side, however, objects to Klíma's comments on Čapek's pragmatism. According to him, Čapek wanted to create his own system of thought in which the first place was to be occupied by man. Pragmatist relativism which allows for the existence of numerous truths attracted the writer by its conciliatory spirit.[378] Klíma concedes Čapek's pragmatism and supports this claim with the notion that no uniform pragmatist philosophy exists. It is above all a method. Pragmatists are connected only through their acceptance of practice as the main criterion of human activity. Only such understanding could allow both the idealist James, and the materialist Dewey to subscribe to pragmatism.[379] Čapek particularly appreciates the individualist aspect which he sees as a requirement of the highest personal responsibility in each individual for his every act: "Čapek sice opakoval pragmatické názory na poznání i pravdu, ale byl si vědom, že *'pragmatism selhává jako teorie poznání; jeho cenný obsah je však jiný, a sice morální.'*"[380] He believes, according to Klíma, that relativism can be a tool for human rapproachement, and a stimulus for moral conduct.[381] One must realize that each individiual has his own truth and therefore no person has the complete truth. People have to trust in people, otherwise the world will be evil.[382] For Klíma, the most unattractive feature of Čapek's writings is the author's concerted effort to separate great ideals and ordinary human activity, his advice to work well as the best contribution for the benefit of humanity.[383]

Josef Branžovský, a scholarly journalist, focuses on the development of Čapek's world view, and its reflection in his literary production. He is particularly interested in the connection of the ideological elements to the pragmatist philosophical system. Branžovský begins with a general exposition of positivism and criticism. According to this critic, Čapek belongs to the generation which seeks to refute the materialistic mechanism: "Po Čapkovi se hází jménem skeptik; nechápe se, že je to idealista, který vede boj proti tísnivému materialismu."[384] The writer's rejection of the mechanistic determination model is just, since even the dialectic materialism opposes the validity of this concept.[385] Unfortunately, the critic continues, Čapek does not find the right—that is the Marxisit—solution. Instead of combining materialism with dialectic, the writer turns to relativism. Bourgeois thought does not gain any confidence in the proximity to absolute truth from the fact that human understanding climbs the steps of relative knowledge, but rather it acquires skepticism that our knowledge is hopelessly relative.[386] American pragmatism, which significantly influenced Čapek, is not different. It also stands under the sign of criticism and freedom, and it is agnostical.[387] Čapek is attracted to this philosophy by its rejection of idealist philosophy's futile speculations, and by its concern for man.[388] Moreover, pragmatism does not have prejudices and accommodates all hypotheses, thus gaining an advantage against positivist empiricism with its antitheological leaning, and against religious rationalism.[389] Conversely, according to Branžovský, the bourgeois criticism disrupts all certainties. Principles and laws are merely approximations, the world is basically unknowable.[390] The absolute world does not allow for human action, for improvement of the world. Specifically, bourgeois humanism notices the shortcomings of the standing order, criticizes capitialism, but arrives at the conclusion that the world can be reformed through individual improvement.[391] Further, Branžovský claims that European pragmatism lacks the active optimism of its American counterpart, because the diversity within the bourgeois society is greater. Hence, the European—that is also Čapek's—pragmatism is more pessimistic.[392] The writer seeks a way out of the crisis which is typical for contemporary European thought. Branžovský observes, however, that he vacillates in his approach to relativity and truth, because absolute and relative moments are contained in each knowledge. The bourgeois thought cannot cope with this because it is not dialectical.[393] Therefore Čapek as a bourgeois thinker cannot determine the right diagnosis or prognosis, and instead of capitalism accuses civilization.[394] With regard to the writer's philosophy, Branžovský notes that pragmatism is lacking unity. There are as many pragmatisms as there are pragmatists. Thus, "Čapek byl výrazný moderní idealista, podstatně ovlivněný americkým pragmatismem osobitě zažitým, se svéráznými rysy pozitivity buržoazního ideologa."[395]

The remaining three monographs were written by literary scholars. The first of them, the Slovak critic Alexander Matuška, is highly praised by Součková for not anxiously following the Marxist blueprint.[396] He writes about Čapek's relationship to other movements in Europe and gives a fair account of how each trend applies to Čapek's work. Similarly, he describes the political-literary milieu which faced the writer. His analysis leads to a claim that " . . . [President] Masaryk's influence on the writer is somewhat exaggerated, because everything that is attributed to it Čapek could have found (and did find) in pragmatism . . . "[397] He establishes that Čapek was acquainted with pragmatist philosophy as early as 1913 and was already then very attracted to it.[398] He liked its spirit of synthesis. " . . . [I]n his [Čapek's] interpretation pragmatism emerged as a philosophy which summarizes, which permeates theory and practice, life and its standards, in order that no antagonism arise in the expounding of an idea and in its realization, between thinking and living."[399] Matuška proceeds to weigh the contradictions with regard to the pragmatism inherent in Čapek's writings, concluding that

> Čapek is a pragmatist if he calls for truth to be personal, gained spontaneously, by an internal experience, if for him truth is a personal event, and the personal event—truth . . . He is a pragmatist if he does not want to pass judgment, to evaluate and choose, but instead to *soften truths*, for he finds some good (and evil) in everything . . . He is a pragmatist if he

substitutes experience for reality, and thus makes the cognition
of objective reality into something subjective. All this and
more is only a segment, the pragmatic facet of Čapek.[400]

Later Čapek begins to overcome pragmatism, although he never
completely overcomes it. " . . . [P]ragmatism ranks first among the
philosophies that formed Karel Čapek. It accompanied him throughout
his life and work, we find it everywhere."[401] His relation to pragmatism
is, however, erratic and full of vacillations. Matuška gives examples
like *Boží muka*, where " . . . truth is pragmatically something personal
(and incommunicable), but the tone in which he speaks of the
impossibility of permanently retaining flashes of absolute truth does
not seem pragmatically optimistic.[402] At the same time, Čapek is
protesting against accusations of pessimism. According to Matuška, he
prides himself on being an optimist.[403] His belief in human work is a
sign of his optimism. "Deeds, activity, work—even the most minor of
efforts, the most insignificant work, this is for Čapek the very moral
essence of man, something that he was constantly exalting . . . "[404]
Matuška, however, finds such sentiment to be ambiguous, and he
concludes that "Čapek is a pessimist searching for sense. He is an
optimist who has—in agreement with pragmatism—every will to believe.
His pessimism is perhaps not tragical. His optimism tends to lack
enthusiasm."[405]

   The same ambiguity is, according to Matuška, evident in the writer's
attitude toward modern technology. He is enchanted, and at the same time
terrified by the dehumanization which technology might impose on human
life.[406] Nature and civilization are conflicting in Čapek's writings.

> Čapek the journalist places "nature" as created by man,
> opposite the "original" nature. Čapek the writer, the man of
> *peasant blood*. On this basis, the return to nature that he
> preaches, and the paradise that he conceives, as opposed to
> the paradise of technical civilization, is not a certitude of the
> past. It is a return to production relations from the pre-
> capitalist period . . . [407]

Matuška uses *Anglické listy* to illustrate Čapek's ambivalence. The writer
admires machines at the British Empire Exhibition:

Jediná dokonalost, které moderní civilisace dosahuje, je
mechanická; stroje jsou nádherné a bezvadné, ale život, který
jim slouží, nebo je jimi obsluhován není nádherný ani lesklý
ani dokonalejší ani sličnější . . . Tato dokonalost hmoty, z níž
neplyne dokonalost člověka, tyto skvoucí nástroje těžkého a
nevykoupeného života mne matou.[408]

Glasgow leaves the same impression on the author with its beautiful factories,
docks and warehouses, chimneys, beam and steel structures, etc., but the life
based on this beauty is not as picturesque: " . . . život, který se z toho rodí,
ulice, lidé, tváře z dílen a pisáren, příbytky lidí, jejich děti a jídlo, život,
jářku, život, který se živí z těch velkých a silných věcí . . . je syrový a
špinavý a lepkavý . . . "[409] Čapek admits that he does not understand these
contradictions of modern life.[410] Matuška compares Čapek's observations
with those made by the young Friedrich Engels who had seen the same, " . .
. with the difference that he did understand, that he did think a thought
through to the end."[411] Matuška agrees with other Marxist critics that Čapek
would always advocate reform and never revolution.[412] He lists a number of
characters in Čapek's works who intend to change the world. Petr's party in
Matka would like to change everything to suit itself. Petr prophesies that
after the war, the people will overthrow their oppressors. This, however, is
not Čapek's opinion. Matuška stresses the message that " . . . of all the great
things in history . . . none has improved the world, none of them makes any
sense. There is plenty of useful work which does not require dying, and life
itself calls for men.[413] From the trilogy Matuška discerns the author's
negative attitude to property and his preference of the small to the large, the
simple and every-day against the exceptional. The trilogy's concluding part,
Obyčejný život, culminates noetic research on the question of how man can
understand the multiplicity of the human universe.[414] "He can understand it,
because he himself is one, and at the same time many, man alone represents
a crowd."[415] In his general evaluation Matuška arrives at a claim that "He
[Čapek] and his generation posed questions that can be summed up into a
single one: How to live?"[416] Some of Čapek's writings do not conform to
this description, and Matuška is aware of it. Hence he comments on one of
his "escapist" works and its reception: "Socialist criticism reproached him,
figuratively speaking, that he did not only write The Garden of Krakonoš
[*Krakonošova zahrada*], but that he also wrote the Gardener's Year
[*Zahradníkův rok*]."[417]

This lack of social involvement is well commented on by Pavel Kohout (now in forced exile), who, as quoted by Součková, in the introduction to his dramatization of Čapek's *Válka s mloky,* writes: "We read quite often: 'What a pity that an author of Čapek's talent was not equipped with the "scientific" weltanschauung [sic]!' It might be so..., yet what a pity that the authors who posses this advantage did not write anything which could match either *První parta* or *Válka s mloky.*"[418]

Oldřich Králík, an outstanding literary historian, collected in a book a number of articles he presented during 1950-1969. The philosophical aspect of Čapek's writings is not his major concern, but the first essay offers an entirely new concept. Králík introduces a possibility that the fundamental categories of Čapek's thought were formed under the influence of French sociology, and particularly the sociologist and philosopher Émile Durkheim. He bases this opinion on the opposition of an individual and a human collective, which is a dualism inherent to Durkheim's social philosophy.[419] Čapek is, according to Králík, constantly on the defensive against the irresistible pressure of collectivity as conceived by Durkheim.[420] In addition to this possible philosophical source, Králík also offers an artistic one. As do Harkins and Matuška,[421] he refers to cubism in Čapek's writings, but unlike them, he goes even further, and offers it as an alternative to relativism: "Snad je v Čapkově tvorbě více kubismu než pověstného relativismu."[422]

The last monograph to be discussed here is written by a Charles University Professor, František Buriánek. He is not the only scholar to believe that efforts to explain Čapek merely on the basis of pragmatist philosophy are rather exaggerated. He deviates from the others, however, in his concentration on Čapek's philosophical dissertation "Objektivní metoda v estetice se zřením k výtvarnému umění." The author's major concern is the possibility for an objective cognizance of an aesthetic object. He believes that, although any aesthetic judgement is necessarily subjective, one can always describe and analyze objectively.[423] Buriánek objects to such a conclusion:

> Zřetel společenského pokroku, který ovšem může být objektivním, vědeckým poznáním určen a hodnocen a může tedy být objektivním kriteriem hodnot, Čapek hodnotil jako subjektivní, jako relativně platný a nepřipouštěl jej jako kriterion objektivního poznání a hodnocení. V tom se zásadně

lišil od marxistického myšlení, od historického a dialektického materialismu.

Čapek nestavěl svou estetiku na základech filozofického relativismu, naopak všechno relativní, co pramení ze subjektivních faktorů, ponechával stranou svého zásadního směřování k "co možná největší objektivnosti." Za tou šel se soustavností a důsledností, kterou můžeme označit jen jako vědeckou.[424]

Hence, according to Buriánek, maximal objectivity is Čapek's aim. Buriánek's analysis of the writer's pragmatism offers no fresh insights. Instead, perhaps, some ideas emerge from a radio broadcast by his political opponent, Peroutka, who also speaks about Čapek's philosophy. He comments on the writer's reception by the communist critics: "Pozorujíc Čapkův vřelý sociální cit, komunističtí kritikové rozhodli, že byl blízek komunismu, že by mu bylo stačilo udělat ještě jeden krok, podívat se trochu hlouběji, aby se stal plnokrevným komunistou."[425] Relativism, according to Peroutka, is an unfortunate misnomer for Čapek's philosophy:

Vykládaje svou filosofii, Čapek pravděpodobně chyboval, když znovu a znovu ji nazýval relativismem. Slovo relativismus bylo značně zdiskreditováno, pro mnohé představovalo filosofii dobrovolné a ochotné nejistoty ve věcech poznání i ve věcech morálních, jakousi kapitulaci myslícího a jednajícího člověka. Jestliže všechno je relativní, nastává trapný zmatek mezi dobrem a zlem.[426]

Čapek's concept as understood by Peroutka is, however, different. As he says:

Čapek hlásal, že pravda je mnohostranná a složitá, že existuje "gotický charakter faktů," o němž mluvil americký filosof William James, a že pravdu je třeba hledat opatrněji a svědomitěji, než jak činí nacionalistické a stranické žurnály a politikové. Velmi jasně vyslovil, komu oponuje jeho relativismus: člověku, "který věří v nějakou část pravdy a myslí, že musí nenávidět člověka, který věří v pravdu poněkud jiné značky." Od komunismu ho tedy dělil ne jen krok, nýbrž dlouhá cesta, kterou nikdy nehodlal podniknout.[427]

Summary

From the foregoing survey of Čapek and Čexovian criticism emerge two basic similarities: first, critics are unable to agree about the two writers' *Weltanschauung*; second, this disagreement seems to indicate other, more fundamental, similarities between the Russian and the Czech authors. A simple juxtaposition of Čapek and Čexovian criticism demonstrates many perceived shared elements in their philosophical attitudes. Despite conflicting views expressed by some of the critics, or rather even within these controversies, the reader can see affinities in their *Weltanschauung*. Nevertheless, this term is already debatable, for both authors are repeatedly accused of having a feeble or nonexistent world view. The dearth of a unifying idea or underlying philosophical outlook, and a lack of direction are *topoi* in critical evaluations of their writings. Moreover, the connection between ideas in Čexov's works is said to be insufficient, while Čapek purportedly utilizes the cubist story form to depict the chaos in a soul without meaningful direction. Čexov, it is maintained, is detached from salient contemporary political and social issues, and Čapek lacks interest in mankind. They are both indifferent, restrained, and cold-blooded. They accept life as it is without calling for positive action. They do not, indeed, offer any solutions to propounded problems. Čexov is compared to a photographer, and Čapek allegedly also strives for the utmost objectivity. The spiritual crisis in the Russia of Čexov's time leads to a gloomy pessimism which becomes a dominant feature in his art. The crisis of idealism permeates literature at the time of World War I, and Čapek's sentiments again parallel those of the Russian writer. The advance of materialism and the destruction of traditional values result in general skepticism, and both authors are even criticized for nihilism. The latter charge, however, is refused even by some of the critics who admit the writers' skepticism. Čapek emerges from post-war nihilism with his humanist relativism, and, like his Russian counterpart, struggles against all dogmatism. That, indeed, is not nihilism. Both writers vehemently oppose generalizations. The unit for Čapek is the individual man, not the collective, and Čexov insists on recognizing the rights of individuals in preference to rhetorics. They both show love and understanding for ordinary people, although this sentiment is questioned by some critics. Thus, the Czech writer is a meliorist but does not trust people, and both, as already mentioned, are dispassionate in their writings. Yet, although both express concern about the dubious nature of human progress, they believe in man's ability to overcome all obstacles. The optimal method for reaching a better tomorrow is to improve one's own life. If every person will work for amelioration of the world, the future will be bright. Thus, both writers develop a link between aesthetics and ethics. Neither of them proposes a revolutionary solution, at least such an interpretation did not appear during their lifetime. Modern Marxist literary scholarship developed a policy according to which the critic, although aware of the author's shortcomings, must select the positive elements in his work. Hence, the pictures of contemporary society become revelations of the criminal nature of the capitalist order, bourgeois justice and morals. Consequently, Čapek and Čexov are seen as budding revolutionaries. Some critics object to such assertions, proclaiming that Čexov warns against revolution, and seeks liberation of art from ideology, while for Čapek communism only desires to rule, not to solve problems; its attitude is too hateful. Neither writer can accept progress based on enmity. Scientific development brings intellectual, not emotional satisfaction, and both writers place love for one's fellow above science. Hence, the philosophy discerned from their works is designated as humanistic. The question of its idealism or materialism remains unresolved. Ontological arguments are of no importance in Čapek's pragmatism. Yet, he is claimed by the materialists, while also called an idealist in the struggle against mechanistic determinism. Similarly, critics note Čexov's observation about the immense expanse between the sayings "God exists" and "There is no God." Nevertheless, Čexov is called a positivist and a materialist, but he is also, consciously or not, a religious man. To complete the scale, he is outside all trends. The only philosophy Čexov takes seriously is positivism, but he struggles against it. Čapek is a pragmatist, therefore this question becomes immaterial, except that his pragmatism is eclectic and, as a result, some critics claim that his philosophy, if any, is not pragmatist.

The difficulty encountered in the attempts at classifying the authors' expressed ideology is consistent with their objections to generalizations and absolutes. They strive to stay outside trends in which people are so absorbed in their own views as to preclude divergent opinions. Such an imposition on freedom is not acceptable to either of the two writers. After all, the reason for their non-acceptance of mechanistic determinism is its denial of freedom. Čapek and Čexov recognize the complexity, and even the protean quality of truth, and find some truth in every statement. Critics disagree whether the two writers believe in the existence of absolute truth, none of their protagonists ever attains it. Both authors are, however, interested in such a possibility. Indeed, the gnoseological theme is a dominant feature in their works. The duality of unreconciled views is prominent throughout Čexov's writing, although the basis for the double perspective changes. Since the author refuses to condemn any point of view, and merely depicts divergent codes of life, each of which represents a partial truth, he is inevitably drawn to relativism. Čapek turns to pragmatism not only because of its practicality, but also for its tolerance. Truth is personal, and since objective truth is beyond the human grasp, the writer concerned with an individual and his conception of the world turns to relativism. Both authors depict ordinary men, not literary titans, but common people endeavouring to orientate themselves in this world. The critical evaluation of Čapek and Čexov's literary production demonstrates a great similarity of arguments and indicates common elements in their philosophy. In the following chapter an attempt will be made to derive a system of thought common to both.

Notes

1. Some important criticisms with purely artistic considerations will be included in order to preserve chronological order.

2. The praise of Čexov's talent is repeated in most reviews published in his lifetime. The review of Čexov's *Pestrye rasskazy* [by M.A. Skabičevskij], published in "Novye knigi," *Severnyj vestnik*, 2, No. 6 (1886), quoted in N.I. Gitovič, *Letopis' žizni i tvorčestva A.P. Čexova* (Moskva: GIXL, 1955), p. 138, is typical. Other such examples will be introduced further in the text. All secondary quotations not available to this author have been checked in other accessible sources.

3. For instance, the above quoted 1886 review by Skabičevskij, the 1887 New Year's issues of Russian periodicals, as cited in Gitovič, p. 148, or L.E. Obolenskij, "Obo vsem," *Russkoe bogatstvo*, 4, No. 12 (1886), 166-96.

4. [N.K. Mixajlovskij], "Novye knigi," *Severnyj vestnik*, 3, No. 9 (1887), 81-85.

5. N.K. Mixajlovskij, *Sočinenija* (S.-Peterburg: Izdanie redakcii žurnala *Russkoe bogatstvo*, 1897), VI, 1044, as cited in Henry Urbanski, "Chekhov as Viewed by his Literary Contemporaries," Diss. New York Univ. 1973, p. 41.

6. R.A. Disterlo, "O bezvlastii molodyx pisatelej," *Nedelja*, 23, No. 1 (1888), ii, 33, as quoted in A.P. Čudakov, *Poètika Čexova* (Moskva: Nauka,1971), p. 178.

7. "Periodičeskija izdanija: *Severnyj vestnik*, fevral' i mart," rev. of Čexov: "Step'," *Russkaja mysl'*, 9, No. 4 (1888),ii, 209-10.

8. R.D. (Disterlo), "Novoe literaturnoe pokolenie," *Nedelja*, 23, Nos. 13 and 15 (1888), ii, 484, as quoted in Čudakov, pp. 178-79.

9. "Na žurnal'noj nive," rev. of Čexov, "Ogni," *Novosti dnja*, 14 June 1888, as quoted in Čexov, (VII, 647).

10. Aristarxov (A.I. Vvedinskij), "Žurnal'nye otgoloski," *Russkie vedomosti*, 1 July 1888, as quoted in Čexov, (VII, 648).

11. D.S. Merežkovskij, "Staryj vopros po povodu novogo talanta," *Severnyj vestnik*, 4, No. 11 (1888), 77-79.

12. "Zadači literaturnoj kritiki," *Russkoe bogatstvo*, 8, No. 12 (1890), ii, 128-40.

13. L.E. Obolenskij, "K predyduščej stat'e," *Russkoe bogatstvo*, 8, No. 12 (1890), ii, 141-44.

14. Sozercatel' (L.E. Obolenskij), "Novyj povorot v idejax našej belletristiki," *Russkoe bogatstvo*, 8, No. 1 (1890), i, 95.

15. Ibid., p. 96.

16. Mixajlovskij, "Ob otcax i detjax i o g. Čexove," *Russkie vedomosti*, No. 104 (1890), rpt. in *Literaturno-kritičeskie stat'i* (Moskva: GIXL, 1957), pp. 599-600.

17. Ibid., p. 598.

18. Ibid., p. 599.

19. Ibid., p. 606.

20. Ibid., p. 607.

21. Ibid., p. 607.

22. A.M. Skabičevskij, *Istorija novejšej russkoj literatury* (S.-Peterburg, 1891), p. 415, as cited in "Narodničeskaja kritika," *Istorija russkoj kritiki*, ed. B.P. Gorodeckij (Moskva: Izd. AN SSSR, 1958), II, 368.

23. M.A. Protopopov, "Žertva bezvremen'ja," *Russkaja mysl'*, 13, No. 6 (1892), ii, 107 and 109.

24. Ibid., p. 113.

25. Ibid., p. 116. Protopopov's quotation is from the "Step'," in Čexov, (VII, 65-66).

26. Ibid., p. 117.

27. Ibid., p. 117.

28. Ibid., p. 121.

29. P.P. Percov, "Iz"jany tvorčestva," *Russkoe bogatstvo*, 11, No. 1 (1893), ii, 44.

30. Ibid., pp. 43-44.

31. D.S. Merežkovskij, "O pričinax upadka i o novyx tečenijax sovremennoj russkoj literatury," (1893; rpt. in *Sobrannye stat'i: Simvolizm,Gogol, Lermontov* (München: W. Fink Vlg., 1912), p. 232.

32. Ibid., p. 234.

33. Ibid., p. 235.

34. Ibid., p. 226.

35. Ibid., pp. 286-88.

36. Ibid., p. 288.

37. Skabičevskij, "Est'-li u g. A. Čexova idealy?" (1895), rpt. in *Sočinenija v dvux tomax* (S.-Peterburg: Ju.N. Èrlix, 1903), 349-80.

38. Skabičevskij, pp. 350-51.

39. Novus (P.B. Struve), "Na raznye temy: 'Mužiki' Čexova," *Novoe slovo*, 4, No. 8 (May 1897), ii, 42-51, as quoted in Čexov, (IX, 518-519).

40. A.B. (A.I. Bogdanovič), "Kritičeskie zametki," *Mir Božij*, No. 6 (1897), ii, 1-9, as quoted in Čexov, (IX, 519).

41. Mixajlovskij, "'Mužiki' g. Čexova," *Russkoe bogatstvo*, 15, No. 6 (1897), ii, 116-26.

42. Ibid., p. 121.

43. Ibid., p. 122.

44. Novus (P.B. Struve), "Na raznye temy: 'Mužiki' Čexova i g. Mixajlovskij," *Novoe slovo*, 4, No. 10 (Oct. 1897).

45. Mixajlovskij, "Literatura i žizn': O strašnoj sile g. Novus'a, o moej robosti, i o nekotoryx nedorazumenijax," *Russkoe bogatstvo*, 15, No. 11 (1897), ii, 123-27.

46. Novus, "Miscelanea," *Novoe slovo*, 4 (Dec. 1897).

47. P.F. Grinevič (P.F. Jakubovič), "Itogi dvux jubileev," *Russkoe bogatstvo*, 16, No. 8 (1898), ii, 88-124.

48. Ibid., p. 101.

49. A.B. (Bogdanovič), "Kritičeskie zametki," *Mir božij*, No. 10 (1898), ii, 9, as quoted in Čexov, (X, 393-94).

50. _____, "Kritičeskie zametki: Pessimizm avtora. Bezysxodno mračnoe nastroenie rasskazov. Sub"ektivizm, preobladajuščij v nix," *Mir božij*, No. 10 (1898), ii, 2, as quoted in Čexov, (X, 376).

51. Skabičevskij, "Tekuščaja literatura: Novye rasskazy A. Čexova: 'Čelovek v futljare,' 'Kryžovnik,' 'O ljubvi,' *Syn otečestva*, 4 September 1898, as quoted in Čexov, (X, 375).

52. _____, *Istorija novejšej russkoj literatury 1848-1898 gg.*, 4th ed. (S.-Peterburg: Obščestvennaja pol'za, 1900), p. 389.

53. D.N. Ovsjaniko-Kulikovskij, "Naši pisateli: A.P. Čexov," *Žurnal dlja vsex*, No. 3 (1899), ii, 263, rpt. *in Sobranie sočinenij* (S.-Peterburg: Obščestvennaja pol'za, Prometej, 1911), V, 129.

54. Ibid., p. 130.

55. M. Gor'kij, "Po povodu novogo rasskaza A.P. Čexova 'V ovrage:' *Žizn'*, Janvar'," *Nižegorodskij listok*, No. 29, 30 Jan. 1900, rpt. in *Sobranie sochinenij v tridcati tomax: Stat'i 1895-1906* (Moskva: GIXL, 1953), XXIII, 317.

56. Ibid., p. 316.

57. Mixajlovskij, "Literatura i žizn': Koe-čto o g. Čexove," *Russkoe bogatstvo*, 18, No. 4 (1900), ii, 119-40.

58. Ibid., pp. 127-28.

59. Ibid., p. 133.

60. Ibid., p. 129.

61. Ibid., p. 129.

62. Ibid., p. 135.

63. Ibid., p. 137.

64. Ibid., p. 138.

65. A. Volynskij (Flekser), "Anton Čexov," in *Bor'ba za idealizm: Kritičeskie stat'i* (S.-Peterburg: N.G. Molostvov, 1900), pp. 334-343.

66. Ibid., pp. 337 and 338).

67. Ibid., p. 340.

68. Ibid., pp. 340-41.

69. The most recent Complete edition of Čexov's works contains only two stories dated later than 1900.(X, 452 and 462).

70. V.G. Podarskij, "Naša tekuščaja žizn'," *Russkoe bogatstvo*, 10, No. 1 (1902), ii, 155.

71. A.V. Lunačarskij, "O xudožnike voobšče i nekotoryx xudožnikax v častnosti," *Russkaja mysl'*, 24, No. 2 (1903), rpt. in *Sobranie sočinenij v vos'mi tomax* (Moskva: Xudož. lit-ra, 1967), VII, 23.

72. Ibid., p. 24.

73. S.N. Bulgakov, *Čexov kak myslitel'*, a public lecture, Jalta and S.-Peterburg, 1904, publ. (Kiev, 1905), p. 4.

74. Ibid., p. 4.

75. Ibid., p. 4.

76. Ibid., p. 8. Bulgakov's quotation is from Čexov, (IX, 185-86).

77. Ibid., p. 11.

78. Ibid., p. 12.

79. A.A. Fadeev, "O Čexove," *Zapisnye knižki: Russkaja literatura* (1944), rpt. in

Sobranie sočinenij (Moskva: Xudož. lit-ra, 1971), VI, 532, and similarly, VI, 535.

80. Bulgakov, p. 13.

81. Ibid., p. 20.

82. Ibid., p. 21.

83. Ibid., p. 23.

84. Ibid., p. 24.

85. B.J. Poplavskij, unpubl. journal, as quoted in S. Karlinsky, ed. *Letters of Anton Chekhov* (New York: Harper and Row, 1973), p. 31.

86. G. Andreev maintains in his article "Zagadka Čexova," *Novyj žurnal*, 34, No. 118 (1975), 63, that Kurdjumov is a pseudonym of Marija Aleksandrovna Kalaš, a writer and a collaborator of *Vozroždenie* in the 1920s.

87. M.G. Kurdjumov, *Serdce smjatennoe: O tvorčestve A.P. Čexova 1904-1934* (Paris: YMCA Press, 1934), p. 20.

88. Ibid., p. 42.

89. Ibid., p. 47.

90. Ibid., p. 48.

91. Ibid., p. 48.

92. Ibid., p. 96.

93. Ibid., p. 49.

94. Ibid., p. 54.

95. Ibid., p. 64.

96. Ibid., p. 65.

97. Ibid., p. 124.

98. Ibid., p. 125.

99. Ibid., p. 125.

100. Ibid., p. 138.

101. Ibid., p. 134.

102. Ibid., p. 145.

103. Kurdjumov, p. 148.

104. Ibid., p. 148.

105. Ibid., p. 178.

106. Ibid., p. 175.

107. Ibid., p. 170.

108. Ibid., p. 170.

109. Ibid., p. 176.

110. S. Karlinsky, ed. *Letters of Anton Čexov* (New York: Harper and Row, 1973), p. 400.

111. G.A. Andreev (Xomjakov), "Zagadka Čexova," *Novyj žurnal,* 34, No. 118 (1975), 59.
He also quotes Fedor Avgustovič Stepun, the long-time chairman of the *Tovariščestvo
zarubežnyx pisatelej,* as praising Zajcev's study (p. 67).

112. Ibid., p. 67.

113. B.K. Zajcev, *Čexov: Literaturnaja biografija* (New York: Izd-vo im. Čexova, 1954),
p. 236.

114. Ibid., p. 88.

115. Ibid., pp. 199-200.

116. Lev Šestov, "Tvorčestvo iz ničego: A.P. Čexov," *Vestnik žizni,* No. 3 (1905), 101-42,
rpt. in *Načala i koncy* (S.-Peterburg: M.M. Stasjulevič, 1908), pp. 1-68.

117. Ibid., p. 3.

118. I.A. Bunin, *O Čexove* (New York: Izd-vo im. Čexova, 1955), p. 116.

119. Andreev, pp. 61-62.

120. Šestov, pp. 30-31.

121. Ibid., p. 32.

122. Ibid., p. 33.

123. N.A. Berdjaev, "Mir tvorčestva; smysl tvorčestva i pereživanie tvorčeskogo èkstaza,"
in *Samopoznanie: Opyt filosofskoj avtobiografii* (Paris: YMCA-Press, 1949), pp. 231-32.
The major part of this passage is quoted in Bunin, pp. 118-19.

124. Šestov, pp. 12-13.

125. Ibid., p. 47.

126. Šestov, p. 50.

127. Ibid., p. 52.

128. Andreev, pp. 62-63.

129. Ibid., p. 63.

130. V.V. Veresaev, "A.P. Čexov," in *A.P. Čexov v vospominanijax sovremennikov* (Moskva: GIXL, 1960), p. 674.

131. Bunin, p. 405.

132. Veresaev, p. 676.

133. V.V. Ermilov, *A.P. Čexov*, rev. ed. (1946; rpt., Moskva: Sovetskij pisatel', 1959), p. 488.

134. Bunin, p. 377.

135. Profan (V.V. Vorovskij), "A.P. Čexov," *Naše slovo*, No. 21, 17 Jan. 1910, rpt. in V.V. Vorovskij, *Literaturno-kritičeskie očerki* (Moskva: GIXL, 1956), p.252.

136. V.V. Vorovskij, "Lišnie ljudi," *Pravda*, No. 4 (1905), rpt. in Vorovskij, *Literaturno-kritičeskie stat'i* (Moskva: GIXL, 1956), pp. 99-140.

137. Profan (Vorovskij), p. 252.

138. G.P. Berdnikov, *A.P. Čexov: idejnye i tvorčeskie iskanija* (Leningrad: Xudož. lit-ra, 1970).

139. Ibid., p. 115.

140. Ibid., p. 137.

141. Ibid., p. 245.

142. Ibid., pp. 334-35.

143. Ibid., p. 378, quoting Čexov, (IX, 230).

144. Ibid., p. 378, quoting Čexov, (IX, 259).

145. Ibid., p. 409.

146. Ibid., p. 480, quoting Čexov, (X, 220).

147. Ibid., p. 480.

148. John Galsworthy, "Four Novelists in Profile," *English Review*, 55 (Nov. 1932), 488.

149. "Chekhov through the Eyes of the World," *Sovetskaja literatura*, No. 1 [382] (1980), 94.

150. "Chekhov through the Eyes of the World," p. 93

151. T. Mann, "Čexov," trans. L. Rudnaja, *Novyj mir*, 31, No. 1 (1955), 212-26.

152. Berdnikov, "Chekhov," p. 10.

153. Mann, "Versuch über Tschechow," *Sinn und Form*, 6, No.5-6 (1954), 789.

154. Ibid., p. 797.

155. H. Auzinger, "Čechov und das Nicht-zu-Ende-sprechen," *Die Welt der Slaven*, 5 (1960), 240.

156. Mann, p. 798.

157. Ibid., p. 800.

158. Ibid., p. 800.

159. Ibid., p. 801.

160. Ibid., p. 801.

161. Karlinsky, p. 21.

162. Ibid., p. 22.

163. Ibid., p. 23.

164. Ibid., pp. 24-25.

165. K. Čukovskij, *O Čexove* (Moskva: Xudož. lit-ra, 1967), p. 153.

166. Karlinsky, p. 25.

167. È.L. Brojde, *Čexov: Myslitel', xudožnik (100-letie tvorčeskogo puti); katastrofa, vozroždenie* (Frankfurt a. M.: n.p., 1980), p. 202.

168. È. L. Brojde, "Čexov-myslitel'," *Grani*, No. 117 (1980), p. 233.

169. _____, *Čexov*, p. 5.

170. Ibid., p. 9.

171. Ibid., p. 17.

172. Ibid., p. 53.

173. Ibid., p. 53.

174. Ibid., p. 36.

175. Brojde, *Čexov*, p. 51.

176. Ibid., p. 74.

177. Ibid., p. 103, quoting Čexov, (VI, 431).

178. Ibid., p. 103, referring to Čexov, (VII, 222).

179. Ibid., p. 138.

180. Ibid., p. 151, referring to "Duèl'."

181. Ibid., p. 135.

182. Ibid., p. 165.

183. K.D. Kramer, *The Chameleon and the Dream: The Image of Reality in Čexov's Stories* (The Hague: Mouton, 1970), p. 53.

184. Ibid., p. 59.

185. Ibid., p. 64, referring to Čexov, (IV, 355).

186. Ibid., p. 77.

187. Ibid., p. 77, referring to Čexov, (VI, 103).

188. Ibid., p. 83, referring to Čexov, (VI, 414).

189. Ibid., p. 99.

190. N.I. Gitovič, *Letopis' žizni i tvorčestva A.P. Čexova* (Moskva: GIXL, 1955), p. 235.

191. Kramer, p. 109.

192. Ibid., p. 153.

193. Ibid., p. 154.

194. Ibid., p. 157.

195. Ibid., p. 158.

196. Ibid., pp. 163-64.

197. Ibid., p. 164.

198. Ibid., p. 164.

199. Ibid., p. 173.

200. V.B. Kataev, *Proza Čexova: problemy interpretacii* (Moskva: Izd-vo Moskovskogo univ., 1979), p. 12.

201. Ibid., pp. 24-25.

202. Ibid., p. 26.

203. Ibid., p. 27.

204. Ibid., pp. 28-29.

205. Ibid., p. 30.

206. Ibid., p. 35.

207. Ibid., p. 45.

208. Ibid., p. 47.

209. Ibid., p. 48, referring to Čexov, (VII, 314).

210. Ibid., p. 52.

211. Ibid., p. 89.

212. Ibid., pp. 111-12.

213. Ibid., p. 112.

214. L.P. Grossman, "Čexov: Naturalizm Čexova," *Mastera slova*, in *Sobranie sočinenij v pjati tomax* (Moskva: N.A. Stoljar, 1928), IV, 204.

215. Kataev, pp. 113-14.

216. Ibid., p. 114.

217. Ibid., pp. 208-09.

218. Ibid., p. 211.

219. R.H. Marshall, "Chekhov and the Russian Orthodox Clergy," *Slavic and East European Journal*, 7, No. 4 (1963), 379, cited in Kataev, p. 284.

220. A.N. Tolstoj, "Da zdravstvuet Gor'kij!" *Polnoe sobranie sočinenij* (Moskva: GIXL, 1949), XIII, 397.

221. G. Ivask, Čechov and the Russian Clergy," in *Anton Čechov 1860-1960: Some Essays*, ed. T. Eekman (Leiden: E.J. Brill, 1960), p. 84.

222. Kataev, p. 318.

223. *Chekhov: The Critical Heritage*, ed. V. Emeljanow (London: Routledge and Kegan Paul, 1981).

224. Articles of the type of J. de Proyat, "Anton Čexov et Herbert Spencer," *Revue des études slaves*, 54, No. 1-2 (1982), 177-93 do not represent a major trend. Moreover, in this particular example the author is concerned with education, rather than philosophy.

225. B. Èjxenbaum, "O Čexove," in *O proze: sbornik statej* (Leningrad: Xudož. lit-ra, 1969), pp. 363-64.

226. V.T. Romanenko, *Čexov i nauka* (Xar'kov: Xar'kovskoe knižnoe izd-vo, 1962)

227. T.G. Winner, "Čechov and Scientism: Observations on the Searching Stories," in *Anton Čexov, 1860-1960: Some Essays*, ed. T. Eekman (London: E.J. Briell, 1960), pp. 325-26.

228. Ibid., p. 326.

229. Ibid., p. 326.

230. Ibid., p. 335.

231. I. Èrenburg, *Perečityvaja Čexova* (Moskva: GIXL, 1960), p. 16.

232. Čapek, rev. of *Červenec* by F.V. Krejčí, *Přehled*, 11, No. 47 (14 Aug. 1913), 773-74.

233. F.X. Šalda, "K dnešní situaci literární," *Česká kultura*, 2, No. 1 (3 Oct. 1913), 19-21, rpt. in *Soubor díla F.X. Šaldy* (Praha: Melantrich and Čs. spisovatel, 1947-63), XVIII, 218.

234. Ibid., p. 218.

235. Šalda, "Karel a Josef Čapkové," *Kmen*, 1, No. 42 (29 Nov. 1917), 1-4 and No. 52 (7 Feb. 1918), 1-3, rpt. in *Soubor*, XIX, 135.

236. Ibid., XIX, 139.

237. Ibid., p. 140.

238. Ibid., p. 141.

239. M. Rutte, "Bratří Čapkové," in *Nový svět: Studie o nové české literatuře 1917-1919* (Praha: Aventinum, 1919), pp. 145 and 147.

240. Ibid., p. 147.

241. Ibid., p. 153.

242. Rutte, "Zklamání z idealismu," in *Nový svět*, p. 12.

243. _____, "Pragmatism—boj o důvěru v život," in *Nový*, p. 16.

244. F. Götz, "Literární kubismus český," in *Anarchie v nejmladší české poesii* (Brno: B. Kočí, 1922), pp. 52-53.

245. A. Novák, "Czech Literature During and After the War," *The Slavonic Review*, 2 (1923-24), 131.

246. Šalda, "Epilog k literární patálii," *Tribuna*, 2, No. 10 (14 Jan. 1923), 3-5, rpt. in *Soubor*, XXI, 139.

247. _____, "Spory literární," *Var*, 3, No. 11 (1 Dec. 1924), 327-34, rpt. in *Soubor*, XXI, 292.

248. Ibid., p. 296.

249. Ibid., p. 297.

250. Götz, *Jasníci se horizont* (Praha: Václav Petr, 1926), pp. 76-77.

251. _____, "Karel Čapek: Věci obecnější," in *Jasníci*, p. 157.

252. Ibid., p. 158.

253. Götz, "Karel," p. 159.

254. Šalda, "Karel Čapek, novinář politický a sociální," in *Šaldův zápisník*, 4 (1931-1932), 409.

255. Ibid., p. 409, quoting Čapek, *O věcech obecných čili Zóon politikon* (Praha: F. Borový, 1932), p. 107.

256. Ibid., p. 409.

257. Ibid., p. 401.

258. F. Peroutka, "Vysvětlení směru," *Přítomnost*, 8, Mos. 19, 20, 22, 23, 25, 26, and 30 (13 May — 29 July 1931), as summarized by Milan Otáhal, in "Ferdinand Peroutka: Muž Přítomnosti," *Svědectví*, 18, No. 70-71 (1983), 346-50.

259. Šalda, "Představitelé tak zvané generace ztracené," *Literární svět*, 1 (Oct. 1927), rpt. in *Soubor*, XXII, 251.

260. S.K. Neumann, "Česká literatura a česká skutečnost," *Listy pro umění a kritiku*, 2 (1934), 52.

261. Ibid., p. 53.

262. Čapek, "Literatura a veřejnost," *Listy pro umění a kritiku*, 2 (1934), 56.

263. J. Mukařovský, "O próze Karla Čapka," *Almanach Kmene*, 5 (1934-1935), 133-34.

264. Ibid., p. 134.

265. Mukařovský, p. 137.

266. Mukařovský, "Úvod," in *Vybor z prózy Karla Čapka*, ed. J. Mukařovský (1934; rpt. Praha: Státní nakl., 1946), pp. 5-37.

267. Ibid., p. 17.

268. Ibid., "Úvod," p. 17, quoting Čapek, *Povídky z jedné kapsy—Povídky z druhé kapsy* (Praha: Čs. spisovatel, 1973), p. 213.

269. Ibid., "Úvod," pp. 27-28, and A.V. Čičerin, *Nerudovskij čtap v istorii kritičeskogo realizma* (Kiev: Izd. AN Ukrainskoj SSR, 1963), pp. 8 and 11.

270. V. Černý, *Karel Čapek* (Praha: F. Borovy, 1936), p. 8.

271. Ibid., p. 11.

272. Ibid., p. 11.

273. Ibid., p. 29.

274. Ibid., p. 30.

275. Ibid., p. 31.

276. Ibid., p. 33.

277. Ibid., p. 35.

278. Ibid., p. 34.

279. J. Hora, "Nové romány," *Rudé právo*, 1 June 1924, rpt. as "Krakatit," in Hora, *Duch stále se rodící* (Praha: Čs. spisovatel, 1981), p. 176.

280. _____, "Nové povídky Karla Čapka," *Literární noviny*, 7 Feb. 1929, rpt. as "Povídky z jedné kapsy," in *Duch*, pp. 376-77.

281. Ibid. p. 377.

282. Hora, "Nový Čapkův román utopistický," *České slovo*, 15 March 1936, rpt. in *Duch*, p. 378.

283. Ibid., p. 378.

284. "Časové otázky naší literatury," *Tradice a modernost: Výbor z díla Bedřicha Vdclavka*, ed F. Valouch and J. Dvořák (Praha. Odeon, 1973), pp. 230 and 256.

285. Z. Nejedlý, "Ze života hmyzu," *Var*, 1, No. 12 (15 May 1922), rpt. in *Sebrané spisy Zdeňka Nejedléno* (Praha: St. nakl. polit. literatury, 1953), XV, 173.

286. _____, "F.X. Šaldovo *Dítě*," *Var*, 2, No. 8 (15 April 1923), rpt. in *Sebrané*, XV, 176.

287. Nejedlý, "Drama českého inteligenta," *Pondělní noviny*, 1, No. 34 (15 Dec. 1924), rpt. in *Sebrané*, XV, 186.

288. _____, "Karel Čapek," *Uèitelské noviny*, No. 20 (1938), rpt. in *Sebrané*, XV, 147.

289. Ibid., p. 150.

290. B. Václavek, Česká literatura XX. století (1934; Praha: Svoboda, 1947).

291. Ibid., p. 93.

292. Ibid., p. 93.

293. Ibid., pp. 94-95.

294. Ibid., p. 95.

295. Ibid., p. 96.

296. Ibid., pp. 96-97.

297. Rutte, "Výpravy za skutečností," in *Mohyly s vavřínem* (Praha: Fr. Borový, 1939), p. 175.

298. Ibid., p. 175.

299. Ibid., p. 172.

300. Ibid., pp. 177-78.

301. Ibid., pp.181-82.

302. Ibid., p. 193.

303. Ibid., p. 200.

304. Ibid., pp. 186-87.

305. Ibid., p. 187, quoting Čapek, *Krakatit* (Praha: Čs. spisovatel, 1968), p. 292.

306. Ibid., p. 187.

307. Ibid., p. 188.

308. Mukařovský, "Významová výstavba a komposiční osnova epiky Karla Čapka," *Slovo a slovesnost*, 5 (1939), 113-31, rpt. *in Kapitoly z české poetiky* (Praha: Melantrich, 1941), II, 517-18.

309. Ibid., pp. 519-20.

310. Černý, rev. of *O lidech*, by Karel Čapek, *Kritický měsíčník*, 3 (1940), 415-16.

311. Peroutka, "Osud Karla Čapka," Radio Broadcast 26 Dec. 1953, rpt. in *Budeme pokračovat* (Toronto: Sixty-Eight Publ., 1984), pp. 40-41.

312. Ibid., p. 41.

313. S.V. Nikol'skij, "Karel Čapek," in Čapek, *Izbrannoe* (Moskva: GIXL, 1950), pp. 3-16.

314. _____, *Karel Čapek*, trans. K. Jiroudková (Praha: Čs. spisovatel, 1952).

315. Černý, *Paměti*, IV (Toronto: Sixty-Eight Publishers, 1983), 401.

316. Ibid., p. 556.

317. Peroutka, "Vítězství Karla Čapka," Radio Broadcast, 28 March 1959, rpt. in *Budeme*, p. 82.

318. Ibid., p. 83.

319. I.A. Bernštejn, "Karel Čapek v Sovetskom sojuze: 20-30-e gody," in *Čexoslovacko-sovetskie literaturnye svjazy* (Moskva: Nauka, 1964), p. 37, quoting I. Klíma, "Karel Čapek v Sovětském svazu," *Praha-Moskva*, 10 (1955), 60.

320. Čapek, *Válka s mloky* (Praha: Čs. spisovatel, 1953), p. 180, cf. 1963 edn., pp. 170 and 171-72. As could be expected, this is also the form of editorship encountered in the Soviet translation of the work. See, e.g., Čapek, *R.U.R.—Sredstvo Makropulosa—Vojna s salamandrami-Fantastičeskie rasskazy* (Moskva: Mir, 1966), p. 419.

321. J. Hájek, "Doslov," in *Povídky z jedné kapsy-Povídky z druhé kapsy* (Praha: Čs. spisovatel, 1955), p. 328.

322. Ibid., p. 332.

323. Milada Součková, "An International Asset," in *A Literary Satelite: Czechoslovak-Russian Literary Relations* (Chicago and London: Univ. of Chicago Press, 1970), p. 53, referring to Nikol'skij, "Karel Čapek," in *Očerki istorii češskoj literatury XIX-XX vekov* (Moskva: AN SSSR, 1963), pp. 503-23.

324. Bernštejn, "Karel," p. 37.

325. Nikol'skij, "Karel Čapek," in *Očerki istorii češskoj literatury XIX-XX vekov* (Moskva: AN SSSR, 1963), p. 503.

326. Ibid., p. 503.

327. Ibid., p. 514.

328. Ibid., p. 514.

329. Nikol'skij, p. 504.

330. Ibid., p. 504.

331. Ibid., p. 505, referring to Čapek, "O čapkovské generaci," in *O věcech obecných*, p. 144, (originally in *Přítomnost*, 9 (1952), 153).

332. Ibid., p. 505.

333. Ibid., p. 506.

334. *Ibid.*, p. 506, referring to W.E. Harkins "Pragmatism and the Czech 'Pragmatist Generation,'" in *American Contributions to the Fourth International Congress of Slavicists: Moscow, September 1958* ('S-Gravengage: Mouton, 1958), p. 120.

335. Ibid., p. 506-07.

336. Ibid., p. 509.

337. Ibid., p. 509.

338. Ibid., p. 517.

339. Ibid., p. 518, referring to an interview with Čapek published as "Čto dlja vas SSSR," in *Ogonek*, 14, No. 8-9 (1936).

340. *Ibid.*, pp. 518-19. The commentary appeared under the title "Zarubežnye otkliki na opublikovanie proekta novoj Konstitucii SSSR: Novyj typ demokracii," in *Pravda*, 18 June 1936, p. 5.

341. Čapek's antifascist stand is the single most important theme in any Soviet critical inquiry. The critics substantiate their conviction about his newly developed (1936) appreciation of the USSR and its constitution by referring to the *Ogonek* interview and the *Pravda* commentary. They expound these views in various articles, including: A.M. Maljarenko, *Istoki češskoj socialističeskoj literatury* (Kiev: Izd. Kievskogo univ., 1966), p. 115, Bernštejn, "Karel Čapek," pp. 47-48, and O. Malevič, "Karel Čapek i Rossija," *Voprosy literatury*, 9, No. 7 (1965), 95.

342. Součková, pp. 51-52.

343. Nikol'skij, 506.

344. Bernštejn, "Čerez prizmu čelovečeskogo soznanija," in Bernštejn, *Češskij roman XX veka i puti realizma v evropejskix literaturax* (Moskva: Nauka, 1979), p. 221.

345. Ibid., pp. 218-19.

346. Ibid., p. 224.

347. W.E. Harkins, *Karel Čapek* (New York and London: Columbia Univ. Press, 1962), p.142

348. Bernštejn, p. 225.

349. Ibid., p. 232.

350. Harkins, "Pragmatism," p. 108.

351. Ibid., pp. 108-09.

352. Ibid., p. 109, paraphrasing Čapek, *Pragmatismus čili filosofie praktického života* (Praha: F. Topič, 1925), pp. 77-82.

353. Ibid., pp. 109-10.

354. Ibid., p. 110.

355. Ibid., p. 112.

356. Ibid., p. 115.

357. Ibid., p. 115.

358. Ibid., "Pragmatism,", p. 116.

359. Ibid., p. 117.

360. Ibid., p. 120.

361. Čapek, *Krakatit* (Praha: Čs. spisovatel, 1968), p. 47.

362. Harkins, "Pragmatism," p. 120, see Nikol'skij, p. 506.

363. Ibid., p. 121.

364. Ibid., p. 122.

365. Ibid., p. 122.

366. Ibid., p. 123.

367. Harkins, *Karel Čapek*, p. 28. The influence of cubism is also discussed on pp. 26-27, 49-50, 59, and 61.

368. Ibid., p. 28.

369. Malevič, *Karel Čapek: Kritiko-biografičeskij očerk* (Moskva: Xudož. lit-ra, 1968), pp. 28-30.

370. Ibid., p. 30.

371. Ibid., pp. 30-31.

372. Malevič, p. 126.

373. Ibid., p. 129.

374. Součková, p. 56.

375. Ibid., p. 56.

376. Harkins, "Supplement: 1945-74," in Arne Novák, *Czech Literature* (Ann Arbor: Michigan Slavic Publications, 1976), p. 353.

377. For example, Miloslav Nosek "Čapkovský esej Ivana Klímy," *Česká literatura*, 10 (1962), 364.

378. Klíma, *Karel Čapek* (1962; rpt. Praha: Čs. spisovatel, 1965), p. 29.

379. Ibid., p. 24.

380. Ibid., p. 31-32.

381. Ibid., p. 32.

382. Ibid., *Karel Čapek.*, p. 52.

383. Ibid., p. 52.

384. J. Branžovský, *Karel Čapek, světový názor a umění* (Praha: Nakl. polit. literatury, 1963), p. 21.

385. Ibid., p. 22.

386. Ibid., p. 25.

387. Ibid., p. 30.

388. Ibid., p. 34.

389. Ibid., p. 39.

390. Ibid., p. 42.

391. Ibid., p. 47.

392. Ibid., p. 115.

393. Ibid., p. 127.

394. Ibid., p. 128.

395. Ibid., p. 131.

396. Součková, p. 61.

397. A. Matuška, *Karel Čapek: An Essay*, trans. Cathryn Alan (London: George Allen & Unwin Ltd., 1964), p. 9.

398. Ibid., p. 42-43.

399. Ibid., p. 45.

400. Ibid., p. 50-51.

401. Ibid., pp. 51-52.

402. Ibid., p. 52.

403. Ibid., p. 106.

404. Ibid., p. 106.

405. Ibid., p. 108.

406.Ibid., *Karel Čapek: An Essay*, pp. 190 and 230.

407. *Ibid.*, p. 221.

408. Čapek, *Anglické listy pro větší názornost provázené obrázky autorovými*, in *Italské listy—Anglické listy—Výlet do Španěl—Obrázky z Holandska* (Praha: Čs. spisovatel, 1960), p. 101.

409. Ibid., pp. 136-37.

410. Ibid., p. 152.

411. Matuška, pp. 242-43.

412. Ibid., p. 223.

413. Ibid., p. 281.

414. Ibid., p. 259 ff.

415. Ibid., p. 265.

416. Ibid., p. 382. The critic's observation about Čapek's repeated reference to the problems which belong in literature, not to be solved, but rather to be well presented, comes to mind here, see p. 297.

417. *Ibid.*, p. 384-85.

418. P. Kohout, "Introduction," in Čapek, *Válka s mloky: musical-mystery*, adapted by P. Kohout (Praha: Orbis, 1963), p. 14, as quoted by Součková, p. 68.

419. O. Králík, *První řada v díle Karla Čapka* (Ostrava: Profil, 1972), p. 17.

420. Ibid., pp. 18-26.

421. Harkins, *Karel*, pp. 26-27, 28, 49-50, 59, and 61; Matuška, p. 20 and 305.

422. Králík, p. 158.

423. F. Buriánek, *Karel Čapek* (Praha: Melantrich, 1978), p. 60, quoting from Čapek's unpublished dissertation.

424. Ibid., p. 61.

425. Peroutka, Radio Broadcast, 21 Dec. 1963, rpt. in *Budeme*, p. 134.

426. Ibid., p. 136.

427. Ibid., p. 137.

‰

THE PHILOSOPHY

Čexov's World View

The voluminous criticism of Čexov's writings, as demonstrated, does not educe a comprehensive philosophy of the author. The reason for this shortcoming is threefold. Firstly, Čexov, in his attempt to achieve objectivity and rejection of tendentiouness, does not make an explicit statement regarding his world view. Secondly, the interpreters utilize this fact which enables them to explain Čexov's works in a manner corresponding (positively or negatively) to their own views. Thirdly, erroneous conclusions are derived through faulty information and, consequently, misapplied logic.

The last is, apparently, the most daring, and, at the same time, the most important claim. It needs, therefore, some substantiation. Thus, for instance, Aleksandr Iosifovič Roskin, a renowned Soviet Čexovian scholar, observes that the " . . . teoretičeskie vozzrenija pozitivista Kloda Bernara javilis' počvoj na kotoroj ukrepljalis' vzgljady molodogo Čexova . . . " and that, as a result, the "Teoretičeskie vzgljady molodogo Čexova na literaturu byli blizki i často polnost'ju sovpadali s pozitivistskimi vozzrenijami Kloda Bernara i Zolja."[1] Thomas Winner speaks of "Čechov's scientific positivism" based on the author's knowledge of Claude Bernard's *Introduction à la médicine expérimentale* and Zola's literary theories. He even refers to the above article by Roskin.[2] Following an analogous train of thought, Leonid Grossman speaks about Čexov's "strogo prozitivnye metody" based on the school of Charles Darwin and Claude Bernard.[3] None of the above critics is a philosopher, and they all incorrectly assume that Bernard was a positivist. The erroneous nature of their premise will be discussed later. However, their assumption contradicts the best reference text available in English, *The Encyclopedia of Philosophy*: "Efforts to enlist Bernard in the cause of vitalism are wide of the mark. Equally mistaken is the attempt to affix a positivist label."[4]

Another claim based on false premises is that Čexov as a physician, well versed in natural sciences, should be necessarily a materialist. Thus, Georgij Berdnikov speaks of the "estestvennonaučnoe vospitanie, vyrabotavšee v nem materialističeskoe mirovozzrenie."[5] Viktor Trofimovič Romanenko is even more insistent in his claim that "medicinskij fakul'tet okazal na Čexova *napravljajuščee* vlijanie, poskol'ku glubokoe oznakomlenie s metodom estestvennyx nauk napravljalo—ne moglo ne napravljat'—v storonu materializma . . . "[6] Yet, for example, Paul Bourget, whose novel *Le Disciple* Čexov criticized for its "pretencioznyj poxod protiv materialističeskogo napravlenija,"[7] studied medicine. Neither is Bourget an exception. William James, an idealist philosopher still to be discussed, received his medical degree fifteen years before Čexov.

Perhaps the most obvious illustration of this type of reasoning is Romanenko's claim that "Čexov pis'menno zajavil, čto on *materialist* po svoim ubeždenijam,"[8] referring to the writer's statement that " . . . esli govorit' ob ego [Vagnera] napravlenii, to skoree vsego on jaryj spiritualist i tolstovec daže. Ja v million raz bol'še materialist, čem on."[9] Romanenko accepts Vladimir Aleksandrovič Vagner's spiritualism, and elaborates on the zoologist's idealism,[10] but it does not prevent him from interpreting Čexov's statement as an admission to materialism.

This cautionary preamble does not deny that the Russian author was greatly influenced by the positivist philosophy, nor does it seek to refute his materialism. But the methods propounded by Claude Bernard probably influenced Čexov precisely because of his objections to Comte's philosophy. Moreoever, neither he, nor Čexov would accept the reasoning exemplified above. The French physiologist does not accept any postulate without a counterproof.[11] The absence of such an examination is a shortcoming of scholastics and systemizers, who, according to Bernard, "never question their starting point."[12] He proceeds to stress the flexibility of the experimenters:

Men of system are also distinguished from men of experimental science by the fact that the first impose their idea, while the second always give it just for what it is worth. . . . . The scholastic who believes himself in possession of absolute certainty comes to naught; this can easily be understood, since by his absolute principle, he puts himself outside of nature, in which everything is relative.[13]

Systems and doctrines necessarily entail certain limitations which Bernard seeks to avoid. Hence, as he says,

[we] must . . . carefully avoid every species of system, because systems are not found in nature, but only in the mind of man. Positivism, like the philosophic systems which it rejects in the name of science, has the fault of being a system. . . . I avoid philosophic systems; but I cannot for that reason reject the philosophic spirit which, without being anywhere is everywhere and, without belonging to any system ought to reign, not only over all science but over all human knowledge. So even while avoiding philosophic systems, I like philosophers and greatly enjoy their converse.[14]

The French scientist requires freedom and independence from any system. Čexov expresses similar feelings in his letter to the editor of *Severnyj vestnik*: "Ja bojus' tex, kto meždu strok iščet tendencii i kto xočet videt' menja nepremenno liberalom ili konservatorom. Ja ne liberal, ne konservator, ne postepenovec, ne monax, ne indifferentist. Ja xotel by byt' svobodnym xudožnikom i—tol'ko, i žaleju, čto bog ne dal mne sily čtoby byt' im.[15] The word "nepremenno" increases in significance when correlated with another of Čexov's admissions, this time in a letter to a renowned writer, Dmitrij Vasil'evič Grigorovič: "Političeskogo, religioznogo i filosofskogo mirovozzrenija u menja ešče net; ja menjaju ego ežemesjačno, a potomu pridetsja ograničit'sja tol'ko opisaniem, kak moi geroi ljubjat, ženjatsja, rodjat, umirajut i kak govorjat."[16] The mutability of the young author's world view seems to be a reflection of Bernard's idea that genuine scientists are flexible enough not to accept any postulate as absolute, or beyond the reach of experiment. All theories are true only until facts are discovered which the theories do not include, or which contradict them."[17] Bernard's previously cited statement about the relativity of everything in nature also finds its way into Čexov's correspondence. He repeats it almost verbatim in a letter to a friend, the children-story writer Marija Vladimirovna Kiseleva: "Vse na ètom svete otnositel'no i priblizitel'no."[18] Thereby, he assumes the position of Bernard's scientist, rather than a scholastic. He further develops the analogy between creative writing and science when stressing objectivity in artistic perception: "Xudožestvennaja literatura potomu i nazyvaetsja xudožestvennoj, čto risuet žizn' takoju, kakova ona est' . . . Ee naznačenie— pravda bezuslovnaja i čestnaja. . . . Dlja ximikov na zemle net ničego ne čistogo. Literator dolžen byt' tak že ob"ektiven, kak ximik; on dolžen otrešit'sja ot žitejskoj sub"ektivnosti . . . "[19] Objectivity alone is not, however, Čexov's basis for comparison of the two branches of human awareness. In a draft of another letter to Dmitrij Grigorovič, Čexov describes his belief that the " . . . čut'e xudožnika stoit inogda mozgov učenogo, čto to i drugoe imejut odni [i te že] celi, [i] odnu prirodu i [u menja togda daže, podobno [tomu] lučam mel'(knulo)] čto, byt' možet, so vremenem pri soveršenstve metodov [oni sol'jutsja] im suždeno slit'sja vmeste v gigantskuju čudoviščnuju silu, kotoruju trudno teper' i predstavit' sebe..."[20] The eventual convergence of art and science is another echo of Bernard's ideas. He implies such a possibility in the *Introduction*,[21] but is explicit in the address he delivered upon entering the French Academy in 1869:

> Letters are the elder sisters of the sciences. It is a law of the intellectual evolution of peoples, who have always produced their poets and philosophers before their scientists. In this progressive development of mankind, poetry, philosophy and the sciences express the three phases of our intelligence, passing through "sentiment," reason and experience; but this procedure must also be followed in reverse, with experience or experiment remounting from facts to their cause, lighting our mind, clarifying our "sentiment," and fortifying our reason. Letters, philosophy and science must join in the search for the same truths.[22]

Shortly after the second letter to Grigorovič, Čexov discussed Petr Nikolaevič Ostrovskij's commentary on Čexov's "Step'." He stresses the critic's knowledge of scholarly methods: "Važno ne to, čto u nego est' opredelennye vzgljady, ubeždenija, mirovozzrenie—vse èto, v dannuju

minutu est' u každogo čeloveka,—no važno, čto on obladaet *metodom*; dlja
analitika, bud' on učenyj ili kritik, metod sostavljaet polovinu talanta."[23]
The French scientist's notion of method includes a progression from the
subjective to the objective, or, in his words, the experimenter advances
" . . . from partial to more general truth, but without ever daring to assert that
he has grasped the absolute truth."[24] Čexov discusses the necessity of
advancement from detail to generality and that it is also valid for creative
literature: "Termin tendecioznost' imeet v svoem osnovanii imenno neumen'e
ljudej vozvyšat'sja nad častnostjami."[25]

Individual problems are, according to Bernard, to be solved by
experimental science, but philosophy shows science the questions torturing
humanity, which it has not yet solved. "For making scientific observations,
experiments and discoveries, [however,] philosophic method and procedure
are vague and powerless; the only means available for that are scientific
methods and procedures that can be known only by experimenters, practicing
some definite science."[26] The Russian writer accepts this limited role of a
guide, when he claims: " . . . ja vsegda nastaivaju na tom, čto ne delo
xudožnika rešat' uzkospecial'nye voprosy. Durno esli xudožnik beretsja za
to čego ne ponimaet. Dlja special'nyx vorprosov suščestvujut u nas specialisty
. . . Xudožnik nabljudaet, vybiraet, dogadyvaetsja, komponuet . . . "[27] The
delineation of the artist's position calls for a comparison with a formula set
by Émile Zola, in his treatise modelled on Bernard's work, "[i]l [le romancier]
lui faudra voir, comprendre, inventer. Un fait observé devra faire jaillir
l'idée de l'expérience à instituer, du roman à écrire, pour arriver à la
connaissance complète d'une vérité."[28] Zola's novelist, imitating Bernard's
experimenter, attempts to apply both components of the experimental
method, namely, observation and experimental reasoning to reach positive
knowledge. The ambition of the Russian writer is limited to the art of
investigation which Bernard calls the cornerstone of all the experimental
sciences.[29] According to the physiologist, observers " . . . must be
photographers of phenomena; their observations must accurately represent
nature."[30] Literary critics do not appreciate this "photographic" practice,
and Zola complains about the contemptible reproaches heaped upon writers
adhering to this method.[31] Čexov, as seen in the previous chapter, is
criticized for this reason by Petr Percov and Nikolaj Mixajlovskij. He is not
dissuaded, however, as corroborated by his expressed opinion that " . . . ne
belletristy dolžny rešat' takie voprosy, kak bog, pessimizm i t. p. Delo
belletrista izobrazit' tol'ko, kto, kak i pri kakix obstojatel'stvax govorili ili

dumali o boge ili pessimizme. Xudožnik dolžen byt' ne sud'eju svoix
personažej i togo, o čem govorjat oni, a tol'ko bespristrastnym svidetelem."[32]
Čexov is firmly convinced that intent observation and correct formulation is
the artist's purpose. He objects to confusion of the two separate notions,
" . . . rešenie voprosa i pravil'naja postanovka voprosa. Tol'ko vtoroe
objazatel'no dlja xudožnika. V *Anne Kareninoj* i v *Onegine* ne rešen ni odin
vopros, no oni Vas vpolne udovletvorjajut, potomu tol'ko, čto vse voprosy
postavleny v nix pravil'no."[33]

    The scientific method seems to have lost some of its reliability when,
only a week later, Čexov comments on Merežkovskij's critical article. As he
notes the reviewer's scientific approach, Čexov expounds the view that,
"[k]to usvoil sebe mudrost' naučnogo metoda i kto potomu umeet myslit'
naučno, tot pereživaet nemalo očarovatel'nyx iskušenij. . . . nynešnim gorjačim
golovam xočetsja obnjat' naučno neob"jatnoe, xočetsja najti fizičeskie zakony
tvorčestva, ulovit' obščij zakon i formuly, po kotorym xudožnik, čuvstvuja ix
instinktivno, tvorit muzykal'nye p'esy, pejzaži, romany i proč."[34] Such
formulae do exist in nature and Čexov believes that "[k]to vladeet naučnym
metodom, tot čuet dušoj, čto u muzykal'noj p'esy i u dereva est' nečto obščee,
čto ta i drugoe sozdajutsja po odinakovo pravil'nym, prostym zakonam."[35] A
scientific approach to creative works will, however, necessarily degenerate
into a search for the "cells" or "centers" governing creative ability, and further
into meaningless analyses and discussions. "Dlja tex, kogo tomit naučnyj
metod, komu bog dal redkij talant naučno myslit', po moemu mneniju, est'
edinstvennyj vyxod—filosofija tvorčestva. Možno sobrat' v kuču vse lučšee,
sozdannoe xudožnikami vo vse veka, i, pol'zujas' naučnym metodom, ulovit'
to obščee, čto delaet ix poxožimi drug na druga i čto obuslovlivaet ix cennost'.
Èto *obščee* i budet zakonom. . . . Značit, èto obščee neobxodimo i sostavljaet
conditio sine qua non vsjakogo proizvedenija, pretendijuščego na
bessmertie."[36]

    Despite the author's familiarity with the scientific method,
Merežkovskij's work does not meet with Čexov's approval. Paul Bourget's
Le Disciple evoked the same response. Čexov, in the previously mentioned
commentary on this novel, describes the French writer as a " . . . talantlivyj,
očen' umnyj i obrazovannyj čelovek. On tak polno znakom s metodom
estestvennyx nauk i tak ego počuvstvoval, kak budto xorošo učilsja na
estestvennom ili medicinskom fakultete."[37] Yet, with all his scientific
knowledge, Bourget takes up arms against materialism. Čexov cannot
accept this attitude since, according to him, it never leads anywhere and

does nothing but introduce needless confusion into the sphere of ideas. His reasoning is simple:

> Prežde vsego materialističeskoe napravlenie—ne škola i ne
> napravlenie v uzkom gazetnom smysle; ono ne est' nečto
> slučajnoe, prexodjaščee; ono neobxodimo i neizbežno i ne vo
> vlasti čeloveka. Vse, čto živet na zemle, materialistično po
> neobxodimosti. V životnyx, v dikarjax, v moskovskix kupcax
> vse vysšee, neživotnoe obuslovleno bessoznatel'nym
> instinktom, vse že ostal'noe materialistično v nix, i, konečno,
> ne po ix vole. Suščestva vysšego porjadka, mysljaščie ljudi—
> materialisty tože po neobxodimosti. Oni iščut istinu v materii,
> ibo iskat' ee bol'še im negde, tak kak vidjat slyšat i oščuščajut
> oni odnu tol'ko materiju. . . . Vospretit' čeloveku
> materialističeskoe napravlenie ravnosil'no zapreščeniju iskat'
> istinu. Vne materii net ni opyta, ni znanij, značit, net i istiny[38]

This panegyric to materialism is in contradiction with Bernard's belief that "[f]or physiological experimenters, neither spiritualism nor materialism can exist. These words belong to a philosophy which has grown old; they will fall into disuse through the progress of science. We shall never know either spirit or matter . . . "[39] The French scientist observes, however, that among naturalists and especially physicians there are still men who " . . . express most erroneous ideas on the subject . . . They believe that study of the phenomena of living matter can have no relations to study of the phenomena of inorganic matter."[40] Čexov joins Bernard in rejection of this vitalist idea. Hence, his understanding for M. Sixte. Bourget's hero, according to Čexov, ventures outside his field and is insolent enough to study the inner man on the basis of cell theory, but the Russian writer accepts this conduct. He reasons: "No čem on vinovat, čto psixičeskie javlenija porazitel'no poxoži na fizičeskie, čto ne razbereš', gde načinajutsja pervye i končajutsja vtorye?"[41] Moreover, toward the end of the letter— perhaps as an afterthought—Čexov abates his materialist soliloquy to approximate Bernard's "we shall never know either spirit or matter:" "Govorit' o vrede i opasnosti mater(ialističeskogo) napravlenija, a tem pače voevat' protiv nego, po men'šej mere preždevremenno. U nas net dostatočno dannyx dlja sostava obvinenija."[42] The first impression from these lines indicates a continuing dedication to science. It seems, however, that the author exhausted his store of praise for science and its methods. Thus, although he decides to go on a scientific expedition to Saxalin, his report on the preparatory work does not show much respect for science: "V svoej saxalinskoj rabote ja javljaju sebja takim učenym sukinym synom, čto Vy tol'ko rukami razvedete. Ja už mnogo ukral iz čužix knig myslej i znanij, kotorye vydam za svoi. V naš praktičeskij vek inače nel'zja."[43] Neither does he see any significance in his own enterprise: "Edu ja soveršenno uverennyj, čto moja poezdka ne dast cennogo uklada ni v literaturu, ni v nauku. . . . Ja xoču napisat' xot' 100-200 stranic i ètim nemnožko zaplatit' svoej medicine pered kotoroj ja kak Vam izvestno, svin'ja."[44] In other words, Čexov gives the impression that he feels under an obligation to do something for science, and is willing to pay his debt. He even confirms it when in 1894, upon completion of *Ostrov Saxalin,* he writes: "Moj 'Saxalin'— trud akademičeskij . . . Medicina ne možet teper' uprekat' menja v izmene: ja otdal dolžnuju dan' učenosti . . . "[45] Moreover, eight years later he still refers to the treatise as *"Ostrov Saxalin* napisan v 1893 g.—èto vmesto dissertacii, kotoruju ja zamyslil napisat' posle 1884 g.—okončanija medicinskogo fakul'teta."[46] The sarcasm about contemporary science which appeared in Čexov's description of preparatory work for the Saxalin trip is also reflected in the writer's involvement in the controversy concerning mismanagement of the research facilities at the Moscow zoo, which Čexov criticized in the 1891 article, "Fokusniki,"(XVI, 246-56) co-authored with Vladimir Vagner. The feeling of duty is stressed by statements like: "Medicina—moja zakonnaja žena, literatura nezakonnaja. Obe, konečno, mešajut drug drugu, no ne nastol'ko, čtoby isključat' drug druga."[47] Finally, when expecting the proofs of his *Ostrov Saxalin,* Čexov is explicit: "Osen'ju brosaju medicinu, k janvarju končaju s 'Saxalinom,' i togda ves' po uši otdajus' belletristike."[48] Yet, in 1899, when he writes his autobiography, Čexov does not denigrate the role of science in his life:

Ne somnevajus', zanjatija medicinskimi naukami imeli ser'eznoe vlijanie na moju literaturnuju dejatel'nost'; oni značitel'no razdvinuli oblast' moix nabljudenij, obogatili menja znanijami, istinnuju cenu kotoryx dlja menja kak dlja pisatelj možet ponjat' tol'ko tot, kto sam vrač; oni imeli takže i napravljajuščee vlijanie, i, verojatno, blagodarja blizosti k medicine, mne udalos' izbegnut' mnogix ošibok. Znakomstvo s estestvennymi naukami, s naučnym metodom vsegda deržalo

menja nastorože, i ja staralsja, gde bylo vozmožno,
soobražat'sja s naučnymi dannymi, a gde nevozmožno—
predpočital ne pisat' vovse. Zameču kstati, čto uslovija
xudožestvennogo tvorčestva ne vsegda dopuskajut soglasie s
naučnymi dannymi . . . No soglasie s naučnymi dannymi
dolžno čuvstvovat'sja v ètoj uslovnosti . . .
K belletristam, otnosjaščimsja k nauke otricatel'no, ja ne
prinadležu, i k tem kotorye do vsego doxodjat svoim umom—
ne xotel by prinadležat'.(XVI, 271-72)

Hence, viewing two decades of his literary career in retrospect,
Čexov reconfirms the evidence presented in his correspondence regarding
the import of science's influence on his writing. The duration, intensity, and
form of its impact is another matter. One of his heroines, a physician,
discusses the problem of non-resistance to evil with her brother, and in the
process describes her notion of proper conduct for a man of letters:

Otnestis' k ètomu voprosu čestno, s vostorgom, s toj ènergiej,
s kakoj Darvin pisal svoe *O proisxoždenii vidov,* Brem—*Žizn'
životnyx,* Tolstoj—*Vojnu i mir.* Rabotat' ne večer, ne nedelju,
a desjat' dvadcat' let... vsju žizn'! Brosit' ètu fel'etonnuju
maneru, i otnestis' k voprosu strogo naučno, s ser'eznoj
črudiciej... Izuči ty istoriju i literaturu voprosa, voz'mi sebe
na pomošč' biologiju, literaturu, filosofiju, estestvennye nauki,
kak èto delajut nastojaščie dobrosovestnye mysliteli. Odni
estestvennye nauki mogut dat' tebe ključ k razgadke!(V, 589)

Émile Zola would certainly subscribe to her idea of the writer's need for a
background in the natural sciences, and Čexov seems to have sided with her
on that issue. Unquestionable, however, is the Russian author's pride in an
accurate description of the physical and mental ailings of his characters,[49]
and the earlier-discussed letters of the 1880s demonstrate his concern with
the scientific method.

   A claim that an influence was exerted by Zola's *Le Roman
expérimental* would be forced. Čexov admired the Frenchman's character,
but was not impressed by his writings. He corroborates these sentiments
when commenting on Zola's death: "Kak pisatelja ja malo ljubil ego, no zato
kak čeloveka v poslednie gody, kogda šumelo delo Drejfusa, ja ocenil ego

vysoko."[50] His esteem for Darwin and Bernard is different. Čexov has
nothing but praise for the English naturalist. Already in 1883 he comments
on his method: "Priemy Darvina. Mne užasno nravjatsja èti priemy!"[51] The
epistolary evidence of Čexov's enthusiasm for Darwin culminates in the
exclamation: "Čitaju Darvina. Kakaja roskoš'! Ja ego užasno ljublju."[52]
Documentation of this type is lacking in the case of Claude Bernard. His
Introduction was, however, a standard reference book for every progressive
physician at the time of Čexov's medical studies.[53] Conseqently, as is to be
expected and as is testified by the echoes of Bernard's work mentioned
earlier, the medical student knew the book well.

Lev Šestov, who is known for his polemic against scientific knowledge
and scientific method, does not mention Bernard in his essay, but its title
"Tvorčestvo iz ničego," which Bunin relates to Berdjaev[54] is reminiscent of
Bernard's *Introduction*, wherein the author defines an artist as a man who
carries out a personal idea or feeling in a work of art.[55] Consequently, for
Bernard, literary and artistic productions are expressions of unchanging
feeling.[56] This reasoning led Bernard to the statement which so enraged
Zola: "In arts and letters, personality dominates everything. There we are
concerned with a spontaneous creation of the mind, that has nothing in
common with the noting of natural phenomena, in which the mind must
create nothing."[57] In other words, Bernard insists that the creative process
takes place entirely in the artist's mind, thus anticipating the concept Šestov
would later apply to Čexov.

In addition to the idea of "Creation from nothing," Šestov correlates
Čexov's thought with that of the French physiologist in his observation that
Čexov rejects all philosophical systems. The only one which he takes
seriously, and therefore struggles against seriously is positivist materialism.[58]
Nevertheless, as previously illustrated, some critics claim that Čexov is a
positivist. The same misnomer is often applied to Claude Bernard. Yet,
indications are scattered throughout his works to the contrary. Moreover,
Bernard's notes on positivism were preserved and published as a part of the
collection *Philosophie: Manuscrit inédit*. Even a quick perusal exposes a
number of exceptions which the scholar takes either to Auguste Comte, or
to positivism in general. Thus, he comments on Comte's three stages of the
history of the sciences: " . . . l'état positif ne détruira pas l'état théologique
comme pense Comte: ils seront séparés, voilà tout."[59] Moreoever, " . . .
l'état positif tel que le comprend Comte sera le règne de la tête et la mort du
coeur. Cela n'est pas possible."[60] Bernard does not accept the absolute

supremacy of science. Feelings, and therefore art also, are coordinates rather than subordinates of science. The sentimental element is, according to Bernard, an indispensable feature of human make-up.[61] Next, Bernard selects Comte's notion that " . . . la fondation de la physique sociale est le but capital de la philosophie positive," and comments: "Quelle étrange illusion, comme si les sentiments de l'homme suivaient sa science!"[62] His notes are reiterated in a condensed form in the conclusion: "Je considère qu'Auguste Comte a raison quand il s'agit de science pure. Mais la grande objection que je lui fais, c'est qu'il s'imagine qu'il va suprimer le côté moral et sentimental de l'homme."[63] Further disagreement between the ideas expressed by Comte and those of Bernard concern specialization in science. Comte finds the division useful for each particular branch of science but believes that it is extremely damaging to the *esprit d'ensemble*. As he says, "[i]l y a donc là un écueil pour la philosophie positive qui doit être encyclopédique et saisir les généralités des sciences."[64] Bernard accepts Comte's idea of necessity for generalities, but absolutely refuses his means. According to the physiologist, only specialization can lead to generality. "L'idée de Comte de considérer la philosophie positive comme les généralités scientifiques est mauvaise. Il faut absolument descendre dans les details."[65] Another one of Comte's ideas which is rejected by Bernard is his demand for the elimination of everything linked with theology and metaphysics from instruction and the replacement of it with scientific generalities. Comte's error in this matter is, according to Bernard, in believing in the existence of such a thing as *positif*, and he adds a *bon mot*: "Toutes les théories scientifiques sont des abstractions métaphysiques."[66] Moreover, Bernard is convinced of a need in man for belief: " . . . il y a une contradiction dans l'homme, le besoin impérieux d'une croyance et l'impossibilité de l'avoir immédiatement. Si les savants se contentent de ces croyance provisoires et se passent de religion, la masse des hommes ne peut pas et ne pourra pas s'en passer sous quelque forme d'ailleurs que se montre la croyance."[67]

An American professor, Reino Virtanen, discussed Comte's influence on Bernard in a 1965 lecture. He does not limit himself to the two works already examined. Thus he can offer better support for his claim that Bernard

> . . . was sincerely opposed to Comte on several important
> points. He was probably unaware of any significant influence.
> From our vantage point we can readily see certain affinities

between them. Claude Bernard believed like Comte that the human mind has no access to the Thing-in-Itself [*Ding-an-sich*]. The Kantian phrase reminds us that Auguste Comte had not invented the idea. Like the leader of Positivism, Bernard believed that we can only study phenomena and their relations. . . . And Bernard agreed with Comte that we cannot reach the ultimate cause of an event, but only the conditions or immediate causes.

But in the context of his time, the differences must have appeared more important to Bernard.[68]

Virtanen proceeds with examples of passages in the *Introduction* directed against Comte. These comments are then followed by other grievances that Bernard apparently harbored against Comte. His critique of vivisection and his teaching that physiology should be separated from medicine and take a frankly speculative flight are examples from the area of science.[69] Beyond this field, as Virtanen observes, Bernard does not find Comte's "Religion of Humanity" to his liking.[70] He cannot accept the idea of suppression of the moral and sentimental features of man. A similar predicament is apparent with regard to the famous law of the three stages of human thought— theological, metaphysical, and positive. Bernard maintains that "[n]ever would the earlier states be left behind by mankind as a whole!"[71] This law serves, however, according to Virtanen, as an obvious model for Bernard's triad of feeling, reason, and experiment.[72] Bernard, as Virtanen points out, imparts quite an original twist to the concept with his inference that

. . . the experimental method . . . leans successively on the three divisions of that unchangeable tripod: sentiment, reason and experiment. In the search for truth . . . feeling always takes the lead, it begets the *a priori* idea or intuition; reason or reasoning develops the idea . . . But if feeling must be clarified by the light of reason, reason in turn must be guided by experiment.[73]

The preceeding discussion demonstrates that Claude Bernard could be considered a positivist only in the very broadest sense of the word. His physiology studies and determines the conditions of the interrelations of phenomena without burdening itself with metaphysical preoccupations on the essence of things.[74] However, it was also shown that Bernard deviates from Comte's philosophy. Moreover, the conclusion to the earlier quoted encyclopedia article on Claude Bernard indicates a closer proximity to modern philosophers than to his coevals:

> He strenuously advocated scientific doubt and self-criticism, and was opposed to all philosophical systems, including the positivist, while not denying the usefulness of the work of philosophers in their own sphere. Bernard's critical method was closer to twentieth-century methods based on the principle of falsifiability used by Karl Popper and others, than to those of many of his contemporaries.[75]

The testimony of the outstanding scholars of his time does, nonetheless, indicate that his work had an immediate impact in philosophy as well as in science. Thus, William James acknowledges Bernard's merits in a review of the *Rapport sur le progrès et la marche de physiologie générale en France:* "It is no small service of M. Bernard that he has put the expression *internal medium* into circulation.[76] Henri Bergson, in a tribute delivered in 1913 on the centenary of Bernard's birth, even compares him with Descartes: . . . l'*Introduction à la médecine expérimentale* est un peu pour nous ce que fut pour le XVIIe et le XVIIIe siècles, le *Discours de la methode.*[77] Reino Virtanen speaks of Bernard's direct influence on Bergson and he develops this idea in a direction which is extremely interesting for our future discussion: "His book *Creative Evolution* was influenced by Bernard's inner milieu. Bergson's relation to pragmatism lends authority to his assertion that Bernard had anticipated the pragmatist theories, notably the doctrine of instrumentalism.[78] Bernard's writings contain numerous statements which point in this direction. For instance, in his *Introduction,* he proclaims: "Our ideas are only intellectual instruments which we use to break into phenomena; we must change them when they have served their purpose, as we change a blunt lancet . . . "[79] The activist element in pragmatism was expressed by Bernard in memorable phrases. Virtanen selects one from *La Science expérimentale:* "Mankind seems to have understood today that its aim is no longer passive contemplation but progress and action."[80] The same sentiment is manifest in the observations in the *Introduction:* "With the help of the active experimental sciences man becomes an inventor of phenomena, a real foreman of creation . . . or "Man can do . . . more than he knows . . . "[81]

Virtanen believes that such formulation may have influenced the pragmatists. According to him, "William James did read the *Introduction* nearly a hundred years ago, before he had began to expound his philosophy.

Nevertheless, Claude Bernard was not a pragmatist either. The anti-intellectualist sense which William James gave to the term would have been disowned by Bernard."[82] Virtanen correctly infers that a conjecture which claims that Bernard is a pragmatist is perhaps even less tenable than his positivism. What is important, however, is that the American scholar found enough evidence to consider such a possibility. Moreover, a concurrence of James's and Bernard's ideas, combined with the Frenchman's influence on Čexov, harbours the possibility of affinities between the Russian writer and the pragmatists. A direct influence exercised by William James or any other pragmatists cannot be established, although William James was well acquainted with Ivan Sergeevič Turgenev, and his biographer, Ralph Barton Perry, speaks of "the Russian circle" in Paris with which brothers James were intimate.[83]

Even without a direct link, however, the similarity of psychological make-up combined with medical education and interest in psychology could induce some affinities in their world views. They both experienced a pivotal crisis which completely transformed their outlooks. This critical moment is, of course, the period of deep depression through which they suffered.

From 1888 onward Čexov's spirits steadily declined until in 1889 they reached a point which David Magarshack refers to as "a year of personal tragedy and literary disaster."[84] Another biographer, Ernest J. Simmons, concurs with this assessment of Čexov's despondency built up over the "whole period of his first success."[85] Thus, already in January 1888, Čexov, reacting to a critical article by Disterlo, writes: "Koe-kakie mysli o našem bessilii, k(oto)roe delikatnyj avtor nazval bezvlastiem, prixodili i mne v golovu. V našix talantax mnogo fosfora, no net železa. My . . . ne orly."[86] Less than three months later, Čexov complains of dissatisfaction with his work, and proceeds to confess: "Ja trus i mnitelen; bojus' toropit'sja i voobšče bojus' pečetat'sja. Mne vse kažetsja, čto ja skoro nadoem . . . Bojazn' èta imeet svoe osnovanie: ja davno uže pečetajus', napečetal pjat' pudov rasskazov, no do six por ešče ne znaju, v čem moja sila i v čem slabost'."[87] At the time, the story "Ogni" is nearing completion. Engineer Anan'ev, one of its protagonists, reflects the author's growing pessimism in statements like: "Kto znaet, čto žizn' bescel'na i smert' neizbežna, tot očen' ravnodušen k bor'be s prirodoj i k ponjatiju o

grexe: boris' ili ne boris'—vse ravno umreš' i sgnieš'..."(VII, 116)
Nevertheless, the story does not satisfy Čexov. He is ashamed of it, but
distasteful as it may be, he needs the money.[88] The same sentiments appear
in his correspondence of August: "Roman moj na točke zamerzanija. On ne
stal dlinnee... Čtoby ne ostat'sja bez groša, spešu pisat' vsjakuju čepuxu."[89]
Unfortunately, the "haste" he refers to is rather slow, and Čexov writes
more letters of complaint than creative works. By September he observes
that rather than living, he is losing his life.[90] Proceeding in the same spirit,
Čexov renounces the literary production of his most successful year: "V
istekšij sezon ja napisal 'Step',' 'Ogni,' p'esu, dva vodevilja, massu
melkix rasskazov, načal roman... i čto že? Esli promyt' 100 pudov ètogo
pesku, to polučit'sja (esli ne sčitat' gonorara) 5 zolotnikov zolota,
tol'ko."[91]Several days later Čexov writes a letter which echoes the
sentiments expressed by his Engineer Anan'ev: "Smertnogo časa nam ne
minovat', žit' ešče pridetsja nedolgo a potomu ja ne pridaju ser'eznogo
značenija ni svoej literature, ni svoemu imeni, ni svoim literaturnym
ošibkam."[92] The end of the year finds the writer pondering the meaning of
his work:

> Byvajut minuty, kogda ja položitel'no padaju duxom. Dlja
> kogo i dlja čego ja pišu? Dlja publiki? No ja ne vižu i v nee
> verju men'še, čem v domovogo: ona neobrazovanna, durno
> vospitana, a ee lučšie èlementy nedobrosovestny i
> neiskrenni po otnošeniju k nam. Nužen ja ètoj publike ili
> ne nužen, ponjat ne mogu. . . . Pisat' dlja deneg? No deneg
> u menja ot neprivyčki imet' ix počti ravnodušen. Dlja
> deneg ja rabotaju vjalo. Pisat' dlja poxval? No oni menja
> tol'ko razdražajut.[93]

Naturally this leads to general dissatisfaction: "Voobšče živetsja mne
skučno, i načinaju ja vremenami nenavidet' čego ran'še so mnoj nikogda ne
byvalo."[94] The same letter contains a reference to Čexov's new story,
"Pari." Again, he feels ashamed for having written the story, and asks
Suvorin not to read it. The narrative presents a hero who after fifteen years
of intensive studies claims to be "umnee vsex," and from this superior
position he confirms Čexov's current sentiments as he proclaims: " . . . ja
preziraju vaši knigi, preziraju vse blaga mira i mudrost'. Vse ničtožno,
brenno, prizračno i obmančivo, kak miraž. Pust' vy gordy, mudry i prekrasny,

no smert' sotret vas s lica zemli naravne s podpol'nymi myšami, a potomstvo vaše, istorija, bessmertie vašix geniev zamerznut ili sgorjat vmeste s zemnym šarom."(VII, 235)

Čexov's depression apparently culminates in the spring. A letter to Suvorin offers some insight to his feelings:

> . . . na ètom svete neobxodimo byt' ravnodušnym. Tol'ko ravnodušnye ljudi sposobny jasno smotret' na vešči, byt' spravedlivymi i rabotat'—konečno, èto otnositsja tol'ko k umnym i blagorodnym ljudjam; ègoisty že i pustye ljudi i bez togo dostatočno ravnodušny.
>
> Vy pišete, čto ja oblenilsja. Èto ne značit, čto ja stal lenivee, čem byl. Rabotaju ja teper' stol'ko že, skol'ko rabotal 3-5 let nazad. . . . Esli že iz moej raboty ne vyxodit po dve povesti v mesjac. . ., to vinovata ne len', a moi psixiko-organičeskie svojstva: dlja mediciny ja nedostatočno ljublju dengi, a dlja literatury vo mne ne xvataet strasti i, stalo byt', talanta. . . . Strasti malo; pribav'te k ètomu i takogo roda psixopatiju: ni s togo ni s sego, vot uže dva goda, ja razljubil videt' svoi proizvedenija v pečati, oravnodušel k recenzijam, k razgovoram o literature, k spletnjam, uspexam, neuspexam, k bol'šomu gonoraru—odnim slovom, stal durak durakom. V duše kakoj-to zastoj. Ob"jasnjaju èto zastoem v svoej ličnoj žizni. Ja ne razočarovan, ne utomilsja, ne xandrju, a prosto stalo vdrug vse kak-to mene interesno.[95]

While in this frame of mind, Čexov receives the news that on June 17, 1889 his beloved brother Nikolaj died of tuberculosis. The writer's affection for his brother was one of the deepest attachments in his life, and Nikolaj succumbed to the same terrible illness which undermined Anton Pavlovič's own health. Overwhelmed by the catastrophe he writes to Savorin: "Bednjaga Nikolaj umer. Ja poglupel i potusknel. Skuka adskaja, poèzii v žizni ni na groš, želanija otsutstvujut i proč i proč."[96] Obviously Čexov has to overcome this crisis but he says little about the course of action to be taken. Nevertheless, the pattern exhibited in Čexov's life is paralleled in that of William James, who does analyze his own depression and descibes his recovery, which was facilitated by an adherence to pragmatist philosophy.

As in Čexov's case James's spiritual decline is gradual. Perry speaks of a deterioration that takes place during the autumn and winter of 1869.[97] The biographer also introduces a letter to James's friend, American physiologist Henry P. Bowditch, as characteristic of both the author's sentiments and correspondence at that time. The following are the relevant excerpts:

> I am a low-lived wretch . . . .. I have been a prey to such disgust for life during the past three months as to make letter writing almost an impossibility. . . . My own condition, I am sorry to say, goes on pretty steadily deteriorating in all respects, in spite of a fitful flash up for six weeks this summer. I have, however, begun to poke about in town and to pay visits in spite of it, which is a great refreshment. But I literally have given up all pretense to study or even to serious reading of any kind, and I look on physiology and medicine generally as dim voices from a bygone time..."[98]

Perry also mentions the acute attack of melancholia which James recounts in his *Varieties of Religious Experience*.[99] Here, James, claiming to be quoting from a letter,[100] describes the following experience:

> Whilst in the state of philosophic pessimism and general depression of spirits about my prospects, I went one evening into a dressing-room in the twilight to procure some article that was there; when suddenly there fell upon me without any warning, just as if it came out of the darkness, a horrible fear of my own existence. Simultaneously there arose in my mind the image of an epileptic patient whom I had seen in the asylum . . . ... There was such a horror of him and such a perception of my own merely momentary discrepancy from him, that it was as if something hitherto solid within my breast gave way entirely, and I became a mass of quivering fear. After this the universe was changed for me altogether. I awoke morning after morning with a horrible dread . . . I dreaded to be left alone.[101]

The association here is with Ivan Dmitrič Gromov, a character in Čexov's "Palata No. 6." The author provides his hero with all the reasons for

the general depression described by James when the same sudden fear
overcomes him:

> V odnom iz pereulkov vstretilis' emu dva arestanta v kandalax
> . . . Ran'še Ivan Dmitrič očen' často vstrečal arestantov i
> vsjakij raz oni vozbuždali v nem čuvstva sostradanija i
> nelovkosti, teper' že èta vstreča proizvela na nego kakoe-to
> osobennoe, strannoe vpečatlenie. Emu vdrug počemu-to
> pokazalos', čto ego tože mogut zakovat' v kandaly . . . Doma
> celyj den' u nego ne vyxodili z golovy arestanty . . . Utrom
> Ivan Dmitrič podnjalsja s posteli v užase, s xolodnym potom
> na lbu, sovsem uže uverennyj, čto ego mogut arestovat' každuju
> minutu. . . . I dlja Ivana Dmitriča nastupili mučitel'nye dni i
> noči.(VIII, 77-78)

Eventually, Ivan Gromov's fear becomes so acute that he has to be confined
to a psychiatric ward.

Although they each dread a different fate, the instantaneity and
groundlessness of their fear is identical. Although, accuracy in the description
of the character's psychological state is subject to Čexov's professional
pride, this does not exclude the possibility of personal experience. Perry's
description of James's crisis suggests further similarities: "The spiritual
crisis was the ebbing of the will to live, for lack of a philosophy to live by —
a paralysis of action occasioned by a sense of moral impotence."[102] This
statement immediately brings to mind criticisms aimed against Čexov
precisely because of the dearth of such a philosophy, admissions of this fact
in his correspondence, and, last but not least, his protagonists' suffering
from the same predicament. The professor in "Skučnaja istorija" is one of
these. He feels the lack of such a general concept of life very acutely:

> . . . vo vsex mysljax, čuvstvax i ponjatijax, kakie ja sostavljaju
> obo vsem, net čego-to obščego, čto svjazyvalo by vse èto v
> odno celoe. Každoe čuvstvo i každaja mysl' živut vo mne
> osobnjakom, i vo vsex moix suždenijax o nauke, teatre,
> literature, učenikax i vo vsex kartinkax, kotorye risuet moe
> voobraženie, daže samyj iskusnyj analitik ne najdet togo, čto
> nazyvaetsja obščej ideej, ili bogom živogo čeloveka.
>   A koli net ètogo, to, značit, net i ničego.(VII, 307)

William James is trying to solve an identical problem. Perry quotes from a notebook in which James recorded his resolve on February 1, 1870 to acknowledge the supremacy of morality.[103] This, however, does not yet solve his personal problem since the existence of evil could drive him to despair. Thus, James speculates:

> Can one with full knowledge and sincerely [sic] ever bring one's self so to sympathize with the total process of the universe as heartily to assent to the evil that seems inherent in its details? . . . If so optimism is possible. Are on the other hand, the private interests and sympathies of the individual so essential to his existence that they can never be swallowed up in his feeling for the total process,—and does he nevertheless imperiously crave a reconciliation or unity of some sort. Pessimism must be his portion.[104]

Perry educes from these words that if one adopts "moralism," " . . . one needs that 'vigor of will' which springs from the belief in its freedom."[105] Another excerpt from James's notebook is relevant here:

> I think that yesterday was a crisis in my life. I finished the first part of Renouvier's second "Essais" [*Essais de critique générale*] and see no reason why his definition of Free Will—"the sustaining of a thought *because I choose to* when I might have other thoughts"—need be the definition of an illusion. At any rate, I will assume for the present—until next year—that it is no illusion. My first act of free will shall be to believe in free will. For the remainder of the year, I will abstain from the mere speculation and contemplative grüblei [sic] . . . After the first of January . . . I may perhaps return to metaphysical study and skepticism without danger to my power of action. For the present then remember: care little for speculation; much for the *form* of my action; recollect that only when habits of order are formed can we advance to really interesting fields of action . . .[106]

Perry is not concerned with James's dismissal of metaphysics in favour of action, and focuses on the opening statement. According to him two things are important: "First, the fact that he [James] experienced a personal crisis that could be relieved only by a *philosophical* insight; and, second, the specific quality of the philosophy which his soul-sickness required."[107]

Perry deduces from this that James's mind was of a decidedly philosophical cast, and that he was seeking a viable philosophical solution to live by. Both of these deductions undoubtably apply to Čexov also. Moreover, James's contemplation of acceptance of the universe as a whole, thus assenting to the existing evil is well illustrated in, for instance, Čexov's story "V ovrage." In addition, this example demonstrates the change in the Russian writer's views regarding work. Thomas Winner notices this change when he observes: "Beauty is seen in this story as useful labour. This concept, which Čexov treated satirically in the earlier peasant stories . . . "[108] The idea is summed up in the words of Kostyl' Elizarov, one of the characters in the story: "Kto truditsja, kto terpit, tot i starše."(X, 163) The old professor in "Skučnaja istorija" represents James's other alternative, namely, an individual whose private interests impede acceptance of the total process, and who craves for a unity of some sort.

The above indicates an affinity in the backgrounds of the two doctors. Their quest for a philosophy of life follows a similar path. This does not mean, however, that their solutions are identical. James's philosophy, grown out of personal need and agitation, offers a philosophical, not an emotional, defense of free will, moralism, and belief.[109] Čexov's concern with moral philosophy is evident in the large number of stories concerned with justice. Naturally, the problem of justice carries with it the question of determinism and free will which, in turn, leads to an examination of the issue of beliefs.

James's ontological contemplation steadily gravitates toward the philosophy he made famous, namely, pragmatism. According to professor Earle, "James rarely wrote anything, early or late, which did not at least imply pragmatism."[110] In other words, the American philosopher's quest culminates in the world view to which Virtanen refers in connection with Bernard's thought. At this point, further direct comparison between James's and Čexov's ideological development yields diminishing returns. It is logical to presume, however, that the Russian writer's search for a philosophy to live by could have followed a path analogous to that taken by James in his quest. If this holds true, the ideas of pragmatism must be found in Čexov's literary production.

A summary of pragmatist thought will now be presented for the purpose of facilitating subsequent discussions. In broad outline, pragmatism is a method of philosophizing which is often regarded as a theory of meaning.[111] It was first developed in the 1870s by Charles S. Peirce (1839-1914), revived and reformulated primarily as a theory of truth in 1898 by William James (1842-1910); further developed, expanded, and disseminated by John Dewey (1859-1952) and Ferdinand C.S. Schiller (1864-1937).

Peirce's pragmatism grew out of his study of the phenomenology of human thought and the uses of language. One of Peirce's lasting ambitions was to work out a general theory of signs that could make communication possible. Thus his pragmatism is a rule for promoting linguistic and conceptual clarity—successful communication. It is a method, the aim of which is to facilitate communication, and in particular cases, the degree to which this is accomplished determines the relevance and justification of the method. One of Peirce's best known statements, also called the maxim of pragmatism, is that "[i]n order to ascertain the meaning of an intellectual conception one should consider what practical consequences might conceivably result by necessity from the truth of that conception; and the sum of these consequences will constitute the entire meaning of the conception."[112] In order to avoid a possible misunderstanding, Peirce insists that "[p]ragmatism solves no real problem. It only shows that supposed problems are not real problems."[113] Peirce's approach appears to embody sound canons of scientific practice. The experimental verification of which he speaks[114] and the idea of "doubt and belief"[115] resemble Bernard's method. Moreover, Peirce proclaims that "[p]hilosophy ought to imitate the successful sciences in its methods . . . "[116] It should be noted that his pragmatism is part of a more general account of "inquiry," many aspects of which were taken up in Dewey's extensive theory of inquiry. Peirce describes the function of thought as a form of behaviour initiated by the irritation of doubt and proceeding to some resolution in a state of belief.[117] Belief is a condition of organic stability and intellectual satisfaction, but these do not determine the truth of beliefs. Peirce outlines a scientific and pragmatic method of clarifying and justifying belief. The contemplation of belief as habit leads to a discussion of volition. According to Peirce,

> [a] rational person . . . can exert a measure of self-control over
> his future actions; which means, however, *not* that he can

impart to them any arbitrarily assignable character, but . . .
that a process of self-preparation will tend to impart to action
. . . one fixed character, which is indicated . . . by the absence
. . . of the feeling of self-reproach, which subsequent reflection
will induce. . . . . [T]here is a tendency, as action is repeated
again and again, for the action to approximate indefinitely
toward the perfection of that fixed character . . . ; and where
no self-control is possible there will be no self-reproach.[118]

The idea of self-control and self-reproach verges on James's thought.
While Peirce's pragmatism had a scientific character, James was first and
foremost a moralist. According to him, "[t]he whole function of philosophy
ought to be to find out what definite difference it will make to you and me,
at definite instants of our life, if this world-formula or that world-formula
be the true one."[119] A simple juxtaposition of this statement with Peirce's
maxim of pragmatism indicates the difference between their respective
versions of pragmatism. Whereas Peirce sought meaning in general concepts
and formulas of action, James sought meaning in experienced facts and
plans of action. James looked to the concrete, immediate, practical level of
experience as the testing ground of our intellectual efforts; for Peirce, the
immediate sensory experience is all but destitute of "intellectual purport."
Pragmatism also serves James as the basis for his definition of truth: "True
ideas are those that we can assimilate, validate, corroborate and verify.
False ideas are those that we cannot."[120] James spoke of truth as what is
good or expedient in our beliefs. Hence the belief that a seeing force and not
a blind one governs the universe, creates optimism, and thus confidence in
the future is the effective pragmatic meaning of the terms "cosmic design"
and "divine creator." Science does not give us any criteria for decision in the
case of metaphysical and theological beliefs. Since the meanings of world
formulae are their effects on the attitude of an individual, the individual is
justified in regarding such formulae as true insofar as they provide him with
vital benefits. Thus, "[o]n pragmatic principles, if the hypothesis of God
works satisfactorily in the widest sense of the word, it is true."[121] The
philosophical community was shocked by James's statement, that "'[t]he
true' is only the expedient in the way of our thinking, just as 'the right' is
only the expedient in the way of our behaving."[122]
      Professor Earle also stresses the importance of the evolutionary
theory for James's philosophy:

James was strongly influenced by the Darwinian theory of
evolution and was therefore predisposed to find in all feelings,
including religious feelings, clues about what the world is
like. Feelings that evolved in the world must somehow reflect
the world. . . .
Evolutionary theory, as James saw it, begins with the
presupposition that each part of reality has a function, that
each part is in some way or other good for something or other.
The strictly useless, according to such a theory cannot endure
. . . Religious experience is not especially justified by evolution
because nothing is *especially* justified. Religion and irreligion,
insofar as they both exist, are exactly equal before the
evolutionary tribunal. . . . The questions must be asked of
religion as it must be asked of everything. How is it that it
came to be what it is? What is it for?[123]

James finds a way, however, of justifying moral and religious belief,
namely, through pragmatism. When, for a given person, a certain belief
answers or satisfies a compelling need, the "vital good" supplied by this
belief in the life of that person justifies the belief. This justification can be
applied only if the option to believe or not to believe is "live," "forced," and
"momentous."[124] Hence, a genuine option, or an option which satisfies
these three conditions, offers a choice in which both hypotheses are live
ones, the option is unavoidable, and it will not be repeated. Thayer observes
that Peirce and Dewey, among others, were extremely critical of this defense
of the will to believe, while it was precisely this side of James that was
enthusiastically received as the moral code of his pragmatism, by for
instance, F.C.S. Schiller. Here also, according to Thayer, James's views
have affinities with those of Henri Bergson.[125]

John Dewey represents a synthesis of Peirce's logical and James's
humanistic pragmatism. For him, this theory bridged the separation of
science and values, knowledge and morals. The inquiry describes the formal
conditions of intelligent action. Richard J. Bernstein summarizes Dewey's
ethics in the following manner:

Man is a creature who by nature has values. . . . Moral choices
and decisions arise only in those situations in which there are
competing desires or a conflict of values. The problem that a

man then confronts is to decide what he really wants and what
course of action he ought to pursue. He cannot appeal to his
immediate values to resolve the situation; he must evaluate or
appraise the situation and the different courses of action open
to him. This process of deliberation that culminates in a
decision to act is what Dewey calls "valuation." . . . It should
also be clear that ethics conceived in this manner blend into
social philosophy. Valuation, like all inquiry, presupposes a
community of shared experience in which there are common
norms and procedures, and intelligent valuation is also a
means of making such a community a concrete reality. Here,
too, ends and norms are clarified, tested, and modified in light
of the cumulative experience of the community.[126]

In view of the impact evolutionary theory had on James, it is of
interest that Dewey presented a lecture in 1909 entitled "The Influence of
Darwinism on Philosophy."[127] Here, Dewey maintains that the Darwinian
principle of natural selection undermined the design argument in the old
problem of design *versus* matter.[128] As a result, "[p]hilosophy forswears
inquiry after absolute origins and absolute finalities in order to explore
specific values and the specific conditions that generate them."[129] According
to Dewey, the effect of Darwinian logic is evident in the intellectual
transformation.

Interest shifts from the wholesale essence back of special
changes to the question of how special changes serve and
defeat concrete purposes; shifts from an intelligence that
shaped things once for all to the particular intelligences which
things are even now shaping; shifts from an ultimate goal of
good to the direct increments of justice and happiness that
intelligent administration of existent conditions may beget
and that present carelessness or stupidity will destroy or
forego.[130]

Hence, Dewey claims that, " . . . the new logic introduces responsibility into
the intellectual life."[131] By idealization and rationalization of the universe
at large, mankind confessed inability to master the course of things, thus
shifting " . . . a burden of responsibility to the more competent shoulders of

transcendent cause. But if insight into specific consequences of ideas is possible, philosophy must in time become a method of locating and interpreting the more serious of conflicts that occur in life and a method of projecting ways for dealing with them . . . "[132] Dewey concludes with an observation that the Darwinian mode of thinking did not settle the conflict between traditional philosophic conceptions and absolutistic philosophies. It is not necessary, according to Dewey, because " . . . intellectual progress usually occurs through sheer abandonment of questions together with both of the alternatives they assume. . . . We do not solve them: we get over them."[133]

In his book on American pragmatism, Edward C. Moore gives a good evaluation of Dewey's role within the school. According to him,

> The most complete statement of Dewey's pragmatism in the tradition of Peirce and James is to be found in his *Essays in Experimental Logic* in the chapter titled "The Control of Ideas by Facts." The title is indicative and informative. For the pragmatist, ideas are controlled by facts. The idea starts from facts and returns to facts, and it is the differences that it makes to the world of fact that indicate its meaning.[134]

Hence, according to Moore, Dewey's definition of pragmatism includes the views of Peirce and James, " . . . but goes beyond them to give pragmatism a wider scope. Dewey defines pragmatism as the doctrine that reality possesses practical character . . . [and] also as the doctrine of the unity of theory and practice."[135] In addition, Moore observes in Dewey's definition " . . . his theory of the meaning of ideas, or instrumentalism, the doctrine that ideas are intellectual instruments for directing our activities when we are dealing with reality."[136]

These are the basics of pragmatism as it was understood by its most prominent advocates at the end of the nineteenth and the beginning of the twentieth centuries. As mentioned earlier, there is no conclusive evidence that Čexov was acquainted with this philosophy. Moreover, a substantial part of it was developed only after the writer's death. He knew, however, the sources of pragmatism as provided, for instance, by the works of David Hume, Adam Smith, and particularly, John Stuart Mill. Čexov's interest in psychology combined with his personal experience contributed, as demonstrated, to determine the direction of his thought. The choice of themes further substantiates the affinity of his outlook with that of pragmatism. As a result, the ideas found in this philosophy can be illustrated by examples from Čexov's writings, and, conversely, the conduct of Čexov's characters can be explained with the aid of pragmatism.

Thus, for instance, Dewey's valuation presupposes a community with common norms and procedures. This is precisely what is missing in stories like "Zloumyšlennik," "Bab'e carstvo," and "Novaja dača." Similarly, James's justification of belief brings to mind Čexov's "Dušečka." The applicability of such a justification can be questioned, since Ol'ga Semenovna's beliefs do not necessarily satisfy the three conditions prescribed by James. It would be very difficult, however, to explain the heroine's behaviour without the aid of Jamesian reasoning. Ol'ga Semenovna goes through four major changes in her life. She alters all her interests and all her views according to the person with whom she lives. This phenomenon has been explained as her need to love. Such a motivation would indicate, perhaps in a remote sense only, that her feelings are hypocritical. But Ol'ga Semenovna is truly convinced of her ideas. She "knows" she is right. Her beliefs are justified by their consequences. The same argument applies, for instance, to the conduct of Očumelov in "Xameleon." It could be simplified as opportunism; a claim can be made that Očumelov does not have the courage of his convictions, that his action is caused by fear of consequences. But, in his case, the option is "live," "forced," and—considering the possibility of recurrence—"momentous." Moreover, he believes what he says in the same way as Unter Prišibeev, in the story of that title, or as Denis Grigor'ev in "Zloumyšlennik' are convinced about their "truth."

The same examples can be used to illustrate Peirce's concept of thought. According to him, "[t]he whole function of thought is to produce habits of action . . . "[137] This is precisely what happens in "Xameleon," "Unter Prišibeev," and "Dušečka." Action is the key word here; a crucial element in pragmatism, this phenomenon, or lack thereof, dramatically gains importance in Čexov's writings after his depression.

The similarity of subjects of thought between the Russian writer and Peirce should also be noted. The philosopher's first concern is the lack of communication, his aim is not to solve problems but rather to expose them, and the fundamental element in his thought is action. Čexov did not follow Peirce's progression, but his writings include all these elements. The phenomenon of action, however, presents in itself the already mentioned but not yet discussed problem of determinism and free will. As a scientist and a disciple of Bernard, Čexov must accept determinism since, according to Bernard, " . . men of science . . . will never deny the absolute determinism of the phenomena; because it is precisely the recognition of determinism that characterizes true men of science."[138] Such a view removes, however, all responsibility from our actions, and the French physiologist himself realized this. Therefore, he modifies his credo by differentiation between determinism and fatalism:

> We gave the name of determinism to the immediate or determining cause of phenomena. We never act on the essence of natural phenomena, but only on their determining causes; and because we act thus, determinism differs from fatalism, on which we cannot act. Fatalism assumes that the manifestation of any phenomenon is necessary and independent of its conditions, while determinism is the condition necessary to a phenomenon, whose manifestation is free.[139]

In James's vocabulary, the two quotations mean a shift from "hard" to "soft" determinism. He applies the term soft determinism to all the theories which affirm that determinism is true and then, by means of what he considers sophistical and contorted definitions, somehow manage to preserve a semblance of moral notions that, according to James, are plainly obliterated by any theory of determinism.[140] James attacks Bernard's view on determinism in Zola's[141] interpretation. He maintains that despite its "scientific" and "analytic" character, such an approach lacks remedies in the hour of satiety with the things of life and in the hour of terror at the world's vast meaningless grinding.[142] Moreover, James sees the determinists, who deny free-will and postulate that individuals originate nothing, but merely transmit to the future the whole push of the past cosmos of which they are so small an expression, as diminishing Man. He is less admirable, stripped of the creative principle.[143] Čexov's post-1889 writings clearly demonstrate that he could not accept the determinist philosophical thesis. A vivid illustration is provided in the story "Gusev," where the hero's humble acceptance of life and death is dramatically emphasized when his body, after being buried at sea, is devoured by a shark. In "Skučnaja istorija," a capable scientist ignores the world around him at first because of his overdedication to science, and later, realizing that science offers no remedy in time of need, he resigns to indifference. The protagonist himself provides an explanatory comment: "Govorjat, čto filosofy i istinnye mudrecy ravnodušny. Nepravda, ravnodušie—èto paralič duši, preždevremennaja smert'."(VII, 306)

The scientist von Koren in the "Duèl'" is active, but he does not use the maxim of pragmatism to assess his world-formula. He claims that his conduct will in the long run benefit humanity.[144] Unfortunately the consideration of a future benefit alone is not satisfactory. James speaks about the "definite difference" that the truth of a world-formula would make at definite instants of our life. Pragmatism, contrary to the popular misconception, does not profess that the ends justify the means. For similar reasons, Čexov rejects von Koren's unscrupulous method promising a future benefit. One of Čexov's letters to Suvorin clearly demonstrates the writer's view in this regard: "Esli naši socialisty v samom dele budut èksploatirovat' dlja svoix celej xoleru, to ja stanu prezirat' ix. Otvratitel'nye sredstva radi blagix celej delajut i samye cely otvratitel'nymi."[145] Laevskij is, until the night of his duel, afraid to face reality, and all his romantic dreams fail. When he, however, abandons his romantic illusions, and accepts a mediocre life of constant work, he is fulfilled. Laevskij, after his metamorphosis, becomes an illustration of Dewey's meliorist view of "direct increments of justice and happiness," while the ultimate goal, the real truth, remains obscure. The same ideas are echoed in other stories of this period and further enumeration would add little to the present argument.

Supporting the affinity between Čexov's outlook and pragmatism is, however, a passage from James's *A Pluralistic Universe*. He displays a liking for Fechner's "daylight view,"[146] and refers to the " . . . great reservoir in which the memories of earth's inhabitants are pooled and preserved, and from which, when the threshold lowers or the valve opens, information ordinarily shut out leaks into the mind of exceptional individuals among us."[147] The only evidence James feels sufficiently decorous to support Fechner is religious experience, which manifests itself in pathological states (split human personality, mediumship, etc.). This points, according to James,

> . . . with reasonable probability to the continuity of our consciousness with a wider spiritual environment from which the ordinary prudential man . . . is shut off. . . . There are resources in us that naturalism . . . never recks of, possibilities that take our breath away, of another kind of happiness and power, based on giving up our own will and letting something higher work for us . . . "[148]

This theory explains beautifully Čexov's "Černyj monax." The story has already been discussed as a quest for the meaning of life. James's conception supplies, however, an explanation for Kovrin's behaviour. Moreover the monk seems almost to be referring to James when he says: "Govorjat že teper' učenye, čto genij, srodni umopomešatel'stvu. . . . Povyšennoe nastroenie, vozbuždenie, èkstaz—vse to čto otličaet prorokov, poètov, mučenikov za ideju ot obyknovennyx ljudej, protivno životnoj storone čeloveka, to est' ego zdorov'ju."(VIII, 242-43) Visions, however, do not solve any problems, and Kovrin fails because he does not act. Truth is created in action, and man, while creating it, will not know it. Truth is measured by the benefit it brings, but above all, it is an act towards achieving the "good." An additional reason for Kovrin's failure is rooted in the nature of his quest. He searches for eternal truth, and truth is relative, mutable.

The story "Student," published only three months after "Černyj movax," also features a contiguity with pragmatism. The hero experiences a moment of intuition described as follows: "I radost' vdrug zavolnovalas' v ego duše . . . Prošloe, dumal on, svjazano s nastojaščim nepreryvnoju cep'ju sobytij, vytekavšix odno ix drugvgo. I emu kazalos', čto on tol'ko čto videl oba konca ètoj cepi: dotronulsja do odnogo konca, kak drognul drugoj."(VIII, 309) The association with pragmatism in this case is indirect. The impromptu ceremony which leads to the above sentiments is a free act as described by Henri Bergson.[149] It is an act which springs spontaneously from the character's whole personality and which carries him back in thought to those unique moments in the past, which will never be repeated. Moreover, the student perceives the dynamic unity of the "durée réelle," the flowing succession of states that melt into each other to form an indivisible process.

The association of Čexov and Bergson[150] is interesting in the light of Perry's observation that "[w]ithout doubt the most important philosophical and personal attachment of James's later years was that which he formed with Bergson."[151] The affinity between the two philosophers is illustrated by the discussions of influence on one another, which Bergson was compelled to deny. An excerpt from his statement can also be applied to Čexov's thought. He speaks about ". . . a movement of ideas which has for some years been in evidence everywhere and which arises from causes that are general and profound. In every country, and with many thinkers, the need has been felt for a philosophy more genuinely empirical, closer to the immediately given, than the traditional philosophy . . . "[152] Further in the discussion of James's relation to Bergson, Perry maintains that

> Both thinkers found the key to metaphysics in a certain
> aspect of conscious experience, namely, its continuity. James
> saw . . . concepts as cuts or excerpts from the continuum, while
> Bergson thinks of them as instantaneous fixation of the flux.
> . . . Both philosophers find that thinking, since it distinguishes,
> specifies, and arrests, is alien to the genius of existence, which
> is interpenetrative and flowing. . . . They measure the
> inadequacy of thought by the standard of intuition. . . . The
> reality which is felt or intuited is a temporal changing
> continuum from which the mind, governed by its practical
> interests, selects what is relevant.[153]

This change of attitude from thought to feeling is clearly that found in
"Skučnaja istorija," "Duèl'," and other stories by Čexov.

Neither Bergson nor James could accept the notion of the "free" act
ex nihilo. The American philosopher realizes that absolute free will would
be connected with extreme volatility of thought and action.[154] No one would
be stable enough to merit either praise or blame. He believes, however, that
instinct and utility can safely be trusted to carry on the social business of
punishment and praise. Free-will, according to him, " . . .pragmatically
means *novelties in the world*, the right to expect that in its deepest elements
as well as in its surface phenomena, the future may not identically repeat and
imitate the past. . . . [Therefore,] persons in whom knowledge of the world's
past has bred pessimism . . . may naturally welcome free-will as a melioristic
doctrine. It holds up improvement as at least possible . . . "[155] Bergson's
concept of free act has been introduced in the discussion of Čexov's story
"Student." The French philosopher speaks about spontaneity at the moment
of action. If this spontaneity is absent, our actions will be simply stereotyped
or mechanical responses. Hence, freedom is far from being absolute: " . . .
la liberté ne presente pas le caractère absolu que le spiritualisme lui prête
quelquefois; elle admet des degrés."[156] For most people free acts are the
exception, not the rule.

Both philosophers believe in free will, but accept limitations to the
idea. The progress of Čexov's thought apparently takes an analogous route,
for the themes of his stories seem not only to reach the point of obvious
confidence in the possibility of improvement, but they illustrate the notions
considered by Bergson and James. Thus, for instance, "Xameleon"
demonstrates remarkable volatility, and the chief magistrate in "Rasskaz

staršego sadovnika" acts as if he follows one of Bergson's attempts at a definition of the free act ("celui qu'on ne saurait prévoir, même quand on en connaît à l'avance toutes les conditions," Bergson, p. 168). In addition, stories like "Gore" and "Skripka Rotšil'da" manifest the judgement of regret which, according to James, prevents deterministic escape from pessimism.[157] Vera in the story "V rodnom uglu" still resigns herself to life fated to her, when she decides that " . . . čtot rjad grubyx ošibok . . . ona budet sčitat' nastojaščeju žizn'ju, kotoraja suždena ej, i ne budet ždat' lučšej..."(IX, 324) Moreover, she decides to accept her past life without regrets, thus gaining an opportunity to escape pessimism. But, as she herself admits, she does not expect to be happy. Then again, as Ivan Ivanyč says in "Kryžovnik," " . . . esli v žizni est' smysl i cel', to smysl ètot i cel' vovse ne v našem sčast'e, a v čem-to bolee razumnom i velikom. Delajte dobro!"(X, 64) The leading character in the story, Ivan Ivanyč's brother Nikolaj manages to achieve his goal and thereby happiness by means of ruthless endeavour. The only good his activity brings is his personal satisfaction. Čexov disapproves of such conduct, concurring with James's statement " . . . [R]egard something else than our feeling as our limit, our master, and our law; be willing to live and die in its service . . ."[158] The "Kryžovnik" reflects this sentiment. Ivan Ivanyč extols action and rejects the self-imposed limits dismissing the law of cause and effect in the process:

> Vy ssylaetes' na estestvennyj porjadok veščej, na zakonnost' javlenij, no est' li porjadok i zakonnost' v tom, čto ja, živoj, mysljaščij čelovek, stoju nado rvom i ždu, kogda on zarastet sam ili zatjanet ego ilom, v to vremja kak, byt' možet, ja mog by pereskočit' čerez nego ili postroit' čerez nego most? I opjat'-tak vo imja čego ždat'? Ždat', kogda net sil žit', a meždu tem žit' nužno i xočetsja žit'!(X, 64)

Doctor Starcev in "Ionyč" is another example of someone who lets his personal feelings limit his action. At the outset of the story, Doctor Starcev is enthusiastic about his work which helps sufferers, about his service to the people. He abandons these ideals in face of a sentimental disillusionment, and concentrates solely on his own profit. The obvious association here is with Dewey's assertion of the supremacy of values that are not connected with individual success, but bind all men equally (social effects).[159]

Nadja in Čexov's last story, "Nevesta," is the rare example of a person who manages to forsake the mediocre past in the vulgar milieu of her youth and asserts her right to a new life hoping for the bright future, the prophetic vision of which is rendered by another character in the story, the young idealist Saša: ". . . vse izmenitsja, točno po volšebstvu. I budut togda zdes' gromadnye, velikolepnejšie doma, čudesnye sady, fontany neobyknovennye, zamečatel'nye ljudi..."(X, 208) The last two stories feature characters who feel the need to work, and it is only through work that such a great future as Saša envisions can materialize. The ultimate goal, as observed by Dewey, can be reached by the direct increments of commonweal, and Čexov believes neither in revolutionary, nor in evolutionary change without human instigation.

Contemplation of the future serves to James as a departure point for his theistic postulate. For, according to him, if materialism and spiritualism are considered pragmatically in the world that is already completed, both theories are identical. They have shown all their consequences, and any dispute is purely verbal.[160] Theism entitles us, however, to predict a future in human experience that contains certain desirable elements for the expectation of which materialism gives no warrant. "Materialism means simply the denial that the moral order is eternal, and the cutting off of ultimate hopes; spiritualism means the affirmation of an eternal moral order and the letting loose of hope."[161] Further, James divides men into those who believe that the salvation of the world is impossible (pessimism), those who believe that it is inevitable (optimism), and midway between the two, he says, there stands the doctrine of meliorism. The last creed treats salvation as neither inevitable nor impossible; "[i]t is clear that pragmatism must incline towards meliorism."[162] In spite of his theistic beliefs, James admits the conditional value of religious faith within pragmatism: "On pragmatistic principles, if the hypothesis of God works satisfactorily in the widest sense of the word, it is true."[163] The relativity of the concept allows James's fellow pragmatist, Dewey, to hold a contrary view. The latter " . . . was convinced that religious ideas cannot function as socially important values, that they block human initiative, people's ability to control their own lives and develop their intelligence, inventiveness, and creativity. In this sense such ideas are 'false'—we have no other criteria for evaluating them."[164]

Pragmatism then does not constrain its adherents in their beliefs. Hence, the following soliloquy of Sof'ja L'vovna in "Volodja bol'šoj i

Volodja malen'kij" is perfectly acceptable: "No ved' bog est', navernoe est', i ja nepremenno dolžna umeret', značit, nado rano ili pozdno podumat' o duše, o večnoj žizni . . . No esli boga net? . . . Bog est' . . . "(VIII, 221) The same heroine utters later, "[k]onečno, ja neverujuščaja i v monastyr' ne pošla by, no ved' možno sdelat' čto-nibud' ravnosil'noe."(VIII, 223) Similar sentiments emerge in the story "V ovrage" from Anisim's conversation with his mother: "Boga-to ved', vse ravno, net, mamaša. Čego už tam razbirat'! . . . Bog, možet, i est', a tol'ko very net,—skazal on.—Kogda menja venčali, . . . ja vse dumal: est' bog! A kak vyšel iz cerkvi—i ničego. Da i otkuda mne znat', est' bog ili net? . . . Tak celyj den' xodiš'—i ni odnogo čeloveka s sovest'ju. I vsja pričina, potomu čto ne znajut, est' bog ili net..."(X, 157-58) Thus, Anisim's contemplation parallels James's reasoning for the necessity of acceptance of the divine existence hypothesis. At the same time, however, both Anisim and Sof'ja proclaim that they do not believe in God.

The question of Čexov's faith—or lack thereof—it seems, cannot be resolved.[165] The note entered in his journal in February 1897 is suggestive: "Meždu 'est' bog' i 'net boga' ležit celoe gromadnoe pole, kotoroe proxodit s bol'šim trudom istinnyj mudrec. Russkij (že) čelovek znaet kakuju-libo odnu iz ètix dvux krajnostej, seredina že meždu nimi ne interesuet ego, i potomu obyknovenno on ne znaet ničego ili očen' malo."(XVII, 224) The indication is clear. Čexov's option is living and momentous, but not forced. He avoids the choice, for he prefers to stay in his metaphorical field.[166] Therefore, the option is not genuine. After all, a decision either way would remove some of the existing possibilities. Hence, such an act would not have a justifiable purpose, and, as Čexov pragmatically observes in one of his notebooks, "[d]ela opredeljajutsja ix celjami . . . "(XVII, 154)

Čapek's World View

The perception of a pragmatist outlook in Čexov's writings is supported by the existence of affinities between the Russian writer and Čapek. Namely, the Czech writer's knowledge of pragmatism cannot be doubted, for not only did he receive his doctorate in philosophy but he wrote a term paper, later published as a book, in which he discusses pragmatist thought in great detail. Moreover, in the second edition of this treatise, Čapek adds an appendix "Sám za sebe," in which he elaborates on his own attitude toward pragmatism. This postscript has already been mentioned in the previous chapter, but it requires a more detailed discussion. Čapek is willing to accept for himself the term pragmatist, provided that the notion is understood according to his specifications, namely, as

1. Nechut' k verbálním řešením, nedůvěra k velkým slovům a snaha zneužívati co nejméně možno intelektuální schopnosti generalisování. Tento poměr k lidskému myšlení se z nějakých nejasnych důvodů nazyvá "skepse" a platí za neobyčejně negativní. . . . Skeptické a negativní je řídit se ve styku s lidmi . . . raději účastnými zkušenostmi než obecnými ideami. Obecné idee mají zvláštní nevýhodu, že si s nimi nic nepočnete v konkrétním případě. . . .

2. Obrat ke skutečnosti; a protože ve filosofii není nic tak pochybného jako právě skutečnost, tedy k obyčejné, vulgární, nepochybné skutečnosti, ve které se nepochybně jí a miluje, nepochybně pracuje a odpočívá a zejména nepochybně sociálně obcuje s ostatními lidmi. . . . skutečnost nám není dána k pozorování, nýbrž k jednání; a protože . . . pohříchu skutečnost se nám jeví v aspektu povážlivě nesystematickém; chcete-li ji sjednotit v nějaký ideový řád, musíte se k ní prostě obrátit zády a dělat svůj systém z obecných pojmů namísto faktů. Je ovšem jiná cesta, jež je trpělivější i dobrodružnější; je to odhodlání vejít v konflikty, jež ve skutečnosti opravdu jsou, a podstoupit je osobně; řešit je jako člověk a ne jako mandatář nějaké obecné zásady. . . .

3. To je zároveň konec subjektivního párání se sebou samotným, neurasthenického subjektivismu a veškeré subtilní vyjímečnosti; je to hrdinné odhodlání stát se obyčejným člověkem. . . . obyčejný člověk na rozdíl od výjimečných bytostí žije ve světě neskonale rozmanitém, protože je to svět objektivní a epický. Neboj se, že ztratíš své "já," obraceje svou pozornost více k tomu, co jest, než k tomu co jsi ty; člověk, ktery bloudí v lese nebo vchází mezi lidi, je v dramatičtějším a aktuálnějším smyslu "já" než ten, kdo z nitra ozařuje stěny své osobnostní ulity.

4. Toto jest individualism, ale individualismus objektivní: jednáš-li . . . jednej vždy sám za sebe . . . Poroučet můžete jménem čehokoliv, . . . ale myslet a upravovat svůj poměr k světu můžete jen svým vlastním jménem; jinak není s vámi co mluvit.

5. Což znamená svobodu ducha, což tedy znamená dramatickou
volnost rozhodnout se na svou vlastní pěst ve všem, co se týká
našeho osobního poměru ke skutečným konfliktům. Chtěl
bych zde říci, jak nádhernou a poutavou věcí je svoboda; ale
je zároveň trýznivá a těžká, nebot' žádá na tobě stálé iniciativy,
stálé nejistoty a často i mučivého kompromisu, jejž cítíš jako
osobní neúspěch. . . .
6. Avšak je-li nám vskutku co činiti s fakty, pak není faktů
filosofických, vysokých a privilegovaných na rozdíl od
faktů nízkých, vulgárních a vůbec nefilosofických; všechny
jsou filosofické a vůči všem záleží na tvém jednání. . . .
zkušenost je velmi demokratická, přijímajíc vše . . .
Obyčejně se považuje za optimism, buduje-li se obraz
světa s aristokratickým ignorováním nebo překonáváním
jeho špatných a triviálních stránek. . . . Starozákonný
Hospodin projevil velmi málo pragmatistický temperament,
když žádal na Sodomě deset dokonale a vybraně
spravedlivých. Kdyby mu stačilo deset tisíc křehkých, ale
poměrně dobromyslných a všedních lidí, mohla stát Sodoma
dodnes, a svět by nebyl o nic hříšnější. V tomto případě se
Hospodin zachoval jako fanatický revolucionář posedlý
jakousi utkvělou myšlenkou. Brát v úvahu největší možný
počet faktů je jako brát v úvahu největší možný počet lidí;
je to sociálnost na poli noetiky. . . .
7. Tak vlastně všechny otázky našeho myšlení jsou v podstatě
otázky našeho chování vůči zkušenostem; . . . našeho
morálního jednání ve světě. Avšak zde nutno se také shodnouti
o slově "svět." Svět pro mne se začíná na mém psacím stole
a ne u zelené tabule ze ženevské konference; . . . náš svět, to
jest náš skutečný, epický, morální svět sahá tak daleko, jak
daleko sahá naše osobní zasahování myšlenkou nebo skutkem.
Nuže, záleží zcela na nás, jakou hodnotu dáme této skutečnosti;
do velké míry záleží na nás, co z toho světa uděláme.
Skutečnost, ve které žijeme, v níž se stýkáme s kýmkoliv a
pracujeme na svých praktických úkolech, je skutečnost morální
a proto vysoce relevantní. . . . "Vysoké etické hodnoty" jsou
velmi krásná věc, jde-li nám o to, abychom hodně s vysoka
soudili, co dělají jiní; ale skutečné mravní jednání má své místo

v prachu země a ve velmi obyčejném, neroztříděném prostředí...
Má-li se těchto několik vět jmenovati "pragmatismus," dobrá:
budu rád, budu-li shledán hodným tohoto jména, nejen podle
slov, ale i podle skutků. Ano, je zcela pravda: toto vše není
ještě filosofie, ale jen jistá metoda uvažování; není to konečná
a vrcholná víra, nýbrž jen jistá otevřená možnost víry.[167]

These stipulations—whether or not they represent pragmatist philosophy—
elucidate Čapek's world view at the time. Moreover, since the treatise was
written at the outset of his literary career,[168] published in 1918 and in
1925, the cited appendix reflects the writer's ideas during this time.
Naturally, the question arises of how Čapek's philosophy developed after
1925. The literary production of this period of his life includes some of his
best known works: *Povídky z jedné a z druhé kapsy, Apokryfy, O věcech
obecných*, the trilogy *Hordubal, Povětroň, Obyčejný život, První parta*,
and *Bajky a podpovídky*. The first of these works is largely noetic—the
concern with cognition of reality corresponds to the pragmatist interests,
although, as Harkins observes, some of the stories " . . . show a new
hesitation to accept a pragmatist epistemology."[169] Nevertheless, even
Harkins admits the presence of pragmatism in the critical attitude of
" . . . a sceptical knife which he [Čapek] uses to cut away the masks of
absolutism and monism with which man invests reality."[170] The truth and
its subjectivity lead him to the themes of justice and responsibility. The
subjectivizing of truth recurrent in all writings by Čapek since *Boží muka*
is of major importance in the *Povídky*. The notion of subjective truth clears
the way for another important concept of pragmatism, namely, relativism.
This term is defined as the ethical principles of individuals which conflict
in a fundamental way.[171] A special form of this is cultural relativism, the
basis of the story "Zločin v chalupě." The relativity of truth is also
prominent in the collection *Kniha apokryfů*. "Pilátovo krédo" can hardly
be surpassed as an exhaustive treatment of this theme. Moreover, the
obvious preference for the practical Martha in the story "Marta a Maria"
further confirms Čapek's pragmatist attitude. The writer also uses this
biblical episode as an example in his article "O relativismu" included in *O
věcech obecných*. Martha is described as a relativist who can learn "many
things," while Mary is a "monomaniac" who listens to one truth only.[172]
The relativism comes forth again in "O skepsi," but, although the article
is published in this book, it is dated 1924 and, therefore, of limited

significance for the post-1925 period. The trilogy demonstrates, however, that Čapek's views did not substantially change. He may indeed abandon the extreme forms of relativism, but never forsakes it entirely. Mukařovský observes that *Hordubal* and *Povětroň* are built on the principle that all realities are equally true.[173] Denying this notion means oversimplification of the actual situation. This becomes clear from Čapek's letter to a reader of *Povětroň*. The writer maintains that, in life as well as in literature, "... nás až příliš často ovládá potřeba prostě přijímat stanoviska, hodnoty a sympatie. ... Skutečnost je strašně složitá, i budiž nám podán její zjednodušený obraz. ... Ukažte nám věci jenom z jedné strany, aby nás nemátly jejich druhé strany a jejich rub. To je zhruba noetický stav, ve kterém žijeme."[174] Naturally, the pragmatic theory of truth and resulting relativism by themselves do not form a sufficient basis to draw any conclusions. Čapek's works of the 1930s display, however, other features of pragmatism. Thus, *Obyčejný život*, "Romeo a Julie," and "Glorie" stress the preference for ordinary life and people rather than exceptional people and romantic heroes. The notion that heroism is not an exceptional romantic deed but unremitting work and fulfillment of one's duties prevails in *První parta*. The constancy of the writer's outlook is further demonstrated by the story "O desíti spravedlivých" based on the biblical analogy which Čapek has used in the sixth clause of his "pragmatist" appendix. Moreover, the pluralistic correlative of pragmatism finds expression in "Sbírka známek," "O fantasii," and *Obyčejný život*.

The assumption of constancy in Čapek's views does not yet show him as a pragmatist. Many historical pragmatists would disagree with a few or with many clauses of the writer's ideological outline. The problem is, however, with the label, not with the philosophy. Pragmatism has never been precisely delimitied, and F.C.S. Schiller claims that even Protagoras was a pragmatist.[175] Lovejoy has counted thirteen distinct pragmatisms,[176] and even this figure does not satisfy Schiller, who claims that " ... Lovejoy has grossly understated their number ... there might be as many pragmatisms as there were pragmatists."[177] This statement is echoed without the conditional by the French philosopher Alfred Foillée.[178] Fortunately, and in the spirit of pragmatism, it is not necessary to decide whether Čapek should actually be labelled a pragmatist. The outline of his ideology has a great deal in common with pragmatism. Moreover, the seven principles in which he specifies his world view indicate a unity of philosophical thought.

Synthesis

Čexov did not epitomize his *Weltanschauung*, but, it seems, Čapek described it for him. Every clause of the outline can be applied to the Russian and illustrated by references to his stories. The affinity of Čexov's philosophy with pragmatism has already been discussed. The conditions under which the Russian writer's outlook developed explain the direction its progress took. The hypothesis of pragmatist content in Čexov's writings is further supported by his literary style. He is often described as an impressionist.[179] As a matter of fact, Arnold Hauser sees Čexov as the purest representative of the movement. He speaks of " . . . das Auftreten eines Schriftstellers wie Tschechow, den man als den reinsten Repräsentanten des ganzen Stils bezeichnen kann."[180] In his discussion of Impressionism, Hauser searches for a theory of cognition which would correspond to this artistic style, and he finds it in pragmatism. He even believes that "[m]an kann sich keine dem Impressionismus entsprechendere Erkenntnistheorie denken."[181] This reaffirms the above hypothesis. Both Čexov and Čapek developed their own philosophy with remarkable affinity to pragmatism. The similarity of their world views and Čapek's explanation of his thought allow one to discern even Čexov's philosophy, the integrity of which has so often been denied.

Notes

1. A.I. Roskin, "Zametki o realizme Čexova," *Literaturnyj kritik*, No. 7 (1939), n.p.; rpt. in *A.P. Čexov: Stat'i i očerki* (Moskva: GIXL, 1959), p. 206.

2. Winner, "Čechov and Scientism," p. 326.

3. Grossman, "Čexov: Naturalizm," p. 204.

4. W.M. Simmon, "Bernard, Claude," *The Encyclopedia of Philosophy*, 1972 rpt. edn.

5. Berdnikov, *A.P. Čexov*, p. 116.

6. V.T. Romanenko, *Čexov i nauka* (Xar'kov: Xar'kovskoe kniž. izd-vo, 1962), p. 8.

7. Letter to A.S. Suvorin, dated May 7, 1889, No. 650 (XXI, *Pis'ma*, III, 207).

8. Romanenko, p. 55.

9. Letter to A.S. Suvorin, dated February 13, 1893, No. 1282 (XXIII, *Pis'ma*, V, 170).

10. Romanenko, p. 57.

11. C. Bernard, *An Introduction to the Study of Experimental Medicine*, trans. H.C. Greene (New York: MacMillan Co., 1927), p. 55.

12. Ibid., p. 50.

13. Ibid., p. 50.

14. Ibid., p. 221.

15. Letter to A.N. Pleščeev, dated October 4, 1888, No. 491 (XXI, *Pis'ma*, III, 11).

16. Letter to D.V. Grigorovič, dated October 9, 1888, No. 496 (XXI, *Pis'ma,* III, 47).

17. Bernard, pp. 49-50.

18. Letter to M.V. Kiseleva, dated January 14, 1887, No. 218 (XX, *Pis'ma*, II, 11).

19. Ibid., pp. 11-12.

20. Letter to D.V. Grigorovič, dated February 12, 1987, No. 231 (XX, Pis'ma, II, 360).

21. Bernard, p. 224.

22. _____, *La Science expérimentale*, 6th edn. (Paris, J.-B. Brilličre, 1918), pp. 405-406, as quoted in R. Virtanen, "Claude Bernard and the History of Ideas," in *Claude Bernard and Experimental Medicine*, eds. F. Grande and M.B. Visscher (Cambridge: Schenkman, 1967), p. 10.

23. Letter to A.N. Pleščeev, dated March 6, 1888, No. 385 (XX, *Pis'ma*, II, 210-11).

24. Bernard, *An Introduction,* p. 27.

25. Letter to A.S. Suvorin, dated October, 18, 1888, No. 507 (XXI, *Pis'ma*, III, 37).

26. Bernard, p. 224.

27. Letter to A.S. Suvorin, dated October 27, 1888, No. 515 (XXI, *Pis'ma,* III, 45).

28. É. Zola, *Le Roman expérimental*, in *Oeuvres complètes*, ed. H. Mitterand (Paris: Cercle du Livre Précieux, 1968), X, 1180.

29. Bernard, *An Introduction*, p. 13.

30. Ibid., p. 22.

31. Zola, p. 1180.

32. Letter to A.S. Suvorin, dated May 30, 1888, No. 447 (XX, *Pis'ma*, II, 280).

33. Letter to A.S. Suvorin, dated October 27, 1888, No. 515 (XXI, *Pis'ma*, III, 46).

34. Letter to A.S. Suvorin, dated November 3, 1888, No. 520 (XXI, *Pis'ma,* III, 53).

35. Ibid., p. 53.

36. Ibid., p. 54. The idea of a common denominator for all great artistic works is examined in Čapek's dissertation "Objektivní metoda v estetice se zřením k výtvarnému umění," see Buriánek's commentary in the previous chapter.

37. Letter to A.S. Suvorin, dated May 7, 1889, No. 650 (XXI, *Pis'ma*, III, 207).

38. Ibid., p. 208.

39. Bernard, p. 66.

40. Ibid., p. 68.

41. Letter to A.S. Suvorin, dated May 7, 1889, No. 650 (XXI, *Pis'ma,* III, 208).

42. Ibid., p. 209.

43. Letter to A.S. Suvorin, dated approximately February 20, 1890, No. 772 (XXII, *Pis'ma,* IV, 31).

44. Letter to A.S. Suvorin, dated March 9, 1890, No. 782 (XXII, *Pis'ma,* IV, 23).

45. Letter to A.S. Suvorin, dated January 2, 1894, No. 1371 (XXIII, *Pis'ma,* V, 258).

46. Letter to S.P. Djagilev, dated December 20, 1901, No. 3587 (XXVIII, *Pis'ma,* X, 145).

47. Letter to I.I. Ostroveskij, dated February 11, 1893, No. 1281 (XXIII, *Pis'ma*, V, 169-70).

48. Letter to A.S. Suvorin, dated August 18, 1893, No. 1334 (XXIII, *Pis'ma*, V, 226).

49. See, for instance, his letter to A.S. Suvorin, dated November 15, 1888, No. 532 (XXI, *Pis'ma*, III, 70).

50. Letter to O.L. Knipper-Čexova, dated September 18, 1902, No. 3837 (XXIX, *Pis'ma*, XI, 41).

51. Letter to Al. P. Čexov, dated April 17 or 18, 1883, No. 39 (XIX, *Pis'ma*, I, 65).

52. Letter to V.V. Bilibin, dated March 11, 1886, No. 157 (XIX, *Pis'ma*, I, 213).

53. Roskin, p. 197.

54. For details see the discussion in the previous chapter.

55. Bernard, *An Introduction*, p. 203.

56. Ibid., p. 142.

57. Ibid., pp. 42-43, cf. Zola, p. 1201.

58. Šestov, p. 52.

59. Bernard, "Cours de philosophie positive (par Auguste Comte): Exposition de la doctrine philosophique," in *Philosophie: Manuscrit inédit*, ed. J. Chevalier (Paris: Boivin, 1937), p. 26.

60. Ibid., p. 27.

61. Ibid., p. 28.

62. Ibid., p. 29.

63. Ibid., p. 29.

64. Bernard's note, p. 30.

65. Bernard, "Cours," p. 31.

66. Ibid., p. 32.

67. Ibid., p. 41.

68. R. Virtanen, "Claude Bernard and the History of Ideas," in *Claude Bernard and Experimental Medicine*, Collected Papers from a Symposium commemorating the centenary of the publication of *An Introduction to the Study of Experimental Medicine*, eds. F. Grande and M.B. Visscher (Cambridge: Schenkman, 1967), p. 14.

69. R. Virtanen, p. 15.

70. *Ibid.*, p. 15. Virtanen refers to Bernard, "Cours," p. 29. The physiologist proclaims that "[l]a religion de Comte est aussi mystique et plus absurde que les autres."

71. Bernard, *Pensées, notes détachés*, ed. L. Delhoome (Paris: J.-B. Baillière, 1937), p. 64, as referred to by Virtanen, p. 15, cf. Bernard, *An Introduction*, p. 32.

72. Virtanen, p. 15, see also Bernard, *An Introduction*, p. 28.

73. Bernard, p. 28, referred to by Virtanen, p. 15.

74. Bernard, p. 82.

75. Simon, "Bernard, Claude," *The Encyclopedia of Philosophy*, 1972, rpt. edn.
    The reference to the falsifiability criterion is not surprising, since Popper, not unlike Bernard, maintains that the formation of a scientific hypothesis is creative exercise of the imagination; it is not a passive reaction to observed regularities. Ther is no such thing as pure observation, for observation is always selective. Moreover, no collection of particular observations can verify a general statement since many theories that are known to be false have an indefinitely large number of confirming instances. Hence, the search for negative instances is of utmost importance.

76. W. James, rev. of *Rapport sur le progrès et la marche de physiologie générale en France*, by C. Bernard, North American Review, 107, No. 220 (1868), 325.

77. H. Bergson, "La Philosophie de Claude Bernard," in *La Pensée et le mouvant: Essais et conférences* (Paris: Félix Alcan, 1934), P. 257.

78. Virtanen, p. 21. The author supports his claim by references to Bergson, "La Philosophie de Claude Bernard;" "La Philosophie," in *La Science française* (Paris: n.p., 1905), p. 12; *L'Evolution créatrice* (Paris: F. Alcan, 1910), pp. 135 and 273.

79. Bernard, *An Introduction*, p. 41.

80. Virtanen, p. 21, referring to Bernard, *La Science expérimentale* (Paris: J.-B. Baillière, 1918), p. 109.

81. Bernard, pp. 18 and 50, respectively.

82. Virtanen, p. 21.

83. R.B. Perry, *The Thought and Character of William James* (Boston: Little, Brown, and Co., 1935), I, 368.

84. D. Magarshack, *Chekhov: A Life* (1953; rpt. Westport: Greenwood Press, 1970), p. 177.

85. E.J. Simmons, *Chekhov: A Biography* (Boston: Little, Brown and Co., 1962), p. 203.

86. Letter to I.L. Leont'ev (Ščeglov), dated January 22, 1888, No. 361 (XX, *Pis'ma*, II, 180).

87. Letter to A.N. Pleščeev, dated April 9, 1888, No. 411 (XX, *Pis'ma*, II, 240).

88. Letter to I.L. Leont'ev (Ščeglov), dated May 3, 1888, No. 431 (XX, *Pis'ma*, II, 262).

89. Letter to A.N. Pleščeev, dated August 13, 1888, No. 470 (XX, *Pis'ma*, II, 312).

90. Letter to I.L. Leont'ev (Ščeglov), dated September 14, 1888, No. 482 (XX, *Pis'ma*, II, 330).

91. Letter to A.N. Pleščeev, dated September 15, 1888, No. 483 (XX, *Pis'ma*, II, 332).

92. Letter to Al.P. Čexov, dated September 15, 1888, No. 486 (XX, *Pis'ma*, II, 335).

93. Letter to A.S Savorin, dated December 23, 1888, N0. 559 (XXI, *Pis'ma*, III, 98).

94. Ibid., p. 100.

95. Letter to A.S. Suvorin, dated May 4, 1889, No. 648 (XXI, *Pis'ma*, III, 203-04).

96. Letter to A.S. Savorin, dated July 2, 1889, No. 665 (XXI, *Pis'ma*, III, 229).

97. Perry, *The Thought*, I, 320.

98. Letter to H.P. Bowditch, dated December 29, 1869, in Perry, I, 320.

99. Perry, I, 322.

100. Henry James, the son of the philosopher, positively identifies his father as the author (and protagonist) of this fictitious correspondence. See, *The Letters of William James*, ed. H. James (1920; rpt. 2 vols. in 1, Boston: Little, Brown, and Co., 1926), I, 145.

101. W. James, *The Varieties of Religious Experience: A Study in Human Nature* (New York: Longmans, Green, and Co. 1920), pp. 160-61.

102. Perry, I, 322.

103. Ibid., I, 332.

104. W. James's notebook, as quoted in Perry, I, 332.

105. Perry, I, 323.

106. W. James's notebook, as quoted in *The Letters of William James*, ed. H. James (1920; rpt. 2 vols. in 1, Boston: Little, Brown, and Co., 1926), I, 147-48.

107. Perry, I, 323.

108. Winner, *Chekhov*, p. 156.

109. See, W.J. Earle, "James, William," *The Encyclopedia of Philosophy*, IV, 241.

110. Earle, IV, 246. Moreover, this idea is generally accepted.

111. This outline is largely based on H.S. Thayer, "Pragmatism," *The Encyclopedia of Philosophy*, 1972 rpt. edn.

112. C.S. Peirce, *Pragmatism and Pragmaticism*, vol. V of *Collected Papers of Charles Sanders Peirce*, ed. P. Weiss (Cambridge: Harvard Univ. Press, 1934), p. 6, par. 9.

113. _____, *Reviews, Correspondence*, and *Bibliography*, vol VIII of *Collected Papers of Charles Sanders Peirce*, ed. H.W. Burks, 2nd edn. (Cambridge: Harvard Univ. Press, 1966), p. 190, par. 259.

114. _____, *Pragmatism*, p. 123, par. 197.

115. Ibid., pp. 229-31, pars. 370-73.

116. Ibid., p. 157, par. 265.

117. Ibid., p. 230, par. 372.

118. Ibid., pp. 279-80, par. 418.

119. W. James, *Pragmatism* (Cambridge: Harvard Univ. Press, 1975), p. 30.

120. Ibid., p. 97.

121. Ibid., p. 143.

122. Ibid., p. 106.

123. Earle, IV, 244.

124. James, "The Will to Believe," in *The Will to Believe and Other Essays in Popular Philosophy* (Cambridge: Harvard Univ. Press, 1979), p. 14.

125. Thayer, "Pragmatism," VI, 434.

126. R.J. Bernstein, "Dewey, John," in *The Encyclopedia of Philosophy*, II, 384-85.

127. J. Dewey, "The Influence of Darwinism on Philosophy," *Popular Science Monthly*, 74, (July 1909); rpt. in *The Influence of Darwin on Philosophy and Other Essays in Contemporary Thought* (New York: Henry Holt & Co, 1910), p. 19.

128. Ibid., p. 11.

129. Ibid., p. 13.

130. Ibid., p. 15.

131. Ibid., p. 17.

132. Dewey, "The Influence," p. 17.

133. Ibid., p. 19.

134. E.C. Moore, *American Pragmatism: Peirce, James, and Dewey* (New York: Columbia Univ. Press, 1961), p. 206, referring to J. Dewey, *Essays in Experimental Logic* (Chicago: Univ. of Chicago Press, 1916), pp. 230-49.

135. Ibid., pp. 261-62.

136. Ibid., pp. 262.

137. Peirce, *Pragmatism*, p. 256, par. 400.

138. Bernard, *An Introduction*, pp. 54-55; cf. pp. 52, 60, and 219.

139. Ibid., p. 219.

140. James, "The Dilemma of Determinism," in *The Will to Believe*, pp.114-40, see also R. Taylor, "Determinism," in *The Encyclopedia of Philosophy*, II, 368.

141. Zola, p. 1190.

142. James, "The Dilemma," p. 133.

143. _____, *Pragmatism*, p. 59.

144. John Tulloch in *Chekhov: A Structuralist Study*, pp. 118-20, applies to von Koren Max Nordau's depiction of a genius who will counteract the evils of degeneracy caused by sudden changes in man's environment. He refers to the following idea expressed in Nordau, *Paradoxe* (Leipzig: Victor Ottman, 1891), p. 198: "Die Organisation eines solchen Urteils- und Willensgenies bringt es mit sich, daß es mehr oder weniger, in äußersten Fällen vollkommen, dessen entbehrt, was man gefühl und künstlerischen Sinn, Schönheits- und Liebesbedürfnis nennt. . . . Von . . . Regungen ist das Genie beinahe ganz frei. Es ist in keiner Weise sentimental."
The comparison is interesting but, as indicated in Čexov's correspondence, he did not read Nordau before "Duèl'" was completed.

145. Letter to A.S. Suvorin, dated August 1, 1892, No. 1207, Čexov (XXIII, *Pis'ma*, V, 101).

146. James devotes an entire chapter of the book to Fechner, refers to him often, and recommends his works in his correspondence.
The *Tagesansicht* (daylight view), according to Gustav Theodor Fechner, means to regard the entire material universe as inwardly alive and conscious.

147. James, *A Pluralistic Universe* (Cambridge: Harvard Univ. Press, 1977), p. 135.

148. Ibid., pp. 135 and 138.

149. H.Bergson, *Essai sur les données immédiates de la conscience* (Paris: Félix Alcan,

1930), pp. 124-32, 177-78 and 183-84.

150. Bergson originally published his *Essai* in Paris in 1889, Čexov visited Paris in April 1891, and the "Student" was written in March 1894. No evidence, however, exists that Čexov was acquainted with Bergson's work.

151. Perry, II, 559.

152. Bergson, as quoted by Perry, II, 600.

153. Perry, II, 601-02 and 603.

154. James, *Pragmatism,* p. 60.

155. Ibid., pp. 60-61.

156. Bergson, p. 127.

157. James, *The Will*, pp. 126 and 129.

158. Ibid., p. 134.

159. See Leszek Kolakowski, *Positivist Philosophy: From Hume to the Vienna Circle*, tr. N. Guterman (Harmondsworth: Penguin Books, 1972), p. 198.

160. James, *Pragmatism*, pp. 50-51.

161. Ibid., p. 55, see also A.O. Lovejoy, "The Thirteen Pragmatisms," in *The Thirteen Pragmatisms and Other Essays* (Baltimore: John Hopkins, 1963), p. 7.

162. James, *Pragmatism*, p. 137.

163. Ibid., p. 143.

164. Kolakowski, p. 199.

165. Cf. Bruford, Ivask, and Marshall.

166. Professor Ivask follows his reference to Čexov's "field" with a discussion of his anti-intellectualism which well compares with similar sentiments expressed by James and Bergson. See Ivask, pp. 84-85.

167. Čapek, *Pragmatismus,* pp. 76-83.

168. For illustration of the similarity of views expressed in Čapek's early theoretical articles, see Buriánek, *Karel*, pp. 40-42; for a discussion of the pragmatist content in his fiction of that time, see Harkins, "Pragmatism," pp. 116-20. Professor Harkins considers *Kritika slov* (1920) to be the highpoint of Čapek's "pragmatism," cf. p. 120.

169. Harkins, "Pragmatism," p. 122.

170. Harkins, p. 122.

171. R.B. Brandt, "Ethical Relativism," *The Encyclopedia*, III, 75.

172. Čapek, *O věcech*, p. 63.

173. Mukařovský, "Vývoj," p. 443.

174. A manuscript from Čapek's estate; rpt. in Čapek, *Poznámky*, p. 103.

175. F.C.S. Schiller, "William James and the Making of Pragmatism," *The Personalist*, 8 (1927), 82.

176. Lovejoy, "The Thirteen Pragmatisms." Already the title of the essay proclaims the existence of several trends under one label. The fact that Lovejoy also wrote on the diversity in descriptions of Romanticism ("The Discrimination of Romanticisms") does not weaken the argument, especially as it is enhanced by the pragmatists themselves. (Cf. the next footnote.)

177. Schiller, p. 92.

178. As cited in Branžovský, *Karel Čapek*, p. 130.

179. This claim was made, among others, by Merežkovskij, Tolstoj, Lunačarskij, and more recently, by H.P. Stowell; Thomas Eekman, attempted to refute the assertion in his recent article entitled "Čechov—an Impressionist?" *Russian Literature: North-Holland*, 15, No. 2 (1984), 203-22.

180. Hauser, *Sozialgeschichte*, p. 972.

181. Ibid., p. 989.

❦

Conclusion

A comparative study examining the affinities between Čapek and Čexov is long overdue. The parallels were first observed almost half a century ago, and commented on *in passim* by no less than seven scholars. According to the critics' allusions, a similarity exists in the quality of the stories, in the artistic method, stylistic structure, language, and in the atmosphere, or mood, inherent in Čapek and Čexov's narratives. The affinity based on the similar treatment of analogous subjects has remained until now an entirely unexplored field.

Yet, numerous stories in the *oeuvre* of the two authors feature identical or very similar themes treated in like manner. Thus, for instance, the atmosphere of heavy melancholy which is, as observed by several critics, common to both writers results from lack of action and passive submission to existing conditions. The reasons for this inertia vary from fear of action as in "Košile" and "Strax" to frustrated endeavour as in "Na zámku" or "Van'ka" and inability to act imposed by external circumstances as in "Historie dirigenta Kaliny" and "V more." The melancholy mood is also evoked by frustrated attempts at communication and by human loneliness. Čapek demonstrates this in "Otcové" and "Pomoc!" Čexov deals with the theme, for instance, in "Toska" and "Bab'e carstvo." Both authors are also concerned with the dearth of feelings in human interrelations. Thus, Čapek stresses the importance of sincere sentiments in the "card game" in his "Pohádka pošt'ácká," and Čexov uses a "card game" to ridicule human relations based solely on professional rank in the story "Vint." One should be compassionate even with criminals. Such is the message of stories like "Hora" and "Vor." Indeed, one should try to understand the motivation of other people's deeds. God, as demonstrated in Čapek's "Poslední soud," cannot judge people because he knows everything, and understands how their actions were induced. Čexov parallels this sentiment when he has one of the characters in "Perepolox" quote Madame de Staeül's "Tout comprendre, tout pardonner." That we know only one side of our fellow beings is illustrated in "Šaty dělají člověka" and "Dvoe v odnom." Čapek elaborates on the relativity of truth in his *feuilleton* "Co je pravda?" Relativism is an important factor in the creative work of both writers. Thus, descriptive relativism is, for instance, defined as the ethical principles of individuals which conflict in a fundamental way.[1] A special form of this is cultural relativism featured in Čapek's "Zločin v chalupě" and in Čexov's "Zloumyšlennik." Both authors express their concern for ordinary people and wish to help them. This cannot be done by beautiful speeches. They demonstrate the emptiness of big words and *clichés*, for instance, in "Jasnovidec" and "Orator."

The most prominent themes in Čexov's literary production are, however, the foursome of freedom, lack of communication, justice, and truth. The selection of the most recurrent themes in the Russian writer's voluminous *oeuvre* precludes the pitfall of selecting from the numerous stories only those with similarities to confirm the hypothesis that an affinity between Čexov and Čapek exists. The analogies in the choice and treatment of major issues rules out the workings of mere chance.

Three groups can be distinguished among the characters in Čexov's exploration of the theme of freedom, the first of the four major topics. Nevertheless, with the exception of his last works perhaps, all these categories point in the same direction: if the heroes desire tranquillity, they cannot do what they want, unless their chosen paths coincide with those fated to them. Thus Olen'ka, the protagonist in "Dušečka," or Očumelov in "Xameleon" can be untroubled, since their wishes change with existing conditions. The other two types of characters in Čexov's writings are frustrated. Either they act as they do not want to do, like Var'ka in "Spat' xočetsja" and Nastas'ja Kanavkina in "Znakomyj mužčina;" or, they act according to their desire and are nevertheless discontented with their choices, as with the former group of heroes. This type can be exemplified by Misail in "Moja žizn'," or Zinaida Fedorovna in "Rasskaz neizvestnogo čeloveka."

Čapek's protagonists, like Čexov's characters, may also be subdivided into three categories. First, the smallest group is formed by the heroes who are happy with their choices, such as Klára in "Modrá chryzantéma," or the cactus collector in "Ukradený kaktus." The second group is made up of those characters whom some force compels to behave differently from what they had originally intended. Thus, the protagonists of *Boží muka* feel constricted and see their life as a prison. The last group, as in Čexov, is that of characters who make their choice but are nevertheless frustrated as a result. Examples of this type are found in "Muž, který se nelíbil," "Ušní zpověď," and "Tribunál."

The theme of freedom is one of the most prominent issues in the works of both writers. Moreover, their heroes who are—as is often stressed—conscious of this freedom rarely find peace of mind as a result of their decisions. They may be prevented from exercising their freedom, for it is far from absolute. While some characters do not act according to their own choosing, others do; their lack of concern for people around them, however, frustrates their activity, and again results in unhappiness. This phenomenon is one of the factors contributing to human isolation, or lack of communication, the second major issue discerned in the writings of Čexov and Čapek.

Freedom of action which is devoid of interest in one's fellows does not suffice to provide happiness, and the misery of the protagonists whose self-determination is limited by external causes reaches its supreme point when combined with lack of communication. Čapek's *Hordubal* and the entire collection *Trapné povídky*, along with Čexov's "Toska" and "Čelovek v futljare," may serve as examples of treatment of this theme. They cannot, however, by themselves encompass the multitude of approaches to the subject employed by the two writers. "Toska" awakens in the reader the same feeling of heavy melancholy as does Čapek's book *Trapné povídky*, while "Doč' Al'biona," similar to "Muž, který se nelíbil" by the Czech writer, is a rather amusing tale. When the effects of lack of communication are considered, Čexov's stories dealing with this theme cover the entire scale of possibilities. Murder results in some of them (e.g. "Barynja), despair in others (e.g. "Toska"), the hero's liberation from the impasse through his own death in still others ("Gore"), or sometimes no resolution ensues ("Doč' Al'biona"). Some characters are even happy in their isolation ("Kryžovnik"), while others find relief because they believe that communication has been established, whether it has or not ("Van'ka"). The narratives dealing with this theme are mostly tragic, but in some stories the outcome is humorous ("Doč' Al'biona"). Similarly, most of Čapek's writings based on human isolation are not comic, but exceptions can be found ("Modrá chryzantéma"). The characters of *Trapné povídky* are desperately alone and unable to escape their isolation. *Hordubal* and the hero of "Ušní zpověd'" find escape only in their own death. In Hordubal's case the death is violent. As in Čexov's stories, lack of communication often leads to crime: for instance, murder in "Zločin v chalupě," "Ubijstvo," *Hordubal*, and "Spat' xočetsja," thievery in "Košile," "Rasskaz neizvestnogo čeloveka," "Ukradený kaktus," and "Zloumyšlennik," embezzlement as in "Muž, který se nelíbil" and "Vor," etc. It is therefore only logical that both authors were also interested in justice. This is illustrated, for example, in their concern with the Dreyfus affair. Čexov often referred to it in his correspondence, and an echo of this case is found in his "O ljubvi." Čapek, because of his youth, was not personally as involved in the affair as his Russian counterpart, but he too wrote a story reminiscent of the Dreyfus affair, the "Případ Selvinův." Miscarriage of justice occurs frequently in the stories by Čapek and Čexov (e.g. "Grófinka," "Sud"), but both writers mainly deal with the imminent possibility of judicial failure (e.g. "Propuštěný," "Palata No. 6"). They are critical of the penal system in their respective countries (e.g. "Věštkyně," "Rasskaz Egora"); both ask for compassion for the convicted criminal (e.g. "Hora," "Vor"); and both find the law incapable of pardon ("Propuštěný," "Rasskaz staršego sadovnika"—only a legend). In the works of both authors there are characters who seem to be above the law ("Zmizení herce Bendy," "Drama na oxote"). Naturally there are some differences in the approach of the two authors to the theme. Čexov presents more cases of miscarried justice and he is more interested in the punishment inflicted. Čapek, on the other hand, is more concerned with the suitability of the verdict and in absolute justice. These slight differences do not change the fact that justice and its administration constitute one of the main issues treated in their respective works.

The concept of justice is inseparable from that of truth: both writers are therefore concerned with this notion. Čapek's story "Pilátovo krédo" is an example of a work in which the two themes are brought together. The fictional Pilate admits that, although Christ was innocent, he handed Him over to death for preaching a new truth. Pilate's question about the essence of truth remains unanswered. The author takes the opportunity, however, to demonstrate how relative the notion is. Čapek's Pilate refuses to accept that each one who makes his own truth can rule out all other truths. He believes that truth exists and that each one of us has a share of it; the man who says yes and the man who says no. If these two were to unite and understand each other, the whole truth would be obtained. Moreover, according to him, man recognizes truth. Indeed, he observes, it would be madness to think that truth is only there for man not to know it. Čexov expresses a similar thought, for instance, in "Duèl'." His characters repeat several times that no one knows the real truth, and conclude through the mouth of one of them that, when seeking truth, people take two steps forward and one back. Passion for truth and stubborn will-power drive them onwards, and—who knows?—perhaps they will attain real truth in the end.

Čapek's approach to the problem is that of a relativist. There are many truths but, however contradictory they may be, they should all be respected because there are people behind them. The noetic problem becomes an ethical one. People need nothing more than mutual understanding. No one should judge a fellow human being; instead, one should try to comprehend that person's own truth. However, as Čapek's Pilate says, everyone who propounds some truth, denies all other truths. People are not really concerned with truth and justice but with their private interests, hence they cannot agree on a single point. The protagonists of *Boží muka* search for truth in vain since they seek the general truth which would elucidate the meaning of life for them. The absolute truth cannot be found, but there are personal truths. If an individual acts according to his own concept of righteousness, he cannot be judged for his transgression of societal precepts. The relativity of truth is recurrent in Čapek's entire literary production. The Russian author is concerned with truth just as much as his Czech colleague is. Čexov remained a seeker for truth throughout his creative life, although his approach to the theme changed. Thus, in "Suščaja pravda," it is amusing how an official is unable to communicate the "truth" to his superior. "Xameleon," with all its humour, already shows the relativity of truth. The stories published before 1889 deal with the problem of communicating truth, the relativity of truth, and social hypocrisy, all of which isolate people. The protagonists of the works which appeared after "Imeniny" are actually in search of truth and the meaning of life. This change of approach is reflected in Thomas Winner's choice of five of the stories from this period, namely "Skučnaja istorija," "Duèl'," "Gusev," "Palata No. 6," and "Černyj monax" to discuss them as "a cycle of psycho-philosophical searching stories."[2]

Although the goal of Čexov's protagonists is specified as truth only in the stories published after 1890, the theme is present in his *oeuvre* from the very beginning. The concept is not and cannot be explained, because of its elusive nature. Truth is relative and volatile. The characters struggle towards it, but they never attain it. Several protagonists ask for advice on how to live, without obtaining any answer. Nevertheless, the hint recurs that one should be interested in one's fellow beings and try to understand them. One should enjoy life and help others to do the same. The best policy for mutual understanding is sincerity, the worst is hypocrisy or putting oneself forward. Čexov stresses human interrelations more consistently than Čapek does, while the process of cognition of truth is of greater concern for the Czech writer. Nevertheless, they are both interested in the theme of truth. For both, the concept is relative and cannot be defined. Perception of reality varies with perspective, and truth encompasses all possible views, including those which seem mutually exclusive. Truth is the objective of the human quest, and the protagonists hope to achieve it, but the concept, with its contradictory elements, is too elusive. Man cannot attain his goal, but, by trying to comprehend the concept and to understand the individual truths of his fellow human beings, he can find happiness in the proximity of truth.

Owing to Čexov's tolerance of conflicting truths, the notion of truth itself becomes relative and therefore ambiguous. In fact, this ambiguity is characteristic of his work as a whole; this explains the great disparity of views found in Čexov criticism. Moreover, the criticism dealing with the Russian author is voluminous and, unfortunately, confusing. References are incomplete or wrong, quotations inaccurate or taken out of context, and the material is selected to illustrate the critic's opinion, rather than to examine views expressed by Čexov. In addition, many of the articles published by his contemporaries are difficult to obtain. Therefore, the survey of Čexovian criticism given in the present work is disproportionately extensive. This author cherishes the hope that the survey chapter with its precise references and quotations—rather than distorted paraphrases—will serve as a dependable research tool for scholars interested in critical views on Čexov's philosophy.

Čapek's writings also tend, if to a lesser degree, to provoke polemics and controversy. Whereas Čexov's world view remains implicit, however, Čapek's is expressed more explicitly, this being a reflection of the latter's philosophical training. Therefore, a typological study not only demonstrates the similarities between the works of the two writers, but also helps to elucidate such a controversial issue as Čexov's philosophy by comparing it with that of an author whose views are akin and more obvious.

Examination of the critical perceptions and commentaries attests to the disagreement of literary scholars regarding the classification of Čapek and Čexov's world views. Nevertheless, the type of difficulties encountered, and the ideologies suggested, indicate other, more fundamental similarities. One exception to the numerous parallels in the critical views is the controversy about Čapek's pragmatism. Since Čapek wrote a treatise on pragmatism, the argument centers around the question of whether he was a pragmatist or not. The opinions cover the entire scale of possibilities from completely denying any trace of pragmatism in his writings to proclaiming him to be a pragmatist philosopher and the leader of the Czech pragmatist generation.

No evidence exists demonstrating Čexov's knowledge of pragmatism. However, his background, interests, and education support the idea of a parallel development. Thus, many biographical similarities between William James, the best known advocate of pragmatism, and the Russian writer provide a basis for the assumption of kindred thought. Moreover, Claude Bernard's influence on Čexov is generally acknowledged and, as Professor Virtanen observes, Bernard's ideas anticipated pragmatist theories.[3] The best argument for kinship between Čexov's *Weltanschauung* and pragmatism is, however, his creative work.

Pragmatism grew out of a concern for proper communication, and its proponents focus on the same topics as Čexov. Individual freedom carries with it the problem of moral responsibility, therefore justice, and truth. Freedom exists, but not in its absolute form. Thus, people are responsible for their deeds. To judge them, however, is difficult, for truth is relative and, from their perspective, their actions may be justifiable. The whole function of thought, according to Peirce, is to produce habits of action. Hence, the maxim of pragmatism is not limited to ideas. Peirce formulates it as follows: "In order to ascertain the meaning of any intellectual conception one should consider what practical consequences might conceivably result of necessity from the truth of that conception; and the sum of these consequences will constitute the entire meaning of the conception."[4] James applies this theorem to the problem of divine existence: "On pragmatic principles, if the hypothesis of God works satisfactorily in the widest sense of the word, it is true."[5]

Many scholars attempt to prove that Čexov is religious, others, that he is not. The former rely more on the writer's biographical data and on some of his stories, the latter on his correspondence and on other stories. The matter of the author's belief is one thing, his writings another. Faith, as depicted in Čexov's writings, can be explained with the aid of the above-quoted statement by James. Religious belief helps, for instance, the protagonist of the "Student," not to feel cold or hunger. This shows that, for him, the hypothesis of God works, and is therefore true. For other characters it does not work, as in "Ubijstvo," for instance; therefore, for them, it is not true. The author himself does not exercise his options and remains in the metaphorical field, which he defines between "God exists" and "there is no God." A decision would not be pragmatically justifiable. Indeed, a decision either way would remove some of the existing possibilities, and, like the pragmatists, Čexov maintains that the results give meaning to the action.(XVII, 42)

Another argument about Čexov's writings concerns his relation to the intelligentsia. Derman, for instance, refutes Sobolev's claim that Čexov is a fierce enemy of the intelligentsia,[6] and he quotes from Čexov's notebook that the strength and salvation of the nation rests in an intelligentsia which sincerely thinks, genuinely feels, and actually works.[7] This statement summarizes the entirety of Čexov's thought. He rejects hypocrisy, as in "Imeniny," dearth of feeling, as illustrated by von Koren in "Duèl'," and passivity, as exemplified by Ragin in "Palata No. 6." Čexov is accused of anti-intellectualism mainly because, like the pragmatists, he refuses to put reason and science before everything else.

Čapek expresses in his writings pivotal ideas often identical to those of his Russian counterpart. It appears that his outlook changes as his interests shift at the time of imminent danger from Hitler's Germany, but his world view remains unchanged. Therefore, the principles which define the Czech writer's beliefs in 1918 apply to his entire creative life. Thus, the first clause of his outline specifies dislike of verbal solutions, big words, and generalizations. "Jasnovidec" and "Orator," for example, demonstrate that both Čapek and Čexov express this notion in their stories. The next clause advocates contact with reality: one should deal with actual conflicts, rather than follow general principles. Several hundred of Čapek's *feuilletons* testify that he practices what he preaches. The same is true for the Russian writer's *feuilletons* and for some of his stories, such as "Mužiki," for instance. This principle for Čapek leads inevitably to the end of subjectivism, which constitutes the next clause. This involves becoming a common man, which takes heroic determination. Thus, in *První parta*, the writer emphasizes that the only real heroism is hard work, and the protagonist of *Obyčejný život* considers his life to be ordinary. Čexov's character, Osip Vardamyč, in "Ubijstvo," advises his employee, Matvej, to do the same: that is, be a common man.(IX, 140) In other words, Čapek asks for objective individualism, which he understands as relating to the world on a personal level, since one can easily hide behind global trends and their slogans. Čapek's heroes accept their responsibility. Many of Čexov's characters do the same. Čapek maintains that such responsibility entails freedom of spirit, the dramatic freedom to decide on one's own about everything which relates to real conflicts. This requires continuous initiative, permanent insecurity, and frequent compromises, which are perceived as failures (e.g. *Povětroň*, "Rasskaz neizvestnogo čeloveka"). The penultimate clause propounds the idea that all facts are of the same value: "high" and "low" facts do not exist. The final clause states that all problems of our thinking are, in practical terms, just problems of our reaction to experiences i.e. of our moral activity in the world. The entire literary production of both writers demonstrates that neither differentiates between "high" and "low" facts. For both, the world begins at their desks, and both are meliorists believing that the future of this world depends on everyone.

The designation of a world view is not important to Čapek. If these stipulations represent pragmatism, he accepts this name for his *Weltanschauung*. The denotation of pragmatism is not very specific, and the views so labeled can differ substantially. Nevertheless, this author prefers not to apply the name to the world views discerned in Čapek and Čexov's writings. It should suffice that both authors demonstrated a consistent and fairly systematic thought, and that their views are similar, showing a strong affinity to pragmatism. This, of course, does not mean that Čexov, preceding Čapek by thirty years, was an original philosopher far ahead of his time. Nor does it mean that the Czech writer was a backward thinker in comparison. Čexov's thought follows a course similar to that of his coevals, which later developed into pragmatism. Čapek, on the other hand, well acquainted with contemporary trends in both art and philosophy, always moved at the head of the stream. His association with pragmatism is a relation to what many considered to be the most progressive systematic thought of the time.

Čapek's progressiveness is attested to by his subscription to the most advanced contemporary artistic movements. Therefore, the critics detect in his writings trends as varied as neo-classicism, expressionism, and cubism. Critics' discussion of Čexov's artistic expression is limited to the question of whether or not he was an impressionist, with the majority believing that he was. Thus, the Russian author's creative method can appropriately be described as that of which Arnold Hauser says: "Der ganze Pragmatismus erwächst aus dem impressionistischen, künstlerisch wandelbaren Erlebnis der Wirklichkeit tatsächlich so, wie diese Philosophie es für die Erfahrung überhaupt annimmt."[8] At the same time, Hauser provides the reader with a link tying expressionism and cubism to pragmatism, namely, the Bergsonian concept of time.[9] This offers a potential topic for investigation, but remains outside the scope of this study, the main consideration of which is the similarity of problems and their treatment by both Čapek and Čexov, which indicates an affinity of thought.

Ulrich Weisstein, in his manual of comparative literature, distinguishes five basic purposes for the use of analogy in literary scholarship.[10] Herein, the use of analogy is justified by the establishment of the affinity between the world views espoused by Čapek and Čexov. This typological study, thus, fills a gap in literary criticism by demonstrating the similarities in their writings, already mentioned by several critics, for the first time in a comprehensive manner. It also, by revealing the affinities apparent in the two authors' ideas supplies a basis for the eduction of Čexov's philosophy, the integrity and even existence of which has so often been denied. A proper understanding of this philosophy provides insight into numerous stories by Čexov which have so far remained unsatisfactorily explained.

Notes

1. R.B. Brandt, "Ethical Relativism," in *The Encyclopedia*, III, 75. The special forms of relativism are also defined and explained in this article.

2. T. Winner, "Čechov and Scientism," p. 325.

3. Virtanen, p. 21.

4. Peirce, Pragmatism, p. 6.

5. James, Pragmatism, p. 143.

6. A.B. Derman, Tvorčeskij portret Čexova (Moskva: Mir, 1929), p. 292, referring to Ju.V. Sobolev, O Čexove (Moskva: 1915), n.p.

7. Ibid., p. 301.

8. Hauser, p. 989.

9. Ibid., p. 1001.

10. U. Weisstein, Vergleichende Literaturwissenschaft: Erste Berricht, 1968-1977 (Bern: Peter Lang, 1981), p. 132.

ॐ

Bibliography

Primary Sources

Čapek, K. *Apocryphal Stories*. Trans. D. Round. London: George Allen & Unwin Ltd., 1949.

_____. *Bajky a podpovídky*. Praha: Čs. spisovatel, 1970.

_____. *Boží muka—Trapné povídky*. Praha: Mladá fronta, 1967.

_____. *Devatero pohádek: a ještě jedna jako přívažek od Josefa Čapka*. *Praha:* Albatros, 1972.

_____. *Hordubal*. Praha: F. Borový, 1939.

_____. *Hovory s T.G. Masarykem*. Souborné vydání. Praha: F. Borový, 1937.

_____. *In Praise of Newspapers and Other Essays on the Margin of Literature*. Trans. M. and R. Weatherall. London: George Allen & Unwin Ltd., 1951.

_____. *Intimate Things*. Trans. D. Round. London: George Allen & Unwin Ltd., 1935.

_____. *Italské listy. Anglické listy. Výlet do Španě l. Obrázky z Holandska*. Praha: Čs. spisovatel, 1960.

_____. *Jak se co dělá—O lidech*. Praha: Čs. spisovatel, 1960.

_____. *Kniha apokryfů* . Praha: Čs. spisovatel, 1964.

_____. *Krakatit*. Praha: Čs. spisovatel, 1968.

_____. "Literatura a veřejnost." *Listy pro umění a kritiku*, 2 (1934), 56-58.

_____. *Loupežník*. Praha: Aventinum, 1931.

230 THE NARRATIVES OF ČAPEK AND ČEXOV

Čapek, K. *Loupežník—R.U.R.—Bílá nemoc*. Praha: Čs. spisovatel, 1983.

_____. *Marsyas čili na okraji literatury: 1919-1931*. Praha: F. Borový, 1941.

_____. *Matka*. Praha: Státní pedagogické nakladatelství, 1966.

_____. *Měl jsem psa a kočku*. Praha: Čs. spisovatel, 1964.

_____. *Místo pro Jonathana!: Úvahy a glosy k otázkám veřejného života z let 1921-37*. Praha: Symposium, 1970.

_____. *Money and Other Stories*. Trans. F.P. Merchant et al. London: Hutchinson & Co. Ltd., n.d.

_____. *Na břehu dnů* . Praha: Čs. spisovatel, 1966.

_____. *O nejbližších věcech: feuilletony*. Praha: Aventinum, 1925.

_____. *O věcech obecných čili zóon politikon*. Praha: Fr. Borový, 1932.

_____. *Obyčejný život*. Praha: F. Borový, 1939.

_____. *Povětroň*. Praha: F. Borový, 1939.

_____. *Povídky z jedné kapsy—Povídky z druhé kapsy*. Praha: Čs. spisovatel, 1961.

_____. *Povídky z jedné kapsy—Povídky z druhé kapsy*. Praha: Čs. spisovatel, 1973.

_____. *Pozdravy*. Praha: MF, 1979.

_____. *Poznámky o tvorbě* . Praha: Čs. spisovatel, 1951.

_____. *Pragmatismus čili filosofie praktického života*. Praha: F. Topič, 1925.

_____. *První parta*. Praha: Naše vojsko, 1958.

_____. *Ratolest a vavřín*. Praha: Dilia, Melantrich, 1970.

_____. Rev. of *Červenec*, by F.V. Krejčí. *Přehled*, 11, No. 47 (14 Aug. 1913), 773-74.

_____. *R.U.R—Sredstvo Makropulosa—Vojna s salamandrami—Fantastičeskie rasskazy*. Trans. N. Aroseva et al. Moskva: Mir, 1966.

_____. *Sloupkový ambit*. Praha: Čs. spisovatel, 1957.

_____. *Spisy*. 20 vols. Praha: Čs. spisovatel, 1980-83.

_____. *Tales from Two Pockets*. Trans. P. Selver. London: George Allen & Unwin Ltd., 1967.

_____. *Three Novels: Hordubal, An Ordinary Life, Meteor*. Trans. M. and R. Weatherall. London: George Allen & Unwin Ltd., 1948.

_____. *Továrna na absolutno: román fejeton*. Praha: Čs. spisovatel, 1962.

_____. *V zajetí slov: Kritika slov a úsloví*. Praha: Svoboda, 1969.

_____. *Válka s mloky*. Praha: Čs. spisovatel, 1953.

Čapek, K. *Válka s mloky*. Praha: Čs. spisovatel, 1963.

_____.*Věc Makropulos: komedie o třech dějstvích s přeměnou*. 2nd edn. Praha: Aventinum, 1922.

_____. *Věci kolem nás*. Praha: Čs. spisovatel, 1970.

_____. *Výbor z prózy Karla Čapka*. Ed. J. Mukařovský. 1934; rpt. Praha: Státní nakl. v Praze, 1946.

_____. *Zahradníkův rok*. Praha: SNKLHU, 1957.

Čapek K. and J. *Krakonošova zahrada—Zářivé hlubiny a jiné prózy— Juvenilie*. Praha: Čs. spisovatel, 1957.

_____. *Ze života hmyzu*. Praha: Orbis, 1958.

Čapek K. and Kohout, P. *Válka s mloky: musical-mystery*. Praha: Orbis, 1963.

Čexov, A.P. *Literary and Theatrical Reminiscences*. Ed. S.S. Koteliansky. London: George Routledge & Sons Ltd., 1927.

_____. *The Oxford Chekhov*. 9 vols. Trans. and Ed. R. Hingley. London: Oxford Univ. Press, 1968-75.

_____. *Polnoe sobranie sočinenij i pisem*. 20 vols. Moskva: OGIZ GIXL, 1944-51.

_____. *Polnoe sobranie sočinenij i pisem v tridcati tomax*. Moskva: Nauka, 1974-83.

_____. *Zaterjannye proizvedenija*. Leningrad: Atenej, 1925.

"Čto dlja vas SSSR." *Ogonek*, 14, No. 8-9 (1936), n.p.

Letters of Anton Chekhov. Ed. S. Karlinsky. New York: Harper & Row, 1973.

Viktor Dyk, St.K. Neumann, Bratři Čapkové: Korespondence z let 1905- 1918. Ed. S. Jarošová, M. Blahynka, F. Všetička. Praha: Nakladatelství ČSAV, 1962.

"Zarubežnye otkliki na opublikovanie proekta novoj Konstitucii SSSR: Novyj tip demokratii." *Pravda*, 18 June 1936, p. 5.

Secondary Sources
On Čapek

Bernštejn, I.A. Češskij roman XX veka i puti realizma v *evropejskix literaturax*. Moskva: Nauka, 1979.

_____. *Karel Čapek: Tvorčeskij put'*. Moskva: Nauka, 1969.

_____. "Karel Čapek v Sovetskom sojuze: 20-30-e gody." In *Čexoslovacko-sovetskie literaturnye svjazy*. Moskva: Nauka, 1964, pp. 35-66.

Bernštejn, I.A. "Talantlivaja kniga o Čapeke." *Voprosy literatury*, 7, No. 3 (1963), 219-22.

Bibliografie Karla Čapka: Soupis jeho díla. Ed. Boris Mědílek a kolektiv. Praha: Academia, 1990.

Bradbrook, B.R. "Chesterton and Karel Čapek: A Study in Personal and Literary Relationship." *The Chesterton Review,* 4 (1978), 89-103.

_____. "Karel Čapek's Contribution to Czech National Literature." In *Czechoslovakia Past and Present.* Ed. M. Rechcigl, Jr. The Hague: Mouton, 1968, II, 1002-11.

Branžovský, J. *Karel Čapek, světový názor a umění.* Praha: Nakl. polit. literatury, 1963.

Buriánek, F. *Česká literatura první poloviny XX. století.* Praha: Čs. spisovatel, 1981.

_____. *Karel Čapek.* Praha: Melantrich, 1978.

_____. "Karel Čapek estetik." *Česká literatura,* 24 (1976), 409-16.

"Čapek, Karel." In *Česká literární bibliografie 1945-1963.* Ed. J. Kunc. Vol. I. Praha: Státní knihovna ČSSR, 1963, pp. 117-49.

Čapková, H. *Moji milí bratři.* Praha: Čs spisovatel, 1962.

"Časové otázky naší literatury," *Tradice a modernost: Výbor z díla Bedřicha Václavka.* Ed. F. Valouch and J. Dvořák. Praha: Odeon, 1973, 230-31 and 256.

Černý V. *Karel Čapek.* Praha: F. Borový, 1936.

_____. "Karel Čapek: 'Kalendář (Jak je rok dlouhý).'" *Kritický měsíčník,* 3 (1940), 256-57.

_____. "Karel Čapek: 'O lidech.'" *Kritický měsíčník,* 3 (1940), 415-16.

_____. "Karel Čapek: *První parta.*" *Kritický měsíčník,* 1 (1938), 37-39.

_____. "Karel Čapek: 'Vzrušené tance.' —Josef Čapek: 'Básně z koncentračního tábora.'" *Kritický měsíčník,* 7 (1946), 342-47.

_____. *Paměti.* Vols. I and IV. Toronto: Sixty-Eight Publishers, 1982 and 1983.

_____. "Poslední Čapkovo tvůrčí období a jeho demokratický humanismus." *Kritický měsíčník,* 2 (1939), 49-56.

_____. "Karel Čapek: *Život a dílo skladatele Foltýna.*" *Kritický měsíčník,* 2 (1939), 178-82.

Elton, O. "Karel Čapek: Later Novels." In *Essays and Addresses.* London: E. Arnold, 1939, pp. 170-90.

_____. "Karel Čapek: Short Tales and Fantasias." In *Essays and Addresses,* pp. 151-69.

Elton, O. "Karel Čapek's Stories." *Life and Letters Today*, 21, No. 22 (1939), 34-42.

Götz, F. *Anarchie v nejmladší česlé poesii.* Brno: B. Kočí, 1922.

_____. *Jasnící se horizont.* Praha: Václav Petr, 1926.

Hájek, J. "Doslov." In *Povídky z jedné kapsy—Povídky z druhé kapsy.* Praha: Čs. spisovatel, 1955, 321-32.

Halík, M. *Karel Čapek: Život a dílo v datech.* Praha: Academia, 1983.

Haller, J. "O slohu Karla Čapka." *Přítomnost*, 14, No. 47-48 (1938), 747-50 and 761-64.

Haman, A., and P.I. Trensky. "Man Against the Absolute: The Art of Karel Čapek." *Slavic and East European Journal*, 11 (1967), 168-84.

Harkins, W.E. *Anthology of Czech Literature.* New York: King's Crown Press, 1953.

_____. "Form and Thematic Unity in Karel Čapek's trilogy." *Slavic and East European Journal*, 15 [1] (1957), 92-100.

_____. *Karel Čapek.* New York and London: Columbia Univ. Press, 1962.

_____. "Karel Čapek: From Relativism to Perspectivism." *History of Ideas Newsletter*, 3, No. 3 (July 1957), 50-53.

_____. "Karel Čapek - poslední období 1935-1938." *Svědectví*, 1, No. 2 (1957), 19-23.

_____. "Pragmatism and the Czech 'Pragmatist Generation.'" In *American Contributions to the Fourth International Congress of Slavicists: Moscow, September 1958.* 'S-Gravenhage: Mouton, 1958, 107-26.

Hora, J. *Duch stále se rodící.* Praha: Čs. spisovatel, 1981.

Howell, Y. "Karel Čapek in 1984." *Cross Currents: A Yearbook of Central European Culture.* Eds. L. Matejka and B. Stolz. Ann Arbor: Univ. of Michigan, 3 (1983), 121-30.

Hrabák, J., Jeřábek, D., Tichá, Z. *Průvodce po dějinách české literatury.* Praha: Orbis, 1976.

Hrubý, A. "Diskuse kolem dramatu 'Ze života hmyzu.'" *Kritický měsíčník*, 8 (1947), 30-31.

Iggers, W. "Karel Čapek: *Apocryphal Stories.*" *Slavic and East European Journal*, 20 (1976), 199-200.

Klíma, I. *Karel Čapek.* 1962; rpt. Praha: Čs. spisovatel, 1965.

_____. "Karel Čapek v Sovětském svazu." *Praha-Moskva*, 10 (1955), 57-62.

Königsmark, V. "Významotvorné možnosti fabulované prózy." *Česká literatura*, 18 (1970), 1-29.

Konrád, Edmond. *Nač vzpomenu.* Praha: Čs. spisovatel, 1967.

Kornelová, M. "Na slovíčko, vážený kruhu oslav Dr. K. Čapka v Malých Svatoňovicích!" *Kritický měsíčník,* 7 (1946), 416-17.

Koželuhová, H. *Josef a Karel: Čapkové očima rodiny.* Frankfurt a. M.: Dialog; Köln: Index, 1984.

Králík, O. *První řada v díle Karla Čapka.* Ostrava: Profil, 1972.

Kučerová, H. "Karel Čapek v roce 1974." *Česká literatura,* 22 (1974), 515-26.

Kudělka, Viktor. *Boje o Karla Čapka.* Praha: Academia, 1987.

Malevič, O. *Karel Čapek: Kritiko-biografičeskij očerk.* Moskva: Xudož. litra, 1968.

_____. "Karel Čapek i Rossija." *Voprosy literatury,* 9, No. 7 (1965), 86-96.

_____. "Úloha literární tradice v knize Karla Čapka *Boží muka.*" *Česká literatura,* 15 (1967), 131-42.

Maljarenko, A.M. *Istoki češskoj socialističeskoj literatury.* Kiev: Izd-vo Kievskogo univ., 1966.

Mathesius, B. "Fort-chabrol, Karle Čapku!" *Kritický měsíčník,* 2 (1939), 24-27.

Matuška, A. *Člověk proti zkáze: Pokus o Karla Čapka.* Praha: Čs. spisovatel, 1963.

_____. *Člověk v slove.* Bratislava: Slov. spisovatel', 1967.

_____. "Karel Čapek." *Plamen,* No. 2 (1960), 67-70.

_____. *Karel Čapek: An Essay.* Trans. Cathryn Alan. London: George Allen & Unwin Ltd., 1964.

Mukařovský, J. *Kapitoly z české poetiky: K vývoji české poesie a prózy.* Vol. II. Praha: Melantrich, 1941.

_____. "O próze Karla Čapka." *Almanach Kmene,* 5 (1934-1935), 130-37.

Nejedlý, Z. *Sebrané spisy Zdeňka Nejedléno.* Vol. XV. Praha: St. nakl. polit. literatury, 1953.

Neumann, S.K. "Česká literatura a česká skutečnost." *Listy pro umění a kritiku,* 2 (1934), 51-54.

_____. "Sociální román relativisty nebo hornický život k pobavení." *Tvorba,* 12 (1937), n.p.; rpt in *O umění,* Praha: Čs. spisovatel, 1958, pp. 498-501.

Nikol'skij, S.V. "Karel Čapek." In Čapek, *Izbrannoe.* Moskva: GIXL, 1950, pp. 3-16.

_____. *Karel Čapek.* Trans. K. Jiroudková. Praha: Čs. spisovatel, 1952.

Nikol'skij, S.V. *Karel Čapek-fantast i satirik*. Moskva: Nauka, 1973.

Nosek, M. "Čapkovský esej Ivana Klímy." *Česká literatura*, 10 (1962), 363-65.

Novák, A. *Czech Literature*. Trans. P. Kussi. Ann Arbor: Michigan Slavic Publications, 1976.

_____. "Czech Literature During and After the War." *The Slavonic Review*, 2 (1923-24), 114-32.

_____. *Stručné dějiny literatury české*. Olomouc: R. Promberger, 1946.

Očerki istorii češškoj literatury XIX-XX vekov. Moskva: AN SSSR, 1963.

Otáhal, M. "Ferdinand Peroutka: Muž přítomnosti." *Svědectví*, 18, No. 70-71 (1983), 339-90.

Páleníček, L., [Gregorec, J., Petrík, J.], *Rukověť' dějin české a slovenské literatury od roku 1918: Česká literatura*. Praha: SPN, 1966.

Peroutka, F. *Budeme pokračovat*. Ed. J. Kovtun. Toronto: 68 Publishers, 1984.

Pohorský, M. "Noetické romány Karla Čapka." *Česká literatura*, 20 (1972), 522-39.

Pujmanová, M. "Sedmero mistrovských ctností Karla Čapka." *Kritický měsíčník*, 2 (1939), 43-44.

Rühle Jürgen. "Die Molche." *Der Monat*, 13, No. 145 (1960), 88-91.

Rutte, M. *Mohyly s vavřínem*. Praha: Fr. Borový, 1939.

_____. *Nový svět: Studie o nové české literatuře 1917-1919*. Praha: Otakar Storch-Marien, Aventinum, 1919.

Růžička, K. "Karel Čapek: 'Bajky a podpovídky.'" *Kritický měsíčník*, 8 (1947), 241-42.

_____. "Na okraj Čapkovy *Knihy apokryfů*.'" *Kritický měsíčník*, 7 (1946), 184-89.

Šalda, F.X. "Karel Čapek, novinář politický a sociální." *Šaldův zápisník*, 4 (1931-1932), 401-17.

_____. *Soubor díla F.X. Šaldy*. Praha: Melantrich and Čs. spisovatel, 1947-1963.

Scheinpflugová, O. *Český román*. Praha: Melantrich, 1969.

Seehaase Ilse. "Gedanken zum Verhältnis Karel Čapeks. *Zeitschrift für Slawistik*, 9 (1964), 114-18.

Součková, M. *A Literary Satellite: Czechoslovak-Russian Literary Relations*. Chicago and London: The Univ. of Chicago Press, 1970.

Strohsová, E. "Karel Čapek." *Česká literatura*, 16 (1968), 14-41.

Václavek, B. *Česká literatura XX. století*. 1934; rpt. Praha: Svoboda, 1947.

Wellek, R. "Karel Čapek." *Columbia Dictionary of Modern European Literature*. Ed. H. Smith. New York: Columbia Univ. Press, 1947.

Wellek, R. "Karel Čapek." *Slavonic and East European Review*, 15 (1936-37), 191-206.

Winner, T. G. "Speech characteristics in Čexov's Ivanov and Čapek's *Loupežník*." In *American Contributions to the Fifth International Congress of Slavists, Sofia*. The Hague: Mouton & Co., 1963, II, 403-31.

On Čexov

A.P. Čexov v vospominanijax sovremennikov. Ed. S.N. Golubova., et al. Moskva: GIXL, 1960.

Aleksandrov, B.I. *A.P. Čexov: Seminarij*. 2nd edn. Moskva: Prosveščenie, 1964.

_____. *Seminarij po Čexovu*. Moskva: Ministerstvo prosveščenija RSFSR, 1964.

Andreev, G.A. (Xomjakov). "Zagadka Čexova." *Novyj žurnal*, 34, No. 118 (1975), 57-71.

Anon. Review of "Step'," by A.P. Čexov. In "Periodičeskija izdanija: *Severnyj vestnik*, fevral' i mart." *Russkaja mysl'*, 9, No. 4 (1888), ii, 208-10.

Anton Čechov, 1860 -1960: Some Essays. Ed. T. Eekman. Leiden: E.J. Brill, 1960.

Anton Čexov as a Master of Story-Writing: Essays in Modern Soviet Literary Criticism. Trans. and Ed. L. Hulanicki and D. Savignac. The Hague: Mouton, 1976.

Auzinger, H. "Čechov und das Nicht-zu-Ende-Sprechen." *Die Welt der Slaven*, 5 (1960), 233-44.

_____. *Die Pointe bei Čechov*. Kempten-Allgäu: Otto Harrassowitz, 1956.

Berdnikov, G. *A.P. Čexov: Idejnye i tvorčeskie iskanija*. Leningrad: Xudož. lit-ra, 1970.

_____. "Chekhov and our Time." *Sovetskaja literatura*, No. 1 [382] (1980), 3-11.

_____. "Social'noe i obščečelovečeskoe v tvorčestve Čexova." *Voprosy literatury*, 26, No. 1 (1982), 124-51.

Bicilli, P.M. *Anton P. Čechov: Das Werk und sein Stil*. München: Wilhelm Fink Vlg., 1966.

Bogatyrev, Š.Š. "Čexov v Čexoslovakii." In *Literaturnoe nasledstvo: Čexov*. Vol. LXVIII. Moskva: AN SSSR, 1960, pp. 747-76.

Bogdanovič, A.I. "Kritičeskie zametki." *Mir božij*, 6, No. 6 (1897), ii, 1-9.

Bogdanovič, A.I. "Kritičeskie zametki." *Mir božij*, 8, No. 2 (1899), ii, 1-10.

Brahms, C. *Reflections in a Lake: A Study of Chekhov's Four Greatest Plays.* London: Weidenfeld and Nicolson, 1976.

Brojde, È.L. "Čexov-myslitel'." *Grani*, 35, No. 117 (1980), 232-60.

_____. *Čexov: Myslitel', xudožnik (100-letie tvorčeskogo puti); katastrofa, vozroždenie.* Frankfurt a. M.: n.p., 1980.

_____. *K problematike Čexovskix universitetov.* N.p.: Izd-vo Svobodnogo Universiteta im. A.P. Čexova, 1982.

Bruford, W.H. *Anton Chekhov.* New Haven: Yale Univ. Press, 1957.

_____. *Chekhov and his Russia: A Sociological Study.* London: Kegan Paul, Trench, Trubner & Co., 1947.

Bukčin, S. *Dorogoj Anton Pavlovič...: Očerki o korrespondentax A.P. Čexova.* Minsk: Nauka i texnika, 1973.

Bulgakov, S. N. "Čexov kak myslitel'." *Novyj put'*, No. 11 (1904); rpt. Kiev: n.p., 1905. Bunin, I.A. *O Čexove: Nezakončennaja rukopis'.* New York: Izd-vo im. Čexova, 1955.

Cervo, N. A. "The Gargouille Anti-Hero: Victim of Christian Satire." *Renascence,* 22 (1970), 69-77.

Čexov. In *Literaturnoe nasledstvo.* Vol. LXVIII. Ed. I.I. Anisimov et al. Moskva: AN SSSR, 1960.

Chekhov: A Collection of Critical Essays. Ed. R.L. Jackson. Engelwood Cliffs, N.J.: Prentice-Hall, 1967.

Chekhov: The Critical Heritage. Ed. V. Emeljanow. London: Routledge and Kegan Paul, 1981.

Chekhov's Art of Writing: A Collection of Critical Essays. Ed. P. Debreczeny and T. Eekman. Columbus, Ohio: Slavica Publishers, 1977.

"Chekhov through the Eyes of the Writers of the World." *Sovetskaja literatura*, No. 1 [382] (1980), 91-103.

Čiževskij, D. *History of Nineteenth-Century Russian Literature.* Vol. II. Trans. R.N. Porter. Nashville: Vanderbilt Univ. Press, 1974.

_____. *Vergleichende Geschichte der slavischen Literaturen.* Vol. II. Berlin: Walter de Gruyter & Co., 1968.

Conradi, Ulrike. "Thomas Mann's Interpretation of Anton Chekhov in his essay 'Versuch über Tschechow.'" Thesis Univ. of Alberta 1968.

Čudakov, A.P. *Poètika Čexova.* Moskva: Nauka, 1971.

Čukovskij K. *O Čexove.* Moskva: Xudož. lit-ra, 1967.

Curtin, C. "Čexov's 'Sleepy:' An Interpretation." *Slavic and East European Journal*, 9 (1965), 390-99.

238   THE NARRATIVES OF ČAPEK AND ČEXOV

Derman, A.B., ed. *A.P. Čexov: Sbornik dokumentov i materialov*. Moskva: GIXL, 1947.

_____. *Tvorčeskij portret Čexova*. Moskva: Mir, 1929.

Düwel, W. *Anton Tschechow: Dichter der Morgendämmerung*. Halle (Saale): Sprache und Literatur, 1961.

_____. "Zum Problem von Inhalt und Form in Čechovs Erzählungen." *Zeitschrift für Slawistik*, 18 (1973), 357-69.

Eekman, Thomas. "Čexov—An Impressionist?" *Russian Literature: North-Holland*, 15, No. 2 (1984), 203-22.

Èjxenbaum, B. "O Čexove." In *O proze: sbornik statej*. Leningrad: Xudož. lit-ra, 1969, pp. 357-70.

Elton, O. "Chekhov." In *Essays and Addresses*, pp. 118-50.

Èrenburg, I. *Chekhov, Stendhal, and Other Essays*. London: MacGibbon & Kee, 1962.

_____. *Perečityvaja Čexova*. Moskva: GIXL, 1960.

Ermilov, V.E. *A.P. Čexov*. Moskva: Sovetskij pisatel', 1959.

Fadeev, A.A. "O Čexove." *Zapisnye knižki: Russkaja literatura*. 1934; rpt in *Sobranie sočinenij*. Vol. VI. Moskva: Khudož. lit-ra, 1971, 532-36.

Galsworthy, John. "Four Novelists in Profile." *The English Review*, 55 (Nov. 1932), 485-500.

Gejdeko, V.A. *A. Čexov i Iv. Bunin*. Moskva: Sovetskij pisatel', 1976.

_____. "Magija kratkosti i prostoty: zametki o masterstve Čexova-rasskazčika." *Voprosy literatury*, 17, No. 7 (1973), 168-83.

Gillčs, D. *Čexov: Observer Without Illusion*. Trans. C.L. Marksmann. New York: Funk & Wagnalls, 1968.

Gippius, Z.N. *Literaturnyj dnevnik: 1899-1907*. 1908; rpt. München: W. Fink Vlg., 1970.

Gitovič, N.I. "Kto byl protiv?—Po sledam propavšix dokumentov." *Voprosy literatury*, 24, No. 1 (1980), 148-55.

_____. *Letopis' žizni i tvorčestva A.P. Čexova*. Moskva: GIXL, 1955.

Gol'denvejzer, A.B. *Vblizi Tolstogo*. Moskva: GIXL, 1959.

Gorbačevič, K.S. "O tekstual'nom izučenii sinonimov: na materiale sinonimičnyx prilagatel'nyx v proizvedenijax A.P. Čexova." *Vestnik Leningradskogo universiteta*, 18, No. 2 (1963), 92-l02.

Gor'kij, M.A. *Sobranie sočinenij v tridcati tomax* Vols. V, X, XXIII, and XXVIII. Moskva: GIXL, 1949-1955.

Gotman, S. "The Role of Irony in Čexov's Fiction." *Slavic and East European Journal*, 16 (1972), 297-306.

Grinevič, P.F. (Jakubovič, P.F.) "Itogi dvux jubileev." *Russkoe bogatstvo,* 16, No. 8 (1898), ii, 88-124.

Grossman, L.P. "Čexov." *Mastera slova. Sobranie sočinenij v pjati tomax.* Moskva: N.A. Stoljar, 1928. IV, 199-244.

Gurvič, I.A. *Proza Čexova: Čelovek i dejstvitel'nost'.* Moskva: Xudož. litra, 1970.

_____. "'Skučnaja istorija:' Rasskaz i rasskazčik u Čexova." *Russkaja literatura,* 13, No. 3 (1970), 125-30.

Hahn, B. Chekhov: *A Study of the Major Stories and Plays.* Cambridge: Cambridge Univ. Press, 1977.

Hingley, R. *A New Life for Anton Chekhov.* London: Oxford University Press, 1976.

Istorija russkoj kritiki. Ed. B.P. Gorodeckij. Vol. II. Moskva: AN SSSR, 1958.

Istorija russkoj literatury. Ed. M.P. Alekseev et al. Vol. IX. Part 2. Moskva: AN SSSR, 1956.

Istorija russkoj literatury XIX v. Ed. D.N. Ovsjaniko-Kulikovskij. Vol. V. Moskva: Mir, 1911.

Istorija russkoj literatury XIX veka (vtoraja polovina). Ed. S.M. Petrov. Moskva: Prosveščenie, 1974.

Ivanov, G.V. "Čexov i Mopassan." *Russkaja literatura,* 20, No. 1 (1977), 175-77.

Ivask, G. "Čechov and the Russian Clergy." In *Anton Čechov,* pp. 83-92.

Karlinsky, Simon. "Russian Anti-Chekhovians." *Russian Literature: North-Holland,* 15, No. 2 (1984), 183-202.

Kataev, V.B. *Proza Čexova: Problemy interpretacii.* Moskva: Izd-vo Moskovskogo univ., 1979.

_____. "Understanding Chekhov's World." *Sovetskaja literatura,* No. 1 [382] (1980), 171-83.

Kirk, I. *Anton Chekhov.* Boston: Twayne, 1981.

Kramer, K.D. *The Chameleon and the Dream: The Image of Reality in Čexov's Stories.* The Hague: Mouton, 1970.

_____. "Cycles in Chekhov Criticism: Impressionism Refurbished." In *Proceedings: Pacific Northwest Conference on Foreign Languages.* Twenty-third Annual Meeting: April 28-29, 1972. Ed. W.C. Kraft. Vol. XXIII. Eugene: Oregon State University, 1972, pp. 268-72.

Kurdjumov M.G. *Serdce smjatennoe: O tvorčestve A.P. Čexova 1904-1934.* Paris: YMCA Press, 1934.

Laffitte, S. *Chekhov 1860-1904*. Tr. M. Budberg and G. Latta. New York: Charles Scribner's Sons, 1973.

Lakšin, V.Ja. *Tolstoj i Čexov*. 2nd edn. Moskva: Sovetskij pisatel', 1975.

Lesňáková, S. "K vývinovej polarite Čechovových poviedok." *Československá Rusistika*, 15 (1970), 28-31.

Lunačarskij, A.V. *Sobranie sočinenij v vos'mi tomax*. Vols. I and VII. Moskva: Xudož. lit-ra, 1963 and 1967.

M. Gor'kij i A. Čexov: Sbornik materialov. Ed. N.I. Gitovič. Moskva: GIXL, 1951.

Magarshack, D. *Chekhov: A Life*. Westport: Greenwood Press Publishers, 1970.

Majakovskij, V. "Dva Čexova." *Novaja žizn'*, 18, No. 6 (1914), n.p.; rpt. in *Polnoe sobranie sočinenij v trinadcati tomax*. Moskva: GIXL, 1955, I, 294-301.

Mann, T. "Čexov." Trans. L. Rudnaja. *Novyj Mir*, 31, No. 1 (1955), 212-26.

_____. *Gesammelte Werke in zwölf Bänden*. Band IX. Frankfurt a. M.: S. Fischer, 1960.

_____. "Versuch über Tschechow." *Sinn und Form*, 6, No. 5-6 (1954), 783-804.

Marshall, R.H. "Chekhov and the Russian Orthodox Clergy." *Slavic and East European Journal*, 7, No. 4 (1963), 375-91.

Martin, David. "Philosophy in Čexov's Major Plays." *Die Welt der Slaven*, 23 (1978), 122-39.

Mašková, A. "'Malý člověk' v díle A.P. Čechova a K. Poláčka." *Česká literatura*, 22 (1974), 136-44.

Merežkovskij, D.S. *Čexov i Gor'kij*. Letchworth: Prideaux Press, 1906.

_____. "O Čexove." *Vesy*, 2, No. 11 (1905), 1-26.

_____. "O pričinax upadka i novyx tečenijax sovremennoj russkoj literatury." 1893; rpt. in *Izbrannye stat'i: Simvolizm, Gogol, Lermontov*. München: W. Fink Vlg., 1912, pp. 207-305.

_____. "Staryj vopros po povodu novogo talanta." *Severnyj vestnik*, 4, No. 11 (1888), 77-99.

Mirsky, D.S. *A History of Russian Literature from its Beginning to 1900*. New York: Vintage Books, 1958.

_____. "Chekhov and the English." *Monthly Criterion*, 6, No. 4 (1927), n.p.; rpt. in *Russian Literature and Modern English Fiction*. Ed. Donald Daire. Chicago and London: The Univ. of Chicago Press, 1965, pp. 203-13.

Mixajlovskij, N.K. "Literatura i žizn': Koe-čto o g. Čexove," *Russkoe bogatstvo*, 18, No. 4 (1900), ii, 119-40.

_____. "Literatura i žizn': O strašnoj sile g. Novus'a, o moej robosti, i o nekotoryx nedorazumenijax." *Russkoe bogatstvo*, 15, No. 11 (1897), ii, 123-27.

_____. *Literaturno-kritičeskie stat'i*. Moskva: GIXL, 1957.

_____. "'Mužiki' g. Čexova." *Russkoe bogatstvo*, 15, No. 6 (1897), ii, 116-26.

_____. *Sočinenija*. S.-Peterburg: Editorial Board of "Russkoe bogatstvo," 1897.

[Mixajlovskij, N.K.] Rev. of *V sumerkax*, by A.P. Čexov. In "Novye knigi." *Severnyj vestnik*, 3, No. 9 (1887), 81-85.

O'Bell, L. "Čexov's skazka: The Intellectual's Fairy Tale." *Slavic and East European Journal*, 25, No. 4 (1981), 33-46.

Obolenskij, L.E. "K predyduščej stat'e," *Russkoe bogatstvo*, 8, No. 12 (1890), ii, 141-44.

_____. "Obo vsem." *Russkoe bogatstvo*, 4, No. 12 (1886), 166-96.

_____. (Sozercatel') "Novyj povorot v idejax našej belletristiki." *Russkoe bogatstvo*, 8, No. 1 (1890), i, 95-113.

O'Toole, L. M. "Structure and Style in the Short Story: Chekhov's 'Student.'" *Slavic and East European Review*, 49 (1971), 45-67.

Ovsjaniko-Kulikovskij, D.N. *Sobranie sočinenij*. Vols. V and IX. S.-Peterburg: Obščestvennaja pol'za, Prometej, 1911.

Papernyj, Z. "Sjužet dolžen byt' nov..." *Voprosy literatury*, 20, No. 5 (1976), 169-89.

Paustovskij, K. "Zametki na papirosnoj korobke." *Literaturnaja gazeta*, 28 January 1960, p. 3.

Percov, P.P. "Iz"jany tvorčestva." *Russkoe bogatstvo*, 11, No. 1 (1893), ii, 39-71.

Petrova, M. "Čexov i 'zloumyšlenniki' iz 'Russkogo bogatstva': fakty i čtenie 'propavšix dokumentov.'" *Voprosy literatury*, 25, No. 7 (1981), 210-24.

Podarskij, V.G. (Rusanov, N.) "Naša tekuščaja žizn'." *Russkoe bogatstvo*, 10, No. 1 (1902), ii, 142-74.

Poggioli, R. *The Phoenix and the Spider*. Cambridge: Harvard Univ. Press, 1957.

Poljak, L. "Tradicii Čexova v sovremennoj novellistike." In *Žanrovo-stilevye iskanija sovremennoj sovetskoj prozy*. Moskva: Nauka, 1971.

Protopopov, M.A. "Žertva bezvremen'ja." *Russkaja mysl'*, 13, No. 6 (1892), ii, 95-122.

_____. "Literaturnye zametki." *Severnyj vestnik*, 8, No. 2 (1892), 177-81.

_____. "Literaturnye zametki." *Severnyj vestnik*, 9, No. 5 (1893), 130-41.

Proyat, J. de. "Anton Čexov et Herbert Spencer." *Revue des études slaves*, 54 (1982), 177-93.

Rayfield, D. *Chekhov: The Revolution of his Art*. London: Paul Elek, 1975.

Rev, Marija. "Specifika filosofskogo rasskaza A.P. Čexova: 'Palata No. 6.'" *Studia Slavica Hung.*, 25 (1979), 327-36.

Romanenko, V.T. *Čexov i nauka*. Xar'kov: Xar'kovskoe knižnoe izd-vo, 1962.

Rosbacher, P. "Nature and the Quest for Meaning in Chekhov's Stories." *Russian Review*, 24 (1965), 387-92.

Rosen, N. "The Unconscious in Čexov's 'Van'ka:' With a Note on 'Sleepy.'" *Slavic and East European Journal*, 15 (1971), 441-54.

Roskin, A.I. *A.P. Čexov: Stat'i o očerki*. Moskva: GIXL, 1959.

Rossbacher, P. "Nature and the Quest for Meaning in Chekhov's Stories." *The Russian Review*, 24 (1965), 387-92.

Sergeenko, P.A. *Tolstoj i ego sovremenniki: Očerki*. Moskva: V.M. Sablin, 1911.

Šestov, Lev. "Tvorčestvo iz ničego: A.P. Čexov." In *Načala i koncy*. S.-Peterburg: M.M. Stasjulevič, 1908, pp. 1-68.

Simmons, E.J. *Chekhov: A Biography*. Toronto: Little, Brown and Co., 1962.

Skabičevskij, A.M. "Anton Pavlovič Čexov." *Russkaja mysl'*, 26, No. 6 (1905), ii, 29-56.

_____. *Istorija novejšej russkoj literatury: 1848-1898 gg.*. 4th edn. S.-Peterburg: Obščestvennaja pol'za, 1900.

_____. Rev. of *Pestrye rasskazy*, by A.P. Čexov. In "Novye knigi." *Severnyj vestnik*, 2, No. 6 (1886).

_____. *Sočinenija v dvux tomax: Kritičeskie ètjudy, publicističeskie očerki, literaturnyja xarakteristiki*. Vol II. S.-Peterburg: Ju.N. Èrlix, 1903.

Skaftymov, A.P. "O povestjax Čexova 'Palata No. 6' i 'Moja žizn'.'" In *Nravstvennye iskanija russkix pisatelej*. Moskva: Xudož. lit-ra, 1972, 381-403.

Šklovskij, V. "A.P. Čexov." In *Zametki o proze russkix klassikov*. 2nd edn. Moskva: Sovetskij pisatel', 1955, pp. 413-59.

Sobolev, Ju.V. *O Čexove*. Moskva: n.p., 1915.

Stowell, H.P. "Chekhov's Prose Fugue: 'Sleepy.'" *Russian Literature Triquarterly*, 11 (1975), 435-42.

_____. "Čexov's 'Steppe:' A Journey through Endless Change." In *Proceedings*. XXIV, 264-69.

_____. "The Prismatic Sensibility: Henry James and Anton Čexov as Impressionists." Diss. Univ. of Washington, 1972.

Stroyeva, M. "Everyone has his own Chekhov." *Sovetskaja literatura*, No. 2 [383] (1980), 138-46.

Struve, G. "On Chekhov's Craftsmanship: The Anatomy of a Story." *Slavic Review*, 20 (1961), 465-76.

Struve, P.B. (Novus) "Miscelanea." *Novoe slovo*, 4 (Dec. 1897).

_____. "Na raznye temy: 'Mužiki' Čexova i g. Mixajlovskij." *Novoe slovo*, 4, No. 10 (Oct. 1897).

Tolstoj, A.N. "Da zdravstvuet Gor'kij!" In *Polnoe sobranie sočinenij*. Vol. XIII. Moskva: GIXL, 1949, 396-98.

Toumanova, N. Andronikova. *Anton Chekhov: The Voice of Twilight Russia*. New York: Columbia Univ. Press, 1937.

Tulloch, J. *Chekhov: A Structuralist Study*. London: MacMillan Press, 1980.

Urbanski, H. "Chekhov as Viewed by his Russian Literary Contemporaries." Diss. New York Univ. 1973.

Volynskij, A. (Flekser). *Bor'ba za idealizm: Kritičeskie stat'i*. S.-Peterburg: N.G. Molostvov, 1900.

_____. "Literaturnye zametki." *Severnyj vestnik*, 9, No. 5 (1893), 130-41.

Vorovskij, V.V. *Literaturno-kritičeskie očerki*. Ed. I.V. Sergeevskij. Moskva: GIXL, 1948.

_____. *Literaturno-kritičeskie očerki*. Ed. I. Černoucan. Moskva: GIXL, 1956.

Winner, T.G. "Čechov and Scientism; Observations on the Searching Stories." In *Anton Čechov*, pp. 325-35.

_____. Chekhov and his Prose. New York, Chicago, and San Francisco: Holt, Rinehart and Winston, 1966.

_____. "Myth as a Device in the Works of Chekhov." In *Myth and Symbol: Critical Approaches and Applications*. Ed. B. Slote. Lincoln: Univ. of Nebraska Press, 1963, pp. 71-78.

Winner, T.G. "Speech characteristics in Čexov's *Ivanov* and Čapek's *Loupežník*." In *American Contributions to the Fifth International Congress of Slavists, Sofia.* The Hague: Mouton & Co., 1963, II, 403-31.

"Zadači literaturnoj kritiki." Signed N.G. *Russkoe bogatstvo*, 8, No. 12 (1890), ii, 128-40.

Zajcev, B.K. *Čexov: Literaturnaja biografija.* New York: Izd-vo im. Čexova, 1954.

Other Sources

Anderson, W. "'Influentia' and 'Influence': The Currents of Maeander." In *Proceedings of the 9th Congress of the International Comparative Literature Association,* Innsbruck, 1979. Innsbruck: Institut für Sprachwissenschaft der Univ. Innsbruck, 1981, I, 35-42.

As William James Said: Extracts from the Published Writings of William James. Ed. E. P. Aldrich. New York: The Vanguard Press, 1942.

Berdjaev, N. *Samopoznanie: Opyt filosofskoj avtobiografii.* Paris: YMCA-Press, 1949.

Bergson, H. *Essai sur les données immédiates de la conscience.* Paris: F. Alcan, 1930.

_____. *L'Evolution créatrice.* Paris: F. Alcan, 1910.

_____. "La Philosophie." In *La Science française.* Paris: n.p., 1905.

_____. "La Philosophie de Claude Bernard." In *La Pensée et le mouvant: Essais et conférences.* Paris: F. Alcan, 1934, pp. 257-66.

_____. *Time and Free Will: An Essay on the Immediate Data of Consciousness.* New York: Harper & Row, 1960.

Bernard, Claude. "Cours de philosophie positive (par Auguste Comte): Exposition de la doctrine philosophique." In *Philosophie: Manuscrit inédit.* Ed. J. Chevalier. Paris: Boivin, 1937, pp. 25-43.

_____. *An Introduction to the Study of Experimental Medicine.* Trans. H.C. Greene. New York: MacMillan, 1927.

_____. *Pensées, Notes détachés.* Ed. L. Delhoome. Paris: J.-B. Baillière, 1937.

_____. *La Science expérimentale.* 6th edn. Paris: J.-B. Baillière, 1918.

Block, H.M. "The Concept of Influence in Comparative Literature." In *Yearbook of Comparative and General Literature*, 7 (1958), 30-37.

Bloom, Harold. *The Anxiety of Influence: A Theory of Poetry.* New York: Oxford Univ. Press, 1973.

Boening, J. "Some Recent Theories of Reception and Influence: Their

Literature Association, Montreal-Ottawa, 1973. Stuttgart: Kunst und Wesen, Erich Bieber, 1980, II, 543-549.

Češsko-ruskie i slovacko-ruskie literaturnye otnošenija: konec XVIII—načalo XX veka. Ed. M. Bakoš et al. Moskva: Nauka, 1968.

Chesterton, G.K. "Introductory Remarks on the Importance of Orthodoxy." In *Heretics.* London: The Bodley Head, 1905, pp. 3-16.

Čičerin, A.V. *Nerudovskij ètap v istorii kritičeskogo realizma.* Kiev: Izd. AN Ukrainskoj SSR, 1963.

Dewey, J. *Essays in Experimental Logic.* Chicago: Univ. of Chicago Press, 1916.

_____. *The Influence of Darwin on Philosophy and Other Essays in Contemporary Thought.* New York: Henry Holt & Co., 1910.

_____. *Studies in Logical Theory.* Chicago: Univ. of Chicago Press, 1909.

D'urišin, D. *O literárnych vzt'ahoch: Sloh, druh, preklad.* Bratislava: Veda, 1976.

_____. *Problémy literárnej komparatistiky.* Bratislava: Slovenská Akadémie Vied, 1967.

The Encyclopedia of Philosophy. 1972 rpt. edn.

Guillén, C. "The Aesthetics of Literary Influence." In *Literature as System: Essays Toward the Theory of Literary History.* Princeton: Princeton Univ. Press, 1971, pp. 21-52.

Hassan, I.H. "The Problem of Influence in Literary History: Notes Towards a Definition." *Journal of Aesthetics and Art Criticism,* 14, No. 1 (1955), 66-76.

Hauser, A. *Sozialgeschichte der Kunst und Literatur.* München: C.H. Beck, 1969.

Hrabák, J. *Literární komparatistika.* Praha: Státní pedagogické nakl., 1976.

Influx: Essays on Literary Influence. Ed. R. Primeau. Port Washington: Kennikat Press, 1977.

James, W. *Essays in Philosophy.* Cambridge: Harvard Univ. Press, 1978.

_____. *The Meaning of Truth.* Cambridge: Harvard Univ. Press, 1975.

_____. *A Pluralistic Universe.* Cambridge: Harvard Univ. Press, 1977.

_____. *Pragmatism.* Cambridge: Harvard Univ. Press, 1975.

_____. Rev. of *Rapport sur le progrès et la marche de physiologie générale en France,* by C. Bernard. *North American Review,* 107, No. 220 (1868), 322-28.

_____. *The Varieties of Religious Experience: A Study in Human Nature.* New York: Longmans, Green, and Co., 1920.

James, W. *The Varieties of Religious Experience: A Study in Human Nature*. New York: Longmans, Green, and Co., 1920.

_____. *The Will to Believe and Other Essays in Popular Philosophy*. Cambridge: Harvard Univ. Press, 1979.

Kolakowski, L. *Positivist Philosophy: From Hume to the Vienna Circle*. Trans. N. Guterman. Harmondsworth: Penguin Books, 1972.

Kuipers, J. *Zeitlose Zeit: Die Geschichte der deutschen Kurzgeschichtenforschung*. Groningen: Wolters-Noordhoff, 1970.

The Letters of William James. Ed. H. James. 1920; rpt. 2 vols. in 1. Boston: Little, Brown, and Co., 1926.

Lovejoy, A.O. *The Thirteen Pragmatisms and Other Essays*. Baltimore: John Hopkins, 1963.

McFarland, T. "Literature and Philosophy." In *Interrelations of Literature*. Ed. J.-P. Barricelli and J. Gibaldi. New York: The Modern Language Association of America, 1982, pp. 25-46.

Mendilow, A.A. *Time and the Novel*. London: Peter Nevill, 1952.

Moore, E.C. *American Pragmatism: Peirce, James, and Dewey*. New York: Columbia Univ. Press, 1961.

Nordau, Max. *Paradoxe*. Leipzig: Victor Ottmann, 1891.

Peirce, Charles Sanders. *Pragmatism and Pragmaticism*. Vol. V of *Collected Papers of Charles Sanders Peirce*. Ed. P. Weiss. Cambridge: Harvard Univ. Press, 1934.

_____. *Reviews, Correspondence, and Bibliography*. Vol. VIII of *Collected Papers of Charles Sanders Peirce*. Ed. H.W. Burks. 2nd edn. 2 vols. in 1. (Vols. VII and VIII.) Cambridge: Harvard Univ. Press, 1966.

Perry, Ralph Barton. *The Thought and Character of William James*. 2 vols. Boston: Little, Brown, and Co., 1935.

Rosenthal, B.G. *Dmitri Sergeevich Merezhkovsky and the Silver Age: The Development of a Revolutionary Mentality*. Hague: Martinus Nijhoff, 1975.

Schiller, F.C.S. *Humanism: Philosophical Essays*. London: MacMillan & Co., 1903.

_____. *Studies in Humanism*. London: MacMillan & Co., 1912.

_____. "William James and the Making of Pragmatism." *The Personalist*, 8 (1927), 81-93.

Spengler, Ute. *D.S. Merežkovskij als Literaturkritiker: Versuch einer religiösen Begründung der Kunst*. Slavica Helvetica, 2. Genève: C.J. Bucher, 1972.

Stevenson, B. *The Home Book of Quotations: Classical and Modern*. New York: Dodd, Mead, 1934.

Thayer H.S. *Meaning and Action: A Critical History of Pragmatism*. Indianapolis: The Bobbs-Merrill Co., 1968.

Twentieth-Century Short Story Explication: Interpretations, 1900-1960 Inclusive, of Short Fiction Since 1800. Ed. W. S. Walker. Hamden: The Shoe String Press, Inc., 1961.

Virtanen, Reino. "Claude Bernard and the History of Ideas." In *Claude Bernard and Experimental Medicine*. Collected Papers from a Symposium commemorating the centenary of the publication of *An Introduction to the Study of Experimental Medicine*. Eds. F. Grande and M.B. Visscher. Cambridge: Schenkman, 1967, pp. 9-23.

Weisstein, U. *Comparative Literature and Literary Theory: Survey and Introduction*. Trans. W. Riggan in collaboration with the author. Bloomington: Indiana Univ. Press, 1973.

————. "Influences and Parallels: The Place and Function of Analogy Studies in Comparative Literature." In *Teilnahme und Spiegelung*. Festschrift für Horst Rüdiger. Eds. B. Allemann and E. Koppen. Berlin and New York: Walter de Gruyter, 1975, pp. 593-609.

————. *Vergleichende Literaturwissenschaft: Erster Bericht: 1968-1977*. Jahrbuch für Internationale Germanistik: Reihe C — Forschungberichte. Band 2. Bern: Peter Lang, 1981.

Wellek, R. "The Revolt Against Positivism in Recent European Literary Scholarship." In *Twentieth Century English*. Ed. W.S. Knickerbocker. 1946; rpt. Freeport, N.Y.: Books for Libraries Press, 1970, pp. 67-89.

Wilde, O. *Lady Windermere's Fan*. In *The Complete Works of Oscar Wilde*. 1963; rpt. London: Hamlyn, 1983, pp. 3-40.

Žirmunskij, V.M. "Les Courants littéraires en tant que phénomènes internationaux." In *Proceedings of the 5th Congress of the International Comparative Literature Association*, Belgrade, 1967. Amsterdam: Swets and Zeitlinger, 1969, pp. 3-21.

————. "On the Study of Comparative Literature." *Oxford Slavonic Papers*, 13, (1967), 1-13.

Zola, É. *Le Roman expérimental*. In *Oeuvres complètes*. Vol. X. Ed. H. Mitterand. Paris: Cercle du Livre Précieux, 1968, pp. 1143-1203.

❦

INDEX